U.S. Policy toward Economic Nationalism in Latin America, 1917-1929

AMERICA IN THE MODERN WORLD
STUDIES IN INTERNATIONAL HISTORY

Warren F. Kimball
Series Editor
Professor of History, Rutgers University

Volumes Published

Lawrence Spinelli, *Dry Diplomacy: The United States, Great Britain, and Prohibition* (1989). ISBN 0-8420-2298-8

Richard V. Salisbury, *Anti-Imperialism and International Competition in Central America, 1920–1929* (1989). ISBN 0-8420-2304-6

Gerald K. Haines, *The Americanization of Brazil: A Study of U.S. Cold War Diplomacy in the Third World, 1945–1954* (1989). ISBN 0-8420-2339-9

Harry Harding and Yuan Ming, eds., *Sino-American Relations, 1945–1955: A Joint Reassessment of a Critical Decade* (1989). ISBN 0-8420-2333-X

Lawrence S. Kaplan, Denise Artaud, and Mark R. Rubin, eds., *Dien Bien Phu and the Crisis of Franco-American Relations, 1954–1955* (1990). ISBN 0-8420-2341-0

Michael L. Krenn, *U.S. Policy toward Economic Nationalism in Latin America, 1917–1929* (1990). ISBN 0-8420-2346-1

Akira Iriye and Warren Cohen, eds., *American, Chinese, and Japanese Perspectives on Wartime Asia, 1931-1949* (1990). ISBN 0-8420-2347-X

U.S. Policy toward Economic Nationalism in Latin America, 1917-1929

Michael L. Krenn

SR
BOOKS

A Scholarly Resources Imprint
WILMINGTON, DELAWARE

The paper used in this publication meets the minimum requirements of
the American National Standard for permanence of paper for printed
library materials, Z39.48, 1984.

Scholarly Resources Inc.
104 Greenhill Avenue
Wilmington, DE 19805-1897

Library of Congress Cataloging-in-Publication Data

Krenn, Michael L., 1957–
  U.S. policy toward economic nationalism in Latin America,
  1917–1929 / Michael L. Krenn.
      p. cm. — (America in the modern world)
  Includes bibliographical references.
  ISBN 0-8420-2346-1
      1. United States—Foreign economic relations—Latin
America. 2. Latin America—Foreign economic relations—United
States. 3. Investments, American—Latin America—History—20th
century. 4. Latin America—Economic policy. 5. Nationalism—Latin
America—History—20th century. I. Title. II. Series.
HF1456.5.L3K74 1990   89–24122
337.7308—dc20   CIP

FOR CORINNE

About the Author

Michael L. Krenn received his Ph.D. in history from Rutgers University in 1985. He is currently an assistant professor of history at the University of Miami. This is Professor Krenn's first book.

Contents

Acknowledgments

Books dealing with historical events, like the events themselves, never occur in a vacuum. To one extent or another, all books are collaborative efforts, and this work is no exception. A number of my colleagues have left their imprints on my scholarship and writing. I am indeed grateful finally to have reached the point at which I can acknowledge their contributions.

This book is an outgrowth of my doctoral dissertation, which was completed at Rutgers University in 1985. To the committee that oversaw its development I owe my first and ardent thanks. I was fortunate to have as my chairman Lloyd C. Gardner, who first suggested the general outlines of the dissertation and guided it, chapter by chapter, to its conclusion. He was never overbearing in his oversight as he encouraged me to push my work beyond self-imposed constraints, nor was he hesitant about pulling me back to the realm of reality and coherence if I pushed too far. As a scholar, he earned my admiration; as a person, he won my friendship; and as a Rutgers football fan, he gained my deepest sympathies.

The other members of that committee also had a marked impact on the original work. Mark Wasserman provided keen insights into Latin American perceptions, and his constant exhortation to "put more Latin America" into the work, while never heeded to his satisfaction, led me to consider more deeply the other side of the picture. His help, both in purely scholarly terms and, perhaps just as important, in terms of what became a developing friendship, has been invaluable. David Oshinsky and James H. Street both came on board on relatively short notice, but that did not deter them from giving my work comprehensive and insightful consideration. Their perceptive comments and suggestions demonstrated a concern with the work that had only positive impact.

Two other members of the Rutgers history department, Samuel L. Baily and Paul Clemens, also helped in the formulation of the dissertation. Dr. Baily's comments improved my understanding of nationalism and economic development in Latin America. Dr. Clemens, exhibiting an interest far beyond the call of duty, gave the work a spirited read-through and asked some probing questions.

Herbert Klein of Columbia University kindly sent me some of his own work, which helped me to define the nature of social constitutionalism in Latin America.

My fellow graduate students at Rutgers University were not only sources of intelligent suggestions and criticisms, but also of friendships that I treasure long after the tribulations of graduate school have faded away. In particular, David Schmitz and John Rossi deserve special note. These two fellow participants in our self-proclaimed "Rutgers School of Diplomatic History" went out of their way to share their knowledge, skills, research notes, criticisms, and suggestions. Most pleasurable of all, however, were their company and friendship. My continuing association with them has kept alive the camaraderie and sense of purpose that developed during the trials of graduate school.

I would also like to extend my thanks and appreciation to the archivists and librarians who aided my research at the National Archives, the Library of Congress, the Baker Business Library at Harvard, and the Yale University Library.

During the rewriting of my dissertation to make it into a book, many of those noted above have helped. In addition, colleagues at the University of Miami have given their time and knowledge. Robert Levine gave the manuscript a thorough and incisive reading, making comments that improved both the mechanical and the scholarly aspects of the work. Greg Bush read parts of the book, and he was especially helpful in his comments on the chapter dealing with racism.

My thanks also go to Richard Hopper and the staff of Scholarly Resources. Always competent, straightforward, and helpful, Richard and the people at Scholarly Resources were also friendly. During the months of rewriting, responding to the readers' comments, and waiting for the final outcome, the last attribute was perhaps the most important. The manuscript arrived at Richard's office in "decent" shape; it is now, I believe, in the shape I had always wanted it to be.

Finally, thanks must go to my long-suffering family. My wife, Corinne Graff-Krenn, postponed her own plans and work to become chief breadwinner and child controller during my graduate school days. Since then she has had to put up with my often single-minded attachment to "the book." Her support has amazed me; her love has held me together. An unforeseen aspect of the past few years has been that I have fallen in love with her again and again. My children, Annaleah, Madelinne, and Summer, have had the great good sense to steer clear of any involvement in what must have seemed to them like madness and have been content to grow into beautiful young ladies.

Introduction

The seeds of the present-day relationship between the United States and the nations of Latin America were sown from 1917 to 1929. This is not to say that the United States had been oblivious to the existence of the continent to its south before that time, nor to imply that it had not used, on more than one occasion, its political and economic might in attempts to influence events in that region. Indeed, prior to its entry into World War I the United States was involved actively in the Caribbean (military occupations of Haiti and Santo Domingo, colonial control over Puerto Rico, and de facto control over Cuba) and in Central America (most demonstrably in its control of the Panama Canal). Before the outbreak of World War I, however, America's political and economic dominance did not extend to the more developed and economically promising nations of South America. There the United States faced the challenges of European powers such as Great Britain, France, and Germany. U.S. trade and investments in these areas, while not insignificant in some instances, as a whole fell far behind the European presence during the early years of the twentieth century. This situation disturbed many U.S. policymakers and businessmen, but with the Europeans, especially the British, so economically entrenched there seemed to be little to do but wait and hope for a change in circumstances.

The Great War in Europe precipitated that change. While the tangled alliances on the Continent proceeded along the path to slaughter, the United States found itself in a pleasantly surprising situation vis-à-vis South America. Almost overnight the war had accomplished what a century of U.S. doctrines and economic policies had failed to effect: the nearly complete removal of the European economic grip on that region.

The American government and business interests rushed to seize this opportunity. Banks and corporations organized massive efforts to fill the vacuum created by the wartime European curtailment of trade and investments in the area. Various government agencies moved quickly to secure the new lines of political and economic influence that the United States was extending southward. An economic conference under the auspices of the Pan American Union was hurriedly called by the United States in 1915 to formalize the new relationship between the United States and all of Latin America. The war years marked a diplomatic and economic turning point.

However, one must be careful about using the word "relationship" to describe what went on between Latin America and the United States during those years. If a relationship means true and meaningful diplomatic intercourse and economic cooperation, then the contacts between the two regions did not qualify. Almost as soon as World War I began, American policymakers defined what the political and economic position of Latin America would be in the postwar world: U.S. diplomatic and economic power would entice or, if necessary, coerce the nations of Latin America into accepting U.S. policy. A number of factors led most American officials and businessmen to ignore, disregard, or disparage the efforts of those nations to determine their own postwar paths of development.[1]

Although publicly they downplayed and ridiculed these efforts, official U.S. observers were well aware that the political and economic autonomy desired by a number of the more-developed Latin American nations was a mortal threat to their goals in that region. The Mexican Revolution, culminating in the promulgation of Mexico's 1917 constitution, released a myriad of forces, the most threatening of which (to the United States) was economic nationalism. As defined by Shoshana Tancer, economic nationalism is the "desire of a nation, within the framework of the world economy, to control its own economic destiny and, within its territorial limits, to exercise its sovereign right over who may exploit natural resources and participate within various sectors of the economy."[2] During the years following the Mexican Revolution, economic nationalism in a variety of forms became an attractive alternative to Latin American nations such as Colombia, Chile, and Argentina, which sought to break free of their economic dependence on the industrialized powers. This alternative did not fit American policymakers' plans for the region. Their perceptions of the proper role of Latin America in the world economy, of U.S. interests in that region, of the challenge posed by economic nationalism, and even of the Latin Americans themselves would guide U.S. policy formation and implementation from 1917 to 1929.

This book closely examines these vital years in the history of U.S.-Latin American relations to determine the bases of U.S. policies and actions during that period and to discover the origins of many of the problems that still plague the relationship between the two regions. Chapter 1 analyzes the rapid economic penetration of Latin America by the United States after the outbreak of World War I. It also sets out the reasons why American officials believed that this penetration was so important to the economic health of the United States and the rest of the world. Chapter 2 provides a brief analysis of the Latin American side of the equation by charting the development of economic nationalism and its various manifestations in selected nations. Chapter 3 looks at the American criticisms of economic nationalism, both a general philosophical distrust of the statism inherent in such a philosophy and a belief that it would endanger not only the important U.S.-Latin American economic connection but also the workings of the entire world capitalist system. These criticisms combined to form a distinctly negative U.S. impression of economic nationalism. In Chapter 4 the roles of communism and racism in the U.S. attitude toward economic nationalism in Latin America are discussed.

Chapters 5 through 7 present case studies of how U.S. antipathy toward economic nationalism translated into specific policies directed at select nations: American efforts to curb that philosophy in Colombia during the periods 1919 to 1922 and 1926 to 1929 are discussed in Chapter 5; relations with the despotic regime of General Juan Vicente Gómez in Venezuela between 1917 and 1929 are analyzed in Chapter 6; and Chapter 7 concerns U.S. efforts to keep Brazil from following the pathway of economic nationalism through a combination of economic rewards and attempts to co-opt the politically important officer corps of the Brazilian navy. Discussions of the U.S. policies toward these nations during and after World War I will enable us to understand the various means by which the United States carried out its battle against economic nationalism. Moreover, a clear grasp of these policies is vitally important to a clearer understanding of the U.S.-Latin American relationship of today, because they became cornerstones of U.S. policies toward its neighbors to the south, a subject discussed in the concluding chapter.

This work focuses on the U.S. side of the story, for this reflects reality. The nations of Latin America were not simply inert pieces of some geopolitical jigsaw puzzle, nor would it be fair to summarize the diplomacy of 1917 to 1929 as U.S. actions merely being met by Latin American reactions. The nations of Latin America were, after all, the initiators of their own programs of economic nationalism. Still, two factors should be kept in mind. First, U.S. policymakers cared little about the opinions of their southern counterparts. When certain Latin American nations tried to implement plans involving economic nationalism, American officials evidenced no interest in discovering why those plans were being put into effect. They were interested only in nullifying those plans by whatever means possible. When the Latin Americans attempted to explain their positions, on occasion backed up by statements from American observers on the scene, they confronted the stony indifference of the U.S. government.

Second, one must keep in mind that economic nationalism in Latin America was essentially a domestic issue. In other words, despite the antiforeign sentiment that usually accompanied their implementation, programs of economic nationalism were not directed against any particular nation. From 1917 to 1929 this created a peculiar situation for the United States which, in essence, had to provide both the action and the reaction. Because the economic nationalism of the Latin American nations was not put forward as a direct attack on the United States, it was up to American officials to perceive and define it as such. Economic nationalism had to be made to seem as threatening as possible; it had to be moved from the arena of domestic policies enacted by sovereign nations to that of international efforts to disrupt and destroy the world capitalist system. Only when economic nationalism was defined in such terms could the United States justify its reactions against it. In effect, the United States reduced the nations of Latin America to mere spectators in this diplomatic ball game: Latin Americans were allowed to throw out the ceremonial first ball of economic nationalism, after which the United States not only defined what that was but also created the policies designed to eradicate it.

This study fits into a growing body of literature dealing with the foreign relations of the United States during the interwar period. Historian Melvyn Leffler has written that "the period 1919 to 1933 remains of great interest to students of American foreign policy because it constituted a transitional phase in the evolution of American diplomacy. During that time policymakers grasped the growing interdependence of the world economy."[3] More accurately, that statement should include the period from 1914 on. Nonetheless, one can hardly disagree with either Leffler's assessment of the diplomatic historian's interest in that period's events or his explanation for that interest. In the last decade a number of excellent monographs have examined this exciting period of U.S. foreign relations, focusing on the attempts of American policymakers to expand their nation's economic, political, and cultural presence around the world.[4]

It is not surprising, considering the European origins of the war that was so instrumental in changing the traditional economic and political structures of the world, that these works have concentrated on U.S. relations with the nations of Europe. All seem to agree that the U.S. policymakers saw as their primary function the expansion of the U.S. economic presence in Europe, both to fulfill domestic needs for foreign markets for American industrial production and to rationalize the often chaotic world capitalist system. To this end, the U.S. government sought to establish a cooperative relationship with American businessmen and bankers to coordinate and plan economic expansion. Indeed, as Michael Hogan has suggested, these efforts at cooperation were extended to include a working relationship with the British to bring about the desired "efficiency" in the world economic system.[5] Although historians differ concerning the level and efficiency of that expansion and rationalizing, such pursuits were the driving force behind most of America's diplomatic efforts.[6]

Various theories have been advanced to explain the rather scattershot American diplomatic efforts of that period. Leffler argues that American policymakers "did not consider export expansionism the only answer, or even the most important solution, to latent economic problems." Domestic solutions to the economic difficulties facing the nation were generally preferred. The acquisition of foreign markets was achieved if it was easily accomplished; if the effort seemed too strenuous, then it was dropped. For, in addition to the relative lack of American interest in actively pursuing foreign outlets, Leffler concludes that the United States simply did not always have the power to enforce its wishes.[7] Other scholars, such as Frank Costigliola and Joan Hoff-Wilson, point to the disunity among the various groups contributing to the making of foreign policy and argue that differences between government officials and businessmen made coordination and continuity difficult if not impossible. Hoff-Wilson concludes that it would be erroneous to believe that "economic and political foreign policies were coordinated with conspiratorial efficiency by government and business leaders."[8]

U.S. relations with Latin America during this period have not undergone such scrutiny. This is unfortunate because, while a study of those relations reveals certain similarities with U.S. policies toward Europe, important differences also exist. Indeed, given the importance of the 1917 to 1929 period in understanding U.S.-Latin American relations and the general interest shown by diplomatic historians in the interwar years, it is surprising to find so little scholarly work on this particular topic. Only two historians have written major works that focus on political and economic affairs concerning the two regions during those years. The first, Joseph Tulchin, took the view in his 1971 work *The Aftermath of War: World War I and U.S. Policy toward Latin America* that U.S. relations with Latin America during that period were basically concerned with the acquisition of cable concessions, oil deposits, and loan opportunities. All of those goals had strategic and not primarily economic ends, the achievement of which would strengthen the U.S. position in the region and prevent European incursions.[9]

Tulchin's work broke ground on this important topic, but it suffers from two main drawbacks. First, the book only covers the period until 1925. His reasoning for that rather arbitrary cutoff point is that U.S. strategic needs in Latin America (oil, markets for loans, and cable concessions) had been satisfied by that time, so American diplomats lost interest in the area. As we shall see, U.S. interest in Latin America did not slacken during the 1920s; indeed, it may have increased. Second, Tulchin overlooks the impact of the Mexican Revolution on U.S. relations with the other nations of Latin America. The battle against economic nationalism, which was paramount in the minds of U.S. policymakers, is therefore ignored.

The only other major work undertaken on this topic is Robert N. Seidel's *Progressive Pan Americanism: Development and United States Policy toward South America, 1906–1931*, which was also published in 1971. Seidel's thesis is that, during the early 1900s, U.S. policymakers "began a search for policies to allay South American mistrust of the United States and to build opportunities for peaceful and mutually profitable economic development." That search resulted in a program that "assumed notable characteristics of American Progressivism."[10]

Seidel builds this interesting thesis around two major points. First, Latin American leaders "who viewed economic progress as crucial for their states recognized the need for the participation of foreign interests and capital, and seemed to accept the secondary status to which Progressive Pan Americanism relegated their countries."[11] While that statement holds true for some nations, notably Brazil, it is hardly an appropriate summation of the South American attitude as a whole, and it is especially erroneous when applied to most of the more developed nations of that region. The leaders of Chile, Argentina, Uruguay, and Colombia may have acknowledged the secondary status that their countries found themselves in, but their programs of economic nationalism, which varied in intensity from nation to nation, demonstrated that they did not accept that status as the natural order of things.

Second, and perhaps more important, Seidel claims that the United States "did not view underdeveloped nations merely as fruitful markets for American business and as objects of the competitive and imperialistic designs of industrial powers." The evidence presented in this study suggests that U.S. leaders took precisely that view of underdeveloped nations, especially in Latin America, often in language that left no room for doubt. Thus, when Seidel writes that the United States "believed that foreign capital, enterprise, and technology would promote economic growth abroad," he is correct only in a very narrow sense.[12] Because U.S. leaders believed that Latin Americans were incapable of constructing workable economies for themselves due to their inherent racial inferiority, they perceived that foreign, preferably American, technology and money were needed to exploit the riches of Latin America. Yet, when Seidel speaks of "economic growth" in terms of "Progressive Pan Americanism," he goes astray. That "economic growth," U.S. business leaders and government officials made quite clear, was to be directed and controlled by the United States primarily for its own benefit. Real progress for Latin America was discussed in vague, futuristic terms, if at all.

Beyond the studies by Tulchin and Seidel, the secondary works on U.S.-Latin American relations during the interwar period take a bilateral approach in which U.S. relations with a particular nation in South America are isolated for study. Few works deal with the three nations used in this study—Colombia, Venezuela, and Brazil.[13] Furthermore, these studies all share a common weakness: By merely recounting the diplomacy between the United States and one particular South American nation, they portray the relations as having occurred in an international vacuum, which was far from the case. A fundamental concept of this study is that one cannot hope to understand the U.S.-Colombian, U.S.-Venezuelan, or U.S.-Brazilian relationships until the larger context of U.S.-Latin American relations is understood.

Mention also should be made of Robert Freeman Smith's *The United States and Revolutionary Nationalism in Mexico, 1916–1932.* Any historian attempting to understand U.S.-Latin American relations during this period owes a debt to Smith's ground-breaking study, which expanded the issues raised by Mexico's revolution into a study of American relations with other Latin American nations. Smith, however, spends much of his effort on U.S.-Central American and Caribbean affairs.[14] This work suggests that a more fruitful approach is to examine U.S.-South American relations, for it was in those nations that economic nationalism developed most strongly after World War I. Consequently, the American view of those nations is much more revealing of the U.S. attitude toward economic nationalism. Smith also underestimates the influence of anticommunism in the American position.

My hope for this work, like that of all historians embarking on scholarly investigations, is that it will both build upon the groundwork of those who have gone before and serve as a takeoff point for those who will follow. In the years since 1929, U.S. relations with South America, and with all of Latin America, have acquired tremendous importance and have been a source of tragedy, regrets, and recriminations. A prelude to changing that situation must start at the beginning by turning to the years from 1917 to 1929.

Notes

1. A recent work by Mark Gilderhus, *Pan American Visions: Woodrow Wilson in the Western Hemisphere, 1913–1921* (Tucson, 1986), argues that Wilson's major aim in Latin America was a "drive for regional integration" that would "bind the nations [of the Western Hemisphere] together in a common purpose and would elevate the conduct of international relations to a higher, more edified plane" (156). This book is an important contribution to a better understanding of the vague phrase "Pan Americanism." However, the research undertaken for this present study comes to very different conclusions regarding U.S. intentions during and after World War I. Notwithstanding Wilson's statements concerning the "natural harmonies and ultimate compatibilities of interest and aspiration" (156) that existed between the United States and Latin America, very little of that rhetoric found its way into U.S. policy. For instance, Gilderhus points to the creation of the International High Commission in 1915 as an example of Wilson's Pan Americanism. It was charged with the "responsibility of devising practical means for achieving the larger goals held in common" between the United States and Latin America (61). This claim underestimates the racist attitudes exhibited by U.S. policymakers and businessmen; see their views on how those "common goals" should be achieved in Chapter 4.

2. Shoshana Tancer, *Economic Nationalism in Latin America: The Quest for Economic Independence* (New York, 1976), 12.

3. Melvyn Leffler, *The Elusive Quest: America's Pursuit of European Stability and French Security, 1919–1933* (Chapel Hill, 1979), 368.

4. Of the many fine works written on American diplomacy during the 1920s, the following especially are recommended: Leffler, *Elusive Quest*; Michael Hogan, *Informal Entente: The Private Structure of Cooperation in Anglo-American Economic Diplomacy, 1918–1928* (Columbia, 1977); Joan Hoff-Wilson, *American Business and Foreign Policy, 1920–1933* (Lexington, 1971); Frank Costigliola, *Awkward Dominion: American Political, Economic, and Cultural Relations with Europe, 1919–1933* (Ithaca, 1984); and Emily Rosenberg, *Spreading the American Dream: American Economic and Cultural Expansion, 1890–1945* (New York, 1982).

5. Hogan, *Informal Entente*.

6. Leffler, *Elusive Quest*, refers to the "elusive" nature of such American efforts concerning France. Costigliola's *Awkward Dominion* concludes that American efforts to influence Europe resulted in an "awkward dominion" at best.

7. Leffler, *Elusive Quest*, 362.

8. Costigliola, *Awkward Dominion;* Hoff-Wilson, *American Business*, xv.

9. Joseph Tulchin, *The Aftermath of War: World War I and U.S. Policy toward Latin America* (New York, 1971).

10. Robert Neal Seidel, *Progressive Pan Americanism: Development and United States Policy toward South America, 1906–1931* (Ithaca, 1971), 1.

11. Ibid., 2.

12. Ibid., 652.

13. For Brazil, one must rely on general histories, the two best of which are Lawrence Hill, *Diplomatic Relations between the United States and Brazil* (Durham, 1932), which is quite out of date; and Roger W. Fontaine, *Brazil and the United States: Toward a Maturing Relationship* (Washington, 1974), a slim volume that offers only one page on the years 1917 to 1929. The situation is better for U.S.-Colombian relations. Two good but very old works are E. Taylor Parks, *Colombia and the United States, 1765–1934* (New York, 1968), which was originally published in 1935; and J. Fred Rippy, *The Capitalists and Colombia* (New York, 1931). Stephen J. Randall, *The Diplomacy of Modernization: Colombian-American Relations, 1920–1940* (Toronto, 1977), is a valuable contribution, although it suffers from the same general weakness of all bilateral studies. I also would question his use of the term "modernization" to describe the goals of U.S. policy in Colombia during those years and, because petroleum plays such a large role in the book, why he begins his study in 1920, when a 1919 Colombian oil decree set the tone for later confrontations with the United States. A more recent work, Richard L. Lael, *Arrogant Diplomacy: U.S. Policy toward Colombia, 1903–1922* (Wilmington, 1987), focuses on the tensions produced by U.S. actions during the Panamanian revolution of 1903 and the subsequent diplomatic efforts to soothe Colombia's indignation. Like Randall's book, it does not expand much beyond its strictly bilateral approach, although it raises some interesting points concerning U.S. strategic concerns in Colombia. Two books published in recent years have explored the relationship between the United States and Venezuela. Sheldon B. Liss, *Diplomacy and Dependency: Venezuela, the United States and the Americas* (Salisbury, 1978), covers the period 1810 to 1977. Its narrative approach fails to put the relationship into the larger context of America's Latin American policy as a whole. Stephen Rabe, *The Road to OPEC: United States Relations with Venezuela, 1919–1976* (Austin, 1982), is an excellent book, although it contains only twenty-two pages on the 1920s. Furthermore, the work is primarily concerned with the Anglo-American competition for oil concessions in Venezuela during those years, failing to consider some larger questions dealing with the U.S. relationship with the Gómez dictatorship.

In addition to these bilateral studies, another group of monographs has attacked the issue of U.S.-Latin American relations during the post-World War I period in a slightly different manner. Gilderhus, *Pan American Visions*, and Kenneth J. Grieb, *The Latin American Policy of Warren G. Harding* (Fort Worth, 1976), use the policies of particular presidents as their points of departure. While it is important to note that differences did exist between the several administrations that served during the years 1917 to 1929, it is perhaps more vital to note the Latin American policy continuities from administration to administration.

14. Robert Freeman Smith, *The United States and Revolutionary Nationalism in Mexico, 1916–1932* (Chicago, 1972).

Chapter One

"Amazing Figures": Growth of the U.S. Economic Presence in Latin America

World War I opened up vast new opportunities for U.S. trade and investment in Latin America, but the years during and after the conflict also brought a sharper definition of the importance and place of the Latin American market in regard to U.S. interests, needs, and worldwide economic goals. This new definition shaped the U.S. response to the challenge of economic nationalism.

In his 1927 work, *The Foreign Expansion of American Banks: American Branch Banking Abroad*, Clyde W. Phelps evaluated the impact of World War I on the foreign trade of the United States. "The rapidly growing foreign trade of the United States had raised our nation by 1913 to a firm position among the greatest foreign trading countries of the world," he wrote, "but for seven years after this date our trade no longer simply grew in value; it leaped into amazing figures." He placed much of the credit for that "leap" on the American expansion into the "neutral" markets of the Far East and, especially, Latin America. In addition, he pointed to the "promising" amount of U.S. investment in Latin America, which had grown to over $4 billion by 1925.[1] "Amazing" and "promising" were but two of the many adjectives used by American businessmen and government officials to describe the growth of the U.S. economic presence in Latin America following the outbreak of the war and into the postwar period.

The onset of the Great War in Europe produced serious dislocations in America's foreign trade structure. E. E. Pratt, chief of the Commerce Department's Bureau of Foreign and Domestic Commerce (BFDC) concluded in a 1915 report that "it is not too much to say that the United States experienced the severest financial strain in her history during those weeks." Foreign trade "came practically to a

standstill . . . and for a few days business stood paralyzed." All of
that brought home the necessity of overseas commerce with
"compelling force."[2] Yet out of that seeming disaster arose a number of
tempting opportunities for American business. Both Pratt and Secretary
of Commerce William Redfield were quick to see that, since Great
Britain, Germany, and France were forced by the exigencies of war to
curtail much of their overseas trade and investment, some other nation
would have to fill that huge economic void. To Redfield the answer
seemed obvious: Only the United States had "the plants, the labor, and
the means to supply the wants of mankind. The nations turn to us."
Pratt spoke of America's new role as an "obligation" to "supply to the
newer countries raw materials, manufactured goods, finances, and
most important of all, enterprise."[3] While the BFDC chief might have
seen the situation as an "obligation" of American business, it was
hardly likely that U.S. business interests viewed it as a particularly
onerous burden. The economic disruption caused by the war opened up
vast new opportunities for American foreign trade, and both business
and government moved quickly to see that they were secured.[4]

One of the most promising areas for the expansion of U.S. foreign
trade and investment was Latin America, especially the larger nations of
South America. Before World War I, U.S. traders and investors found
themselves confronted with a formidable competitor for those markets:
Great Britain. In 1913, for example, Great Britain had exported over
$300 million worth of products to South America and had nearly $4
billion invested in the region. The United States, in stark contrast,
exported only $178 million worth of goods to the area, and its
investments totaled a mere $173 million.[5]

The war drastically altered that situation. In Latin America, as in the
United States, the economic repercussions of the war were hard felt.
Indeed, as a Commerce Department report noted, the effects in America
were "scarcely to be compared in importance and severity with the
situation which was forced upon the various countries of Latin-
America." The American ambassador in Chile, Henry P. Fletcher,
provided an eyewitness account in 1914 of the impact of the war on the
economy: "This country, which depended almost entirely upon
revenues derived from export duties on nitrate and its import tariff
duties, is very severely affected. . . . This war undoubtedly offers to us
a great opportunity in this market and I believe that our business men at
home are fully alive to the situation. But our trade will not be built up
on speeches at banquets and wishes."[6] Businessmen, bankers, and
government officials back in the states obviously agreed with Fletcher's
assessment, and they actively worked together not to let that golden
opportunity pass by them.

Officials in the Commerce, Treasury, and State departments were
all eager to aid and encourage the expansion of America's foreign trade

and investment, especially that portion of it dealing with Latin America, both during and after the war. Just two months after the outbreak of the conflict, Secretary Redfield wrote about the great contribution the Department of Commerce was making toward promoting American commerce with Latin America. He listed an impressive number of accomplishments including the sending of "trained commercial attachés" to the South American cities of Lima, Buenos Aires, Santiago, and Rio de Janeiro; the establishment of branch offices of the BFDC in Boston, New York, Chicago, Seattle, San Francisco, New Orleans, and Atlanta; a congressional appropriation of $50,000 to the BFDC for promoting trade with Latin America; and the ever-increasing work of the BFDC in disseminating commercial data to American businessmen.[7] The Commerce Department was convinced that such encouragement was needed during the war, because businessmen might lose sight of the "greatest opportunities" awaiting them in Latin America by concentrating their attention on the European war trade. This would be disastrous, for the United States would be "foregoing the permanent markets of the world to make a few extra dollars of immediate profit," as a 1915 BFDC report stated. Redfield, for one, was delighted at the prospect of business and government both striving to build America's foreign trade structure. He wrote in 1916 that "it is one thing to criticize and correct business evils. It is another and a happier thing to give to business a helping hand. It is well that the latter has come to be the prevailing practice."[8]

William Gibbs McAdoo, secretary of the treasury, was equally vocal in his support and encouragement of America's foreign trade, and promoting U.S.-Latin American commerce became a personal goal for the secretary. In February 1917, McAdoo wrote to Thomas Lamont of J. P. Morgan and Company concerning Lamont's impending visit to the department to discuss a loan to Argentina. McAdoo was overflowing with praise for the bankers' plans, and he promised to "lend whatever influence I possess to every worthy effort in that direction." He dramatically concluded that "no American's vision is large enough if it does not comprehend Latin America within its scope."[9]

In addition to aiding American businessmen and bankers in Latin America through his personal work and influence, McAdoo also believed that the Inter-American High Commission (IAHC), established in 1915 by the Pan American Union (PAU) to study economic questions, might be useful. As McAdoo explained in a 1915 letter to Leo S. Rowe of the PAU, "the main task" of expanding U.S. trade with Latin America "rests with the business men of the country. The most that the national government can do is create a favorable environment." For McAdoo, strong business and banking representation on the American Section of the IAHC would go far toward creating that "favorable environment." The secretary therefore worked to enlist those representatives.[10]

Writing to John H. Fahey, president of the Chamber of Commerce of the United States, in June 1915, McAdoo asked him to consider a position in the American Section. The secretary proceeded to list the names of others who had already joined: Elbert Gary of U.S. Steel; George Reynolds, president of Continental and Commercial National Bank; Henry Davison of J. P. Morgan and Company; and McAdoo himself. Outlining the functions of the IAHC for Fahey, McAdoo declared that "the main objects we have in view, namely, the strengthening of financial, commercial and political relationships with our sister American Republics, can be accomplished." In 1920 an American member of one of the IAHC's conventions, Paul Warburg, explained the purposes of the commission to Norman Davis in blunter terms: "The work of the Commission is not worth while doing, unless it is in charge of people who believe in the 'long shot.' The banking and finance problems involved had to be approached from the point of view of the ultimate ideal. That was: The United States established as a highly developed banking center, to which the entire American hemisphere should look as its logical point of support."[11]

As the war began to draw to a close, the State Department started to suggest ways in which the United States could retain and even enlarge its economic presence in Latin America. In a May 1918 memorandum concerning a proposed American mission to Latin America, the roles to be played by the members of such a mission were clearly spelled out. Since new trade treaties would be needed, at least two "commercial experts, appointed perhaps by the National Chamber of Commerce," would be required. A banker would be a desirable member of the mission, as he could discuss "the making of loans . . . and their banking problems." Even the military representative of such an entourage would have an important commercial task: He should "encourage the purchase in the United States of warships and military supplies."[12]

Members of the department also were keenly aware of the value of improved lines of communication to the markets to the south. Writing to Bernard Baruch in October 1918, Gordon Auchincloss of the department noted that steel and copper were needed for the construction of cable lines to Argentina and Brazil. He was aware that these materials were vital to the war effort, but he hastened to point out the benefits, primarily those accruing from the "commercial aspect" of the cables. "This aspect is important at present," Auchincloss continued, "but it will be many times more important at the close of the war."[13]

Congressional actions also indicated a deep and intense interest in securing and furthering America's trade and investments during and after World War I. Two pieces of legislation in particular, the Webb-

Pomerene Act passed in 1918 and the Edge Act of 1919, illustrate that interest. The former, also known as the Export Trade Act, exempted business combinations for export purposes from antitrust requirements. The latter was designed to aid the formation of banking enterprises involved in the export trade. Both acts sought to aid America's export activities in the postwar commercial system.[14]

The 1920s saw no slackening of government interest in expanding America's foreign trade and investment. This was especially true for the Department of Commerce. In June 1921, during the latter part of the postwar depression, chief of the BFDC Julius Klein saw his bureau as meeting the "increased demands of American manufacturers who are planning to hold and extend their markets abroad," especially those interests concerned with Latin American trade since, while America's foreign trade as a whole had declined during the depression, trade with Latin America had generally increased. In 1922, with business conditions in the nation showing general improvement, Secretary of Commerce Herbert Hoover reported on a conference held with 150 representatives of commerce and industry. Calls had been issued there for the reorganization of the foreign trade service, with the specific suggestion that the BFDC should have divisions specializing in information on particular products that might be exported.[15]

By 1923, however, and the return of full prosperity to the nation, Commerce saw its role in a different light. Indeed, the prosperity of the nation was seen as something of a threat to its growing foreign trade, as the department believed that wealth might breed apathy toward foreign commerce. To counteract "such untoward developments," the BFDC in particular presented to American businessmen the "advantages of unremitting exertion in the foreign markets." In 1928 the bureau proudly pointed out that the "keen interest that has been manifested in our commercial relations with Latin America during the past decade continues unabated." As proof the BFDC noted that, while business requests for aid in trading matters in other areas of the world had decreased in recent years, requests for such aid for Latin American activities had actually increased 10 percent since 1923.[16] It was evident that the government's active encouragement and aid to American businessmen and investors for the expansion of foreign commerce had not been in vain. Furthermore, right up to the year before the Great Crash, government officials were still calling for "unremitting exertion" in the growth of that commerce, especially with Latin America.

Such calls were hardly necessary, for American banking and business interests, from the beginning of the war, had been very aware of the opportunities for investment and trade in Latin America. Some good indications of the fervent interest in developing those opportunities are found in the pages of *The Americas*, a monthly magazine put out by the National City Bank of New York. Not coincidentally, the publication first appeared in October 1914, just two months after World War I had begun. Articles with colorful titles such as "The Friendly Brazilian and His Country" and "The Amazing Argentine" attempted to portray Latin America as a gold mine of commercial opportunities waiting to be developed by ambitious and farsighted American interests.[17]

Those interests responded enthusiastically to calls such as those emanating from *The Americas* and the BFDC. Trade with South America was a vital topic at the Trade Conference held in Atlanta, the New York Merchants' Association, the Jacksonville Board of Trade, the Business Men's League in St. Louis, the American Exporters' Association, the Machine Tool Builders' Convention, the American Hardware Association, and the New England Jewelers' Association.[18]

Banking interests were also alive to the possibilities in Latin America. Early in World War I representatives of some of the largest banks in America were calling for investment in and extension of dollar credits to Latin America. James H. Perkins, vice president of the National City Bank, argued in July 1915 that American bankers "must be prepared to go out into the world and invest capital in other countries in order to obtain a control over their markets." The manager of the Foreign Department of Crocker National Bank made the same point when he urged the loaning of $500 million to Latin America to "create a corresponding increase in our trade with them." He also argued strenuously that a good knowledge of Spanish was vital for that trade and should be made compulsory in American schools.[19]

At first there was a difference of opinion between American bankers and businessmen over the best way to approach the Latin American market. Businessmen argued that "trade follows investment," while bankers argued just the opposite.[20] Eventually both groups were able to see that trade and investment in Latin America went hand in hand. When they decided to work together, they did so in a big way. The November 1915 issue of *The Americas* announced the formation of "The New Machinery for American Financing Abroad," the American International Corporation (AIC). Armed with $50 million for "directing and promoting a larger participation by this country in the world's commerce and constructive work," the AIC included some of the largest banking and business concerns in America. On its original board of directors sat representatives of Armour and Company; General Electric; W. R. Grace and Company; Great Northern Railways; Kuhn, Loeb and Company; American Telephone and Telegraph; Union Pacific; Standard Oil; Anaconda Copper; Guaranty Trust Company; Ingersoll-Rand; and National City Bank.[21]

The AIC quickly made its presence known, especially in Latin America. In December 1915 the corporation purchased the remaining seven ships of the Pacific Mail Steamship Company, which served

Central America. In 1917 the AIC published figures on the number of investing and trading propositions concerning Latin America that had been referred to its research department, figures that were well ahead of those for any other geographical division, including Europe. By 1918 the corporation had noted that it had entered into a multimillion dollar arrangement in Uruguay for the construction of public works. In 1919 the AIC proudly announced the acquisition of G. Amsinck and Company, a large import-export firm with offices throughout Latin America. Its subsidiaries were active in 1919–1921, building docks in Colombia and railroads in Bolivia.[22]

The AIC was not the only participant in the race for commercial advantages in Latin America. A number of other interests were aware that the disruption brought about by the war could work in their favor. Daniel Guggenheim, president of the American Smelting and Refining Company, wrote to Dwight Morrow of J. P. Morgan and Company in 1916 about the possibilities opened up in Chile by the war, specifically in the nitrate industry. "The opportunity is now presented," he claimed, "of organizing this great nitrate field into a modern, up-to-date, American industry." Thomas Lamont, in response to McAdoo's encouraging letter concerning the expansion of American investment and trade into Latin America, assured the secretary that "an informal group of banks and bankers formed for the purpose of cultivating such business in South America" had been quite active in the field. Some of its major accomplishments had been loans of over $100 million to Argentina, the purchase of $18 million worth of securities in two railroads, and preliminary negotiations with the governments of Chile and Uruguay concerning loans.[23]

Banking interests also participated in a more direct fashion in aiding U.S.-Latin American commerce by setting up branch banks in the nations to the south. The Federal Reserve Act, passed in 1913, had authorized the establishment of such branches, but, as Clyde Phelps noted, "the Federal Reserve Act *permitted*, but the abnormal world credit situation created by the war *impelled* the striking expansion in American foreign banking facilities after 1914."[24] The withdrawal of many of the large European investment houses, together with the influx of new and expanding American concerns into Latin America, made the establishment of branch banks imperative to provide up-to-the-minute data and expedite U.S.-Latin American commercial intercourse. As the *Journal of the American Banking Association* put it in 1917, South America was the "natural field" for U.S. banks run by "large visioned managers. . . . With such a program, . . . the post-war possibilities for the expansion of our banking business in South America are infinite."[25]

The encouragement and aid of the government combined with avid banking and business interests to bring a dramatic growth in the economic penetration of South America by U.S. concerns during the war and postwar years. From the 1913 figure of $178 million, U.S. exports to South America grew to $465 million in 1927; total U.S.-South American trade had reached nearly $1 billion by then, a 160 percent increase from 1913. American trade with Argentina rose from $96 million in 1913 to $260 million in 1927; for Colombia, the figures were $22 million to $136 million. Equally encouraging was the fact that the United States had surpassed the British in terms of trade with South America. Although Great Britain's trade with that region increased 24 percent from 1913 to 1927, its total South American trade amounted to just under $750 million, far below the American figure. Furthermore, it had lost its trading lead to the United States in Chile, Paraguay, Peru, Uruguay, and Venezuela.[26]

The effect of the increase in U.S.-South American trade on the nation's foreign trade figures was quite evident to informed observers. John Williams, an assistant professor of banking at Northwestern University, wrote in 1921 concerning the new trend in American foreign trade that "the percentage of exports to Europe had diminished rapidly, reaching the lowest figure in our history." It was Canada, Asia, and South America that were responsible for "the remarkable increase in our imports since the armistice." The annual report of the Commerce Department in 1924 plainly stated the facts: "The gain in our total trade over the fiscal year 1913 is largely accounted for by the marked increase in our trade with Asia, Oceania, and South America."[27]

The increase in American investment in South America was even more spectacular and, in many ways, more important. By 1929 the United States had $2.29 billion invested in South America, a 1226 percent increase from 1913. While this was still far behind the total British investment in South America of $4.4 billion, it should be noted that nearly half of the British investment was in one nation, Argentina. In Chile, Colombia, Ecuador, Peru, and Venezuela the United States had taken the lead from the British in investments.[28] More significant, perhaps, than the sheer magnitude of the American investments in South America by 1929 was the sort of investments they were. They were not simply government loans; by and large, American investments in South America during the postwar years were direct investments, primarily in mining and agricultural activities. From platinum mines in Colombia, to oil fields in Venezuela, to coffee plantations in Brazil, to Chilean nitrate fields, American money was heavily involved in diverse extractive industries in South America.

The U.S. investment in mining concerns in South America, excluding oil, more than doubled between 1914 and 1929, going from over $220 million to nearly $530 million. Much of that increase was due to American participation in the Chilean copper industry, but American money also financed the mining of gold, silver, lead, tin, zinc, manganese, vanadium, tungsten, nitrates, platinum, iron ore, coal, bauxite, and a variety of precious stones. It was oil, however, that saw the most dramatic increase in American investment. From a mere $22 million investment in 1914 in the three most promising nations in South America for oil development (Peru, Colombia, and Venezuela), there grew a $444 million investment by 1929. These are astronomical figures compared to the $170 million American investment in manufacturing concerns in South America in 1929. Only 44 branches of American interests had been set up in Argentina, Brazil, Chile, and Uruguay by 1929, compared to 821 established in Europe and Canada by that time.[29] The message was clear enough: American investors in South America looked upon that region primarily as a reservoir of raw materials waiting to be developed. Indeed, when some American interests began to argue that U.S. loans to and investments in Latin America had given an "impulse" to competing local manufacturers, the *Journal of the ABA* countered by stating that "the industrial development in Latin America, however, is not likely to affect for a long time to come the exportation of goods that make up the bulk of our export trade."[30]

Other indications of the U.S. financial interest in Latin America were the numerous trading and selling organizations and branch banks established there after 1914. The expansion of selling organizations in South America was particularly striking. Established to encourage the import-export trade and to make important and profitable foreign business contacts, there were only $20 million worth of those organizations in South America in 1914. By 1929 there were over $94 million, second only to the figure for Europe. Branch banks also appeared everywhere in Latin America. By 1926 sixty-one had been set up in that area, with twelve of those in South America. In Europe there were only twenty-five branches, and in Asia there were twenty-one.[31]

As impressive as all of those numbers were, they were not so important in and of themselves. During the war, and especially during the postwar years, the American economic position in Latin America (and in the Far East as well) was seen by U.S. policymakers as a vital key to the structural health of both the national and international economic systems. The prevailing view in government and business circles came to be that this economic interaction was not simply profitable but absolutely necessary to the well-being of the nation. Commenting in September 1915 on the great opportunities for American trade and investment in South America, W. S. Kies of the National City Bank concluded that "the people of this country must be taught that a large foreign commerce means permanent prosperity." The Commerce Department emphatically agreed. In 1917 it equated "loans abroad, investments abroad, sales abroad, services abroad" with "employment, activity, occupation" at home.[32]

That view gained meaning during the economic crisis of 1919–1921. The postwar crunch led BFDC Director Roy S. MacElwee to state the problem in no uncertain terms:

> The only real insurance that will spread the risks of the depression between the crests of the waves of domestic demand is the allotting of a substantial quota of the firm's product for foreign commerce and the building up in the world's markets of a selling organization and clientele that will not necessarily fluctuate with the waves of demand at home. Many American firms recognize that the quota of their production set aside for the purpose of firmly establishing their foreign business is the best insurance against depressions at home.

Latin America, in addition to the Far East, was an especially important element of that equation because, as MacElwee noted, it was one of the "logical markets for our surplus products."[33] In 1928, one year before the collapse, the BFDC was still painting a dismal picture of what would happen if America's vital foreign trade were "suddenly cut off." "A great army of workers" would be left jobless, and "hundreds of thousands of those who are producing for purely domestic consumption" also would find themselves unemployed.[34] Clearly America's foreign trade, and particularly its Latin American trade, required protection to prevent such ugly episodes.

More was involved in the equation, however, than American exports to Latin America. Of equal, if not more importance, were the goods that the United States imported from the nations of that region, particularly from resource-rich South America. American demand for, and reliance on, the mineral and agricultural resources of South America increased from 1914 to 1929. The changing role of imported raw materials in the industrial complex of the United States was reflected in American imports from 1875 to 1925. In 1875 raw materials for manufacturing comprised just 14.8 percent of America's total imports. By 1913 the figure had risen to 35.05 percent, and by 1925 it was 40.7 percent.[35]

The natural resources of South America were viewed by Americans as key import goods. An article in a 1914 issue of *The Americas* stated that "the United States now imports over $750,000,000 worth of tropical and subtropical products annually, a very large part of it of the class which South America produces and can produce in increasing quantities." A vibrant import-export trade with that region was essential, since the goods that South America could provide were those that "the United States requires for use in its factories, fields and homes." This belief was more fully laid out in a 1918 report entitled "Relations between United States and Other Countries regarding Important Materials" prepared by the American Section of the Allied

Maritime Transport Council. This document described the resource needs of the United States and how Latin America could meet them. Among the materials that the report said would come primarily from South America were bismuth, coffee, copper, hides and skins, iodine, manganese, monazite sand, nitrate of soda, platinum, and wool. Manganese, from Brazil, was crucial to the American steel industry. Imports of the mineral had risen from 72,000 tons in 1914 to 541,000 tons in 1917. Chile provided nitrate of soda, which was needed for fertilizer and explosives, and it was then the only nation that could provide iodine. And, "while Russia is in chaos," the report noted, Colombia would be the largest source of platinum.[36]

The BFDC was so impressed with the need to secure natural resources in tropical areas that in 1920 it outlined the necessity for an "Institute of Tropical Research." As this draft explained, "the development of the tropics [is] where the greatest future development in the world will take place and in which the U.S. must have a part."[37] In 1921, William Redfield, then the president of the American Manufacturers' Export Association, summed up the importance of imported raw materials for the United States: "Exclude rubber, palm oil, tin, hides, manganese and many other necessary articles and great industries close till a new supply is found."[38]

Oil was by far the single most important natural resource that Latin America provided after World War I, when a number of U.S. officials became convinced that the nation was exhausting its domestic supply. Van H. Manning, director of the Bureau of Mines, pointed out in a March 1920 meeting of the Council of National Defense that American reserves would soon be depleted; the United States would be forced to look to foreign fields for its supply. He concluded that Persia, Mexico, Colombia, and Venezuela were the most likely areas for American participation in oil development. The latter two nations were "very promising." Secretary of War Newton Baker, writing to President Woodrow Wilson, commented on Manning's presentation and agreed that America would have to enter the foreign race for the oil that was so "important to America for the supply of our Navy and our industries, including shipping."[39]

Latin America continued to be a high priority in America's search for oil during the administrations of Warren Harding and Calvin Coolidge. The secretary of state under President Harding, Charles Evans Hughes, felt it necessary in 1921 to write personally to all American diplomatic offices in Latin America concerning oil. Because of the competition for the Latin American oil fields, particularly from the British, Hughes asked U.S. representatives to report fully on the situation and to offer legal aid to American interests when such aid seemed appropriate.[40]

The intense U.S. interest in developing American-owned oil properties in Latin America led to an embarrassing moment during the tenure of Secretary of State Frank B. Kellogg. The trouble began in 1926 when the Federal Oil Conservation Board (FOCB) issued a release stating that oil fields in Mexico and South America could be a "supply under the control of our citizens." That statement raised some suspicions in those regions, so in 1927 the secretary of the interior tried to make amends by claiming that the FOCB release had been misunderstood. It had meant to "urge our citizens to seek production abroad in order to better adjust conditions of world supply and demand by supplying local markets." At the State Department, one official concluded that this did "not explain *away* the former statement. It is impossible to do that because the former statement admits to very little explanation."[41]

Not unexpectedly, a consensus developed among American businessmen and government officials that the export of U.S. manufactured goods to Latin America in return for raw materials was a natural and completely favorable product of the world economic structure. As the *Journal of the ABA* put it in 1917, "We have what they need in manufactured goods, and they have what we are coming more and more to need in the way of raw materials."[42]

This system seemed to be obvious, necessary, and beneficial, for it met the demands of both the United States and Latin America. As BFDC Director MacElwee stated in 1920, "The tropical and subtropical raw materials that they [Latin America and Asia] produce are indispensable to our factories. On the other hand, they are in need of our manufactured products, and an exchange is therefore mutually profitable." Redfield, in analyzing foreign and domestic commerce, concluded that "the interdependence of these two forms of our general commerce goes deeper. One cannot exist without the other." The *Journal of the ABA* commented approvingly in 1928 on the U.S.-Latin American economic relationship: "The United States found in the Latin-American markets an excellent outlet for its surplus production. It found countries rich in natural resources which could be conveniently exploited in the interest of American industries."[43]

For the United States, then, trade with Latin America served vital needs of the American national economy by providing "convenient" and "logical" markets for surplus manufactures which lessened the chances for depression in the United States while also providing the "indispensable" raw materials that fueled those same manufacturing concerns. The system seemed to form a coherent, viable, profitable whole. The system also could prove to be a vicious circle, but in the financially heady days of the 1920s no one in the United States seemed to notice.

American concerns for the development and protection of the U.S. economy coincided and overlapped with the drive for a viable and "open" world economy. Following the war's catastrophic economic effects, a consensus grew among American policymakers that it was increasingly difficult to separate the two, that the national and world economies were complexly intertwined and the healthy development of one was necessary for the other. Speaking in 1919, Woodrow Wilson drove home this point: "I believe that our business men, our merchants, our manufacturers and our capitalists will have the vision to see that prosperity in one part of the world ministers to prosperity everywhere: that there is in a very true sense a solidarity of interest throughout the world of enterprise."[44]

This belief in the interdependence of the world economy was echoed both by Norman Davis, a former undersecretary of state, in 1926 and by Secretary of Commerce Hoover in 1928. Davis, speaking to a group of journalists, noted that the "tides of commerce" were "overflowing the lands of every nation" and cautioned that the "delicately adjusted . . . machinery" should not be disturbed by international conflict. Hoover also pictured the world economic system as a "machine" that had to be "kept in tune."[45] Keeping the machinery of world capitalism running required equal access to markets, equal opportunities for trade and investment, and equal access to raw materials. And it required that each cog of that machinery perform the roles best suited to it.

The postwar international capitalist system, however, faced some serious challenges to its finely tuned workings. When DeWitt C. Poole, American counselor in Russia, wrote in 1919 that the "vital problem" for America was to lead the nations of the world "between the Scylla of reaction on the one hand and the Charybdis of Bolshevism on the other," he was describing a problem both political and economic.[46]

The monstrous Scylla of reaction was embodied in the postwar economic plans of nations such as Great Britain and France, plans that called for closed preferential economic systems in sharp contrast to the open market system desired by America. That the Allies might embark on such a path had become plain during the war, when representatives from France, Great Britain, and Russia met to discuss economic matters. As historian Lloyd C. Gardner has described it:

> Among other recommendations, the Allies called upon one another to make themselves totally independent of the enemy countries. Resolutions calling for government sponsored and subsidized industries, and for extensive revisions of tariffs and pre-war trade treaties, served as a warning to neutrals as well as enemies that an economic revolution against the largely free trade or laissez-faire system was gaining momentum.[47]

In a memorandum to Secretary of State Robert Lansing in 1916, Henry Fletcher claimed, with some concern, that "the Paris Conference [the above-mentioned wartime meeting of the Allies] and the trend of certain sections of public opinion in England and Europe would seem to indicate a possibility—at least, of the extension of the present military alliance of the Entente Powers to cover the economic field as well." Lansing was quite concerned and wrote to President Wilson on 23 June 1916. The plans made by the Allies at Paris would "cause a serious, if not critical, situation for the nations outside the union by creating unusual and artificial economic conditions," and would "materially affect our industrial and commercial life." Edward House, who had been sent a copy of the memorandum, also was alarmed. House, one of Wilson's most trusted advisers, attempted to convince the president of the dangers inherent in such closed systems. In October 1917 he wrote to Wilson that trade restrictions of all sorts should be removed, as they constituted a "menace to peace." The end of tariffs, subsidies, and the establishment of freedom of the seas would mean that "the world could look with confidence to the future." He added that "there should be no monopoly by any nation of raw materials, or the essentials for food and clothing."[48]

Just three days after writing to Wilson, House met with the president to advise Wilson to "lay down the doctrine that nations should be equally unselfish regarding commerce. There should be complete freedom of commerce upon the seas, no preferential tariffs or transportation rates upon land, making the staple products and raw materials of the world accessible to all." House recorded in his diary that his plea had made quite an impression on the president; by the end of his talk, Wilson had tears in his eyes.[49] Wilson became convinced that the economic policies of the European nations, especially those of Great Britain, posed a major problem for the postwar world. In 1920 he wrote that "we are on the eve of a commercial war of the severest sort."[50]

While the economic policies of England and France were seen as possible danger spots, the far more serious Charybdis of bolshevism threatened to pull the entire capitalist structure into its whirlpool of destruction and anarchy.[51] Poole put it menacingly in his 1919 memorandum: "It is the essence of the Bolshevik movement that it is *international and not national in character*." The Bolsheviks were "pure destructionists" bent on the "subversion of all Governments." One of their major goals, revealed in a 23 January 1919 call for the Third International, was the "immediate expropriation of capital and the elimination of the private right of owning the means of production through making them common property." Poole concluded that liberal leaders such as Wilson needed to give a "clear warning" about this danger to save the world from "barbaric reversion."[52]

In Latin America, however, neither the danger that the region would become enmeshed in Europe's closed systems nor that it would fall prey to bolshevism's anarchy was the primary threat to the American economic position in that region and to the world economic order that the United States was trying to fashion. Certainly the idea that the European powers might attempt to enclose Latin America within the folds of a closed or preferential system had occurred to American policymakers. Henry Fletcher had warned Lansing in his 1916 memorandum that the Europeans might "be able to force preferential tariff treatment in the great consuming markets of South America." He even proposed an American Economic League to prevent this. Yet, while Wilson and others believed that a "commercial war" would take place for world markets, even observers such as Fletcher doubted that attempts by Great Britain and other nations to recover their lost markets in South America would be successful. He believed that, in South America, a European Economic Alliance would not be a "workable arrangement."[53] Echoing Fletcher's assessment, in 1916, BFDC Chief Pratt doubted very much that "an economic struggle" would be waged in Latin America, because America's position after the war would be so sound and secure. By 1917 he was even more confident that "our trade with South America . . . will not be too seriously interfered with and that we may reap in the future the benefits of having cultivated those markets so assiduously and intelligently during the past few years."[54]

Even some British observers agreed. Speaking before a meeting of the Council on Foreign Relations in 1921, P. W. Wilson, a reporter for the *London News*, wondered if a "friendly demarcation" of "spheres of influence" was possible. Wilson added that "to the United States would naturally fall under the Monroe Doctrine, all the shores between Alaska, around Cape Horn and back to Greenland, with Australasia and waters implied as included."[55] Although Wilson's rather generous offer probably would have induced apoplexy among British officials, he was closer to the truth than he perhaps imagined. The United States was already putting the finishing touches on the "friendly demarcation" of its sphere of influence in Latin America.

Despite Poole's warning, the danger of international bolshevism did not spread to Latin America to any significant degree. The Communist parties that sprang up following 1917 were small, factionalized, and politically impotent. While American fears that bolshevism might find a resting place in Latin America continued through the 1920s, especially during the tenure of Secretary of State Kellogg, the Communist "threat" in that region was insignificant at most.[56]

Still, the United States faced a significant challenge, both to its direct economic interests in Latin America, especially in South America, and to its view of the proper world order and Latin America's place within that order. This real challenge was often confused with the nonexistent dangers noted above, for American observers were convinced that it combined the worst aspects of Scylla and Charybdis. That challenge was economic nationalism, and the history of U.S. relations with Latin America from 1917 to 1929 is largely concerned with the attempts of American policymakers to discover exactly what it was and how it could be stopped.

Notes

1. Clyde William Phelps, *The Foreign Expansion of American Banks: American Branch Banking Abroad* (New York, 1927), 112–14, 124.

2. U.S. Department of Commerce, *Reports of the Department of Commerce, 1915: Reports of the Secretary of Commerce and Reports of Bureaus* (Washington, 1916), 237–38 (hereafter cited as CD, *Reports of the CD*, with year).

3. Ibid., 18–19, 237.

4. A number of monographs have discussed in detail aspects of the expansion of American foreign trade both during and after World War I. John J. Broesamle, *William Gibbs McAdoo: A Passion for Change, 1863–1917* (Port Washington, 1973), discusses Secretary of the Treasury McAdoo's ardent support of foreign trade, especially with Latin America. Both Burton I. Kaufman, *Efficiency and Expansion: Foreign Trade Organization in the Wilson Administration, 1913–1921* (Westport, 1974); and Jeffrey J. Safford, *Wilsonian Maritime Diplomacy, 1913–1921* (New Brunswick, 1978), offer valuable insights into the bureaucracy that shaped and planned American foreign trade. Carl Parrini, *Heir to Empire: United States Economic Diplomacy, 1916–1923* (Pittsburgh, 1969), covers the development of foreign trade into the Harding administration and analyzes the U.S. competition with other powers for that trade. Tulchin, *Aftermath of War*, is a general account of postwar economic and political relations between Latin America and the United States, but it only covers the years up to 1925 and is very selective in its coverage.

5. Max Winkler, *Investments of United States Capital in Latin America* (Boston, 1929), 274–85.

6. CD, *Reports of the CD, 1915*, 238; Henry P. Fletcher to Edward House, 3 October 1914, Box 44, Folder 409, Edward House Papers, Yale University Library, New Haven (hereafter cited as House Papers).

7. William Redfield, "The Government's Work for Trade Expansion," *The Americas* 1 (October 1914): 9–11. The $50,000-appropriation, specifically for Latin American trade promotion, was over one fifth of the total 1914 BFDC budget of $224,000. See also CD, *Reports of the CD, 1914* (Washington, 1915), 21.

8. CD, *Reports of the CD, 1915*, 241; *Reports of the CD, 1916* (Washington, 1917), 22.

9. McAdoo to Thomas Lamont, 8 February 1917, Box 81, Folder 27, Thomas Lamont Papers, Baker Library, Harvard University, Cambridge (hereafter cited as Lamont Papers).

10. McAdoo to Leo S. Rowe, 10 December 1915, Box 25, Record Group 43, Records of U.S. Participation in International Conferences, Commissions, and Expositions: Records of the Inter-American High Commission, National Archives, Washington (hereafter cited as RG 43, Records of IAHC).

11. McAdoo to John H. Fahey, 23 June 1915, Box 24, RG 43, Records of the IAHC; Paul Warburg [?] to Norman Davis, 12 February 1920, Box 28, Folder 426, Papers of Frank Polk, Yale University Library, New Haven (hereafter cited as Polk Papers). That Warburg was likely the author is suggested by the letter's reference to the writer's work with Archibald Kains, president of the American Foreign Banking Corporation, on the International Gold Clearance Fund Convention of the IAHC. Warburg figured prominently in that convention and worked closely with Kains.

12. Division of Latin American Affairs, memorandum on "Proposed American Mission to Certain Latin America Countries," 31 May 1918, Box 28, Folder 420, Polk Papers.

13. Gordon Auchincloss to Bernard Baruch, 22 October 1918, Box 4, Folder 52, Papers of Gordon Auchincloss, Yale University Library, New Haven (hereafter cited as Auchincloss Papers).

14. Cleona Lewis, *America's Stake in International Investments* (Washington, 1938), 186, 195.

15. U.S. Department of Commerce, *Ninth Annual Report of the Secretary of Commerce, 1921* (Washington, 1921), 50–51; *Tenth Annual Report of the Secretary of Commerce, 1922* (Washington, 1922), 4 (hereafter cited as CD, *Annual Report of the Secretary*, with year).

16. CD, *Eleventh Annual Report of the Secretary, 1923* (Washington, 1923), 99; CD, *Sixteenth Annual Report of the Secretary, 1928* (Washington, 1928), 94.

17. *The Americas* 1 (October 1914): 6, and (November 1914): 11–13, 29–31.

18. Ibid. (November 1914): 19.

19. *Journal of the American Banking Association* 8 (July 1915): 75, and (August 1915): 136 (hereafter cited as *Journal of the ABA*).

20. Ibid. (July 1915): 10.

21. *The Americas* 2 (November 1915): 1–3.

22. Ibid. (December 1915): 16; *The Bulletin of American International Corporation* 1 (October 1917): 17–18, (May 1918): 6–7, and 2 (February 1919): 7–10 (hereafter cited as *Bulletin of AIC*); Lewis, *America's Stake*, 372–73.

23. Daniel Guggenheim to Dwight Morrow, 11 January 1916, Box 87, Folder 6, Lamont Papers; Lamont to McAdoo, 21 February 1917, Box 81, Folder 27, Lamont Papers.

24. Phelps, *American Branch Banking*, 3 (emphasis in original).

25. *Journal of the ABA* 10 (November 1917): 396.

26. Winkler, *Investments in Latin America*, 274–85.

27. John H. Williams, "Our Foreign Trade Balance since the Armistice," *Journal of the ABA* 13 (February 1921): 571; CD, *Twelfth Annual Report of the Secretary, 1924* (Washington, 1924), 8–9.

28. Winkler, *Investments in Latin America*, 284–85.

29. The figures for American investment are found in Lewis, *America's Stake*, 583–88, 595–99. For descriptions of the varied enterprises in which American money participated see Lewis, *America's Stake*; Winkler, *Investments in Latin*

America; and Grosvenor Jones, "Our Stake in Latin America," *Journal of the ABA* 21 (March 1929): 853–55, 925.

30. *Journal of the ABA* 14 (July 1926): 3.

31. Lewis, *America's Stake*, 578; Phelps, *American Branch Banking*, 212.

32. W. S. Kies, "Branch Banking in South American Trade," *Journal of the ABA* 8 (September 1915): 280; CD, *Reports of the CD, 1917* (Washington, 1918), 56.

33. CD, *Reports of the CD, 1920* (Washington, 1920), 247, 252–53.

34. CD, *Sixteenth Annual Report of the Secretary, 1928*, 94.

35. Phelps, *American Branch Banking*, 90.

36. *The Americas* 1 (October 1914): 25–26; Allied Maritime Transport Council, American Section, Statistical Division, "Relations between United States and Other Countries regarding Important Materials," c. 1918, Box 9, Folder 226, Auchincloss Papers.

37. A. F. Fisher, temporary draft, "An Institute for Tropical Research," 10 August 1920, 430.0, Records of the Bureau of Foreign and Domestic Commerce, Record Group 151, National Archives, Washington (hereafter cited as RG 151 with file number).

38. William Redfield, "You and Our Foreign Trade," *Journal of the ABA* 13 (February 1921): 515–16.

39. Van H. Manning, "Memo on Meeting of Council of National Defense, March 8, 1920," Box 32, Folder 615, Polk Papers; Newton D. Baker to Woodrow Wilson, 9 March 1920, Papers of Newton D. Baker (microfilm edition), Manuscripts Division, Library of Congress, Washington (hereafter cited as Baker Papers).

40. Charles Evans Hughes to American diplomatic offices in Latin America, 26 August 1921, 810.6363/5, Department of State, Record Group 59, National Archives, Washington (hereafter cited as RG 59 with file number).

41. E. B. Rochester to Frank B. Kellogg, 9 July 1927; Stokeley Morgan to Francis White, 12 July 1927, 810.6363/20, /23, RG 59 (emphasis in original).

42. *Journal of the ABA* 10 (November 1917): 396; O. P. Austin, "Development of the Tropics—A Probable Result of the War's Lessons," *The Americas* 4 (June 1918): 25.

43. CD, *Reports of the CD, 1920*, 252–53; Redfield, "You and Our Foreign Trade," *Journal of the ABA* 11 (September 1928): 243.

44. Ray Stannard Baker and William E. Dodd, eds., *The Public Papers of Woodrow Wilson*, 6 vols. (New York, 1925–1927), 5:489–90.

45. Davis, address to the Latin American delegates of the Pan-American Congress of Journalists, 22 April 1926, Box 16, Papers of Norman Davis, Manuscripts Division, Library of Congress, Washington (hereafter cited as Davis Papers); Herbert Hoover, cited in Melvyn P. Leffler, "Herbert Hoover, the 'New Era,' and American Foreign Policy, 1921–1929," in *Herbert Hoover as Secretary of Commerce: Studies in New Era Thought and Practice*, ed. Ellis Hawley (Iowa City, 1981), 152.

46. Poole's memorandum is enclosed in Joseph Tumulty to Baker, 23 October 1919, Baker Papers. This memorandum was circulated among many high officials in the Wilson administration.

47. Lloyd C. Gardner, "Commercial Rivalry with One's Allies as Well as with One's Enemies," in *The Shaping of American Diplomacy*, ed. William Appleman Williams, 2 vols. (Chicago, 1970), 2:54.

48. Memorandum, Fletcher to Robert Lansing, 13 November 1916, enclosed in Fletcher to House, 14 November 1916, Box 44, Folder 411, House Papers; Lansing to Wilson, 23 June 1916, U.S. Department of State, *Papers Relating to the Foreign Relations of the United States: The Lansing Papers, 1914–1920,* 2 vols. (Washington, 1939–40), 1:311–12 (hereafter cited as *FRUS: Lansing Papers*); House to Wilson, 27 October 1917, Box 121, Folder 280, House Papers.

49. House diary, 24 October 1917, House Papers.

50. Wilson to Polk, 4 March 1920, Box 14, Folder 511, Polk Papers.

51. For a more detailed discussion of the U.S. perception of the Bolshevik threat see Arno Mayer, *The Political Origins of the New Diplomacy, 1917–1918* (New Haven, 1954); idem, *Politics and Diplomacy of Peacemaking: Containment and Counterrevolution at Versailles, 1918–1919* (New York, 1967); and N. Gordon Levin, *Woodrow Wilson and World Politics: America's Response to War and Revolution* (New York, 1968). Lloyd C. Gardner, *Safe for Democracy: The Anglo-American Response to Revolution, 1913–1923* (New York, 1984), does an excellent job of relating the American and British response to the Bolshevik Revolution to other revolutionary activities around the globe, especially those occurring in China and Mexico.

52. Memorandum enclosed in Tumulty to Baker, 23 October 1919, Baker Papers (emphasis in original).

53. Enclosed in Fletcher to House, 14 November 1916, Box 44, Folder 411, House Papers.

54. CD, *Annual Reports of the CD, 1916,* 268–69; *Annual Reports of the CD, 1917,* 288.

55. P. W. Wilson, 16 February 1921, Records of Meetings, vol. 1, Archives of the Council on Foreign Relations, New York (hereafter cited as Records of Meetings, Archives of CFR).

56. For a discussion of the early Communist parties in Latin America see Rollie Poppino, *International Communism in Latin America: A History of the Movement, 1917–1963* (New York, 1964).

Chapter Two

"Stale Ideas and False Mirages": Economic Nationalism, Radicalism, and Anti-Americanism

Just as, from 1914 to 1929, the United States attempted to more clearly define goals and problems in its economic relationship with Latin America, so too did Latin America try to cope with significant problems and formulate future directions. Indeed, for Latin America, perhaps even more so than for the United States, World War I brought important problems and changes including trade problems which, while important, were relatively short-lived. The more dramatic and lasting change for Latin America's trade lay in the new direction it was taking.

In 1913 the United States accounted for 25 percent of all imports to Latin America, followed closely by Great Britain (24.4 percent) and Germany (16.6 percent). But by 1917 the U.S. share of the import trade had risen to 54 percent, while Britain's share had dropped to 14.9 percent and Germany's had fallen to negligible levels. The effects on Latin America's export trade were nearly as dramatic, although even before the war the United States had a clear edge over its competitors. In 1917 the United States had 51.7 percent of the total export trade of Latin America, an increase of nearly 21 percent over the 1913 figure which came largely at the expense of Germany.[1] The increase in U.S. investment was equally spirited, although Great Britain continued to hold the lead in that field.[2]

The Latin Americans were well aware of how the war had affected their traditional trade patterns. As the flow of funds and manufactured goods from Great Britain, Germany, and France dried up, Latin America was forced to turn to the United States, both as a market for its goods and as a supplier of its needs. A number of Latin Americans felt a distinct uneasiness about this. For, at the same time that U.S. businessmen and government officials began to covet the markets that the Europeans were abandoning, the Latin Americans were engaged in a serious reevaluation of their nations' roles in the world economy. For them World War I became not an opportunity for trade expansion, but rather a symbol of their dissatisfaction with the roles assigned them in the world trade structure.

Of prime importance in the development of that dissatisfaction was the war's impact on the nascent nationalism in Latin America. An all-inclusive definition of nationalism is, as Arthur Whitaker and David Jordan have pointed out, "elusive." A dictionary would describe nationalism as a "national spirit or aspirations; devotion to the interests of one's nation; desire for national advancement or independence."[3] Nationalism operates in a variety of forms in Latin America, and its focus can be on political, social, cultural, or economic issues. By World War I, however, a "new bourgeois" nationalism characterized Latin America, a nationalism centered around the more specific notion of economic nationalism.[4] Economic nationalism sought national economic growth through freeing the domestic economy from the constraints imposed on it by uncontrolled foreign ownership of land and resources and the dictates of what was perceived as an unfair world trade system.[5]

Latin America's modern role in the world market system developed in the mid-1800s. As the economist Celso Furtado has noted, it was then that Latin America "began to enter the channels of expanding international trade."[6]

The way in which most nations in Latin America entered those "channels" was hardly surprising. The independence movements that rocked Spanish America during the first quarter of the nineteenth century were reactions not only against Spain's political control of the colonies but also against the rigidly closed economic system that the Spanish rulers forced upon their colonial outposts. When they were finally freed from that control, the newly independent nations opened their trading doors to all the world by embracing the concept of free trade.[7] Two major reasons lay behind this decision. First, the Latin American leaders had before them the most shining example of how free trade could work: Great Britain, the world's greatest proponent of it, had risen to the pinnacle of world economic and political power. It was not unnatural that Latin Americans believed that the same might hold true for them if they followed the free trade path.[8]

Perhaps more important, as Aníbal Pinto has explained, nineteenth-century Latin Americans "were not protectionists for the simple reason that they had little to protect." In other words, the primary Latin American producers—those in mining and agriculture—as well as the import-export entrepreneurs saw little use for tariffs or other impediments to free trade. The goods they produced needed no "protection" from foreign competitors, and the goods they imported were necessary or at least desirable. Adherence to laissez-faire seemed logical.[9] As they were to discover, however, free trade carried a substantial price tag.

Latin America's participation in the world trade structure of the nineteenth century was strictly defined and limited.[10] International trade during that period operated under what a number of scholars have referred to as a "division of labor."[11] Furtado divides the nineteenth-century world economy into the "nucleus" of developed, industrialized nations, which produced profitable consumer goods, and the non-nucleus nations, such as those in Latin America, that relied on the export of primary products in exchange for those goods. André Gunder Frank has a more radical view of a much more exploitative system of "metropolises" and "satellites."[12] Whatever the phraseology, the nineteenth century witnessed the delineation of international economic "roles": Developed nations such as Great Britain provided consumer goods and capital to underdeveloped regions in return for agricultural and mineral raw materials.

The basic outline of the economic relationship between Latin America and the developed center, or metropolis, or nucleus, was established. Typically concentrating their resources on the production of one particular crop or mineral resource, the nations of Latin America sought to develop viable import-export trades based on the exchange of those goods for consumer products from the developed center. Under the auspices of free trade policies, this system allowed the center nations of Great Britain and the United States to reap great wealth but exacted a great toll in Latin America.

One immediate consequence of this system was that the Latin American markets were flooded with imported goods. Unable to compete with the technologically advanced exporting nations of Europe and the United States, Latin American craftsmen were often driven from the marketplace. Pioneering industrialists in nation after nation were swept from the field by foreign competition.[13] Any development of a national industrial base was seriously retarded.

A second, and perhaps more serious, consequence arose from the Latin American nations' reliance on monoresource economies. When world demand for coffee, for example, was high, coffee-producing nations such as Brazil and Colombia did well on the exchange market. When demand dropped, due to unforeseen economic crises, overproduction, or change in consumer tastes or needs, those nations suffered drastic financial difficulties.[14]

Furthermore, in most cases the development of Latin America's monoresource export economies had rapidly attracted the attention of foreign investors who were interested in projects that would bring quick and tidy profits. Not coincidentally, they concentrated their monies in those export commodities for which the particular Latin American nation was deriving most of its income. While some in Latin America, such as Porfirio Díaz and his *científico* supporters in Mexico, encouraged this investment as the best way to develop their resources, the result was foreign control over those resources. Chile provided a sobering example. In 1900, Chileans owned 95 percent of the nation's copper industry; by 1920 foreign interests controlled over 90 percent of that same industry.[15]

All of that was a high price to pay, but the real question to be asked is: What was Latin America paying for? Free trade and closer contact with the developed, industrial nations brought little in the way of real economic or social development in Latin America. In addition to retarding national industry, subjecting national development to the whims inherent in a monoresource economy, and denationalizing natural resources, Gerhard Masur has theorized that "the impact of high capitalism" on Latin America "tended to strengthen the stratified society rather than to moderate it."[16] The sectors of the Latin American populace that had always controlled the economic, political, and social life of their respective nations were the beneficiaries of dependency.

Among many Latin Americans significant resentment and disenchantment emerged during the latter years of the nineteenth century, and the criticisms that issued forth contained powerful strains of nationalism.[17] Critics began to turn their fire on the foreign interests that seemed to threaten the economic, political, and even cultural well-being of Latin America. Europe was the special target of Latin American nationalists, although, as U.S. money and trade began to play a growing role in the region, barbs were tossed at the "Colossus of the North" with equal zeal. Some examples demonstrate the depth and emotional content of such criticisms.

Juan Justo, who founded the Argentine Socialist party, issued this condemnation of British investment in 1896: "English capital has done what their arms could not do. Today our country is tributary to England . . . the gold that the English capitalists take out of Argentina . . . does us no more good than the Irish got from the revenues that the English lords took out of Ireland."[18] Others, while not sharing Justo's radicalism, agreed with his general assessment. In 1894, Luis Aldunate, the former Chilean minister, expressed his disappointment over the effects of European investment in his nation. "It is not wise," he wrote, "but on the contrary very dangerous for us to let the interests of a foreign monopoly grow up into the clouds. . . . We are letting ourselves be colonized . . . without noticing that we are the victims of stale ideas and false mirages."[19]

Increasingly, however, it was the United States that was attacked by the Latin American nationalists. Many had a special fear of the North American giant, since its growing economic penetration of the region seemed to be coupled with territorial acquisitiveness. One of the leaders of the Cuban independence movement, José Martí (who would become a martyr to the cause in 1895), put forth his views about the 1889 Pan American Conference called by the United States. He first argued that a careful study should be made of "this invitation which the powerful United States—replete with unsaleable products and determined to

increase its rule over America—extends to the less powerful nations."
He then charged that the people of the United States were "thoroughly
rapacious" and sought only to guarantee a market in Latin America for
their "false production." Latin Americans should "place in their way as
many restraining obstacles as can be forged," for "there can be no
Cains in our America. Our America is One!"[20]

By far the most influential work reflecting the growing anti-U.S.
spirit in Latin America was José Enrique Rodó's *Ariel*, published in
1900. In it Rodó, a Uruguayan, attacked the United States on several
levels, but his primary thrust was pointing out the dangers of allowing
the northern power too much influence on Latin America's economic,
political, and, more important, cultural life. As he put it, "I see no good
in denaturalizing the character of a people—its personal genius—to
impose on it identity with a foreign model to which they will sacrifice
the originality of their genius." Rodó went on to condemn the United
States for its hardheaded materialism and lack of spirituality, creativity,
and beauty, and he chided Latin Americans who looked to such a model
as an ideal.[21]

These angry and eloquent denunciations of the foreign presence in
Latin America, especially the economic presence, expressed a rising
mood of dissent in the region. Not only did powers such as the United
States seem to be threatening the territorial sovereignty of the area's
nations, but the boom/bust economic cycle of the late nineteenth century
also made them painfully aware of the consequences of their dependent
status. But it was not until the first three decades of the twentieth
century, and most especially during World War I, when new political
and economic groups—a middle class, an industrial working class, and
radical political groups—rose to positions of political power, that
programs to control foreign interests in Latin America could be put into
effect. How the war catalyzed this is best summarized by economist
Bill Albert:

> There were many other changes brought about or stimulated by the
> war. For example, foreign influence over national financial systems
> became more of an irritant and began to be challenged.
> Manufacturing industry experienced some expansion, but came up
> against a number of constraints imposed by the fact that these
> economies were so heavily dominated by primary exports and
> dependent on imports. This in turn was important in fueling the
> economic nationalism which was eventually to offer alternatives to
> the pattern of nineteenth-century primary export capitalism.[22]

Economic nationalism was pushed most vociferously by the
developing middle and working classes in Latin America early in the
twentieth century. The major impetus for their development lay in what
Fernando Cardoso and Enzo Faletto have called the "diversification" of
the Latin American economies in that period, during which export

economies "developed not only important financial and mercantile sectors, but also the initial stages of an urban-industrial society."[23] That diversification was speeded by the impact of the war. The reduction of consumer goods brought about by the interruption of normal trade with Europe led to greater savings within Latin America generally. These retained savings, in turn, provided the capital that financed the new industrialization that grew up to meet the consumer demand. This produced both a nascent middle class and a growing working class.[24]

There were many differences between these new classes and the old oligarchic elites who for years had controlled the economic, political, and social power of many Latin American nations. Most important, as Masur describes it, "these people were less tradition-conscious than the old elites; they were more sensitive to outside influences, whether European or North American; they were willing to recognize backwardness at home and to search for new models of social advancement."[25] At the core of these differences was the growing economic nationalism of the new classes.[26]

Some scholars have concluded that economic nationalism played a powerful role in Latin America from 1900 to 1930, a time when the middle sectors were able to obtain real political power in several nations.[27] The goals of the economic nationalists during that period centered around four major desires: first, to protect and to regulate the exploitation of their nations' natural resources; second, to regulate the activities of foreign businesses and investors; third, to substitute domestically produced goods for foreign imports by economic diversification and protective legislation such as tariffs; and fourth, to have government play a more active, positive role in directing the economy for the common good.[28]

Those goals reflected the pressures for change from the new sectors of Latin American society. For the middle class, as Louis Snyder describes it, "A smooth economy became its lifeblood." Dissatisfied with the wild economic fluctuations caused by their nations' reliance on foreign trade and traders, they attacked the "imperialism-via-investments" of the foreign powers as well as the *vendepatrias*, the local elites who "had sold out to the imperialists."[29] As for the industrial workers, protection and import substitution were necessary for their very existence. Both groups demanded that their nations "organize their economies by adding the stimulus of the domestic market to that of the external sector."[30]

In addition, new and radical political philosophies were making an impression in Latin America, especially among the working class. Many of the immigrants pouring into that region during the late nineteenth and early twentieth centuries were from Europe and were not strangers to communism and other radical ideologies. While those ideologies never gained the acceptance of society at large, the radicalism emanating from the small but vocal and largely literate proletariat produced specific ideas that were compatible with the nationalists' agenda.[31] Although the radical European ideologies were ostensibly antinationalistic, both they and the Latin American version of economic nationalism rejected the liberal capitalist model of development in favor of state ownership or control of at least some portion of both the primary and secondary sectors.

During the first thirty years of the twentieth century, programs of economic nationalism were established or experimented with in a number of Latin American nations. The first nation to construct a cohesive program was Uruguay under the brilliant leadership of José Batlle y Ordóñez. As the dominant political figure in Uruguay from 1900 to 1929, and as president from 1903 to 1907 and 1911 to 1915, Batlle pushed for both social democracy and economic nationalism with a great deal of success.[32]

Batlle's rise to political power also meant a rise in the fortunes of his Colorado party. That Batlle should have become a member of the party that found its primary support among urban merchants (as opposed to the Blanco party, which relied mainly on large landowners in the interior for its base of power) was not surprising. His grandfather had been a businessman in Montevideo and his father had served as president of Uruguay as a Colorado from 1868 to 1872.

For Batlle the late 1800s was a time of battle not only against the Blancos but also against what he perceived as increasingly reactionary elements of his own party. In 1886 he established his own newspaper, *El Dia*, which became the voice for his reformist program. As Cardoso and Faletto explain, to gain the political power that he needed to implement the changes he desired, "Batlle first attempted to gain control of the Colorado party by incorporating and enlisting the support of the urban middle and popular classes as well as the farmers."[33] Greater contact with developed nations such as Great Britain together with waves of immigrants had transformed Uruguay into an increasingly urban, industrial nation. Batlle and his supporters were quick to see that this new constituency, especially the workers, could become a potent political force. In 1903, Batlle was elected president of Uruguay. His courting of the industrial and middle classes was not merely a political expedient. As political scientist Martin Weinstein points out, "Throughout his lifetime, Batlle remained faithful to the cause of labor and workers' rights."[34]

Once he was in power, Batlle demonstrated that he had two major goals: first, to build a more democratic and just social order; and, second, to construct a viable economy supported by his brand of economic nationalism. The first goal would allow and encourage greater political participation by the middle sectors; the second would ensure their support by providing the economic protection they desired.

Batlle fought for, and secured, a number of laws aimed at bettering the lives of working-class people and making the political system of Uruguay more open and responsive. Between 1903 and 1929, Uruguay enacted legislation widening the scope of suffrage, lessening press and speech censorship, expanding the nation's school system, and granting women the right to seek divorces. For the workers, bills were passed setting up eight-hour days, minimum wages, provisions for unionization, and the rudiments of a social security system.

More striking was Batlle's program of economic nationalism. He made his stance on this in no uncertain terms. Speaking in 1911, he stated that

> the modern state unhesitatingly accepts its status as an economic organization. It will enter industry when competition is not practicable, when control by private interests vests in them authority inconsistent with the welfare of the state, when a fiscal monopoly may serve as a great source of income to meet urgent tax problems, when the continued export of national wealth is considered undesirable. State socialism makes it possible to use for the general good that portion of the results of labor which is not paid to labor.[35]

Batlle saw to it that state-owned corporations were set up in a number of different fields. A state insurance bank was put into operation in 1912. By the end of the 1920s the government was involved in running railroads, docks, power plants, communication systems, banks, meat-packing plants, and even alcohol production. Batlle also established protective tariffs for Uruguayan industry.

One of Batlle's primary goals was the freeing of Uruguay from domination by foreign investors. Uruguay's reliance on loans was always a "considerable sacrifice," as Batlle stated in 1913. Once the national government could mobilize the internally generated capital, funds could be raised more efficiently and less painfully by state-controlled enterprises.[36]

Argentina's economic and social development from 1900 to 1930 paralleled Uruguay's in a number of ways.[37] There, too, the effects of the import-export trade had created a growing middle class and the beginnings of an industrial class. And there, too, a party captured the support of those groups, rose to political power, and succeeded in implementing a program of economic nationalism, albeit not as wide-ranging a program as Batlle's in Uruguay.

Argentina in 1890 was experiencing severe financial difficulties, as it was wracked by the economic depression that was shaking the rest of the world. A group of young intellectuals formed the Unión Cívica Radical, which began to challenge the ruling class Conservatives by calling for free elections and honest government. By 1891 the group had become the Radical party.

Between 1891 and 1916 the Radical party worked to gain the support of the working- and middle-class sectors, especially the immigrants among them, who were virtually barred from the electoral process. Their efforts were largely successful at a time when an influx of radical political and economic ideas and a greater stridency among labor groups for reform resulted in more strikes and an increased level of political education among the masses.[38]

The Conservative party attempted to go on the political offensive by enacting a number of changes in Argentina. First, a new voting law in 1912 allowed universal suffrage and secret balloting. Second, new laws provided for greater conservation of the nation's natural resources. And third, in an effort to placate German and Italian immigrants, the Conservatives maintained strict neutrality when World War I began.[39]

Nevertheless, the Radicals, aided greatly by the 1912 voting law, attained political power in 1916. Their leader, Hipólito Yrigoyen, was no Batlle to be sure. But he was very popular, especially among the working class, which believed that his election would end oligarchic control and achieve greater freedom for labor. Their hopes were largely illusory. On numerous occasions the Yrigoyen regime used military force to crush strikes, labor rallies, and student meetings. Cardoso and Faletto explain this by pointing out that "the election of Irigoyen signified the victory of an alliance of power in which the electoral base differed significantly from the elite directing it." Incorporated into the government, the elite "remained strong enough to react against the rising pressures from below."[40] Benjamin Keen and Mark Wasserman have summed up the Radical position: "The operating mechanism of the Radical government was a conservative fiscal policy and political stability, in return for which the oligarchy was to allow the middle class wider access to the governmental bureaucracy and the professions."[41]

This situation led to stalemate and little social and economic reform in Argentina during Yrigoyen's rule. Yet, as some scholars have noted, Yrigoyen did manage to move Argentina along the path of economic nationalism from 1916 to 1922. The effects of World War I allowed him to increase the size of some key industries, such as textiles; he also managed to nationalize the railroads.[42] But Yrigoyen's most radical act of economic nationalism came in 1922 when he established a state-owned oil company, Yacimientos Petrolíferos Fiscales (YPF).[43]

These actions reflected a growing feeling in Argentina that it must break its dependency on foreign nations. A 1920 editorial from the newspaper *La Unión* stated that "we must learn slowly, painfully perhaps to develop our own industries, and not to cede one of the chief sources of our wealth [petroleum] to selfish strangers." *La Nación* in that same year was even more strident in denouncing Argentina's reliance on foreign coal and iron. In an editorial entitled "Industrial Subservience" the paper declared that "two years ago, we indicated to the Government the convenience of not counting on foreign coal, and that meant the absolute necessity of working its own deposits as thereon depends our definite emancipation in economic matters."[44] The establishment of YPF was one of the first steps taken to answer those calls for economic nationalism.

In Chile the election of Arturo Alessandri Palma in 1920 marked the beginning of economic nationalism as a real force there.[45] Alessandri had been elected on the Liberal Alliance ticket, a party of reform that had arisen in response to general disillusionment with the two major parties, the Liberals and the Conservatives.[46] As in Uruguay and Argentina, the new middle and working classes had become disenchanted with their political and economic status. World War I had been, for them, a breaking point. Although sales of Chilean nitrate and copper had boosted the income of mine owners and some workers, it also had sent prices spiraling. The postwar period was even more disastrous. While foreign interests, particularly those of the United States, steadily took over the nation's copper resources, the bottom fell out of the nitrate market.[47] The U.S. ambassador to Chile, Joseph Shea, wrote in 1919 that the Chileans were exhibiting a good deal of ire over the situation. He paraphrased an editorial from *La Nación* that had angrily claimed that "while Allied doors are shut against Chile all these powers are doing their best to penetrate economically into Chile and that Chile is on the brink of very hard times."[48]

In that climate Alessandri came to power. He promised a great deal, including the complete separation of church and state, greater rights for women, cheap housing, improvement in education, and more workers' rights. On the economic side Alessandri advocated nationalization of the nitrate mines, state control of insurance companies and banks, development of a state-run merchant marine, and what the new U.S. ambassador to Chile, William Collier, called "prohibitive tariffs." All of those proposals, according to Collier, were part of "a plan of economic defense," which the Chilean press was calling for. As reports from the U.S. embassy indicate, all of those plans, with the exception of the nitrate nationalization, were enacted in one form or another.[49]

Against a still well-entrenched oligarchy, however, Alessandri was not completely successful. In 1924 reformist elements in the military, angered by the parliament's delays in enacting Alessandri's programs, revolted and ordered that those programs be passed. Alessandri declared that he would not share his rule with the military and went into exile. He returned in 1925 when the military offered to step aside, and in that year a new constitution for Chile was written and adopted. One of the more notable aspects of the document, Jay Kinsbruner points out, was that "the nineteenth-century liberal concept of private property rights was overturned: private property rights were subject to a broader social interpretation; they could be limited when social progress made it necessary."[50] Later in 1925 new elections were held, and Emiliano Figueroa was elected president. But the real power in the government was Minister of War Colonel Carlos Ibáñez del Campos, who was "elected" president in 1927 after Figueroa's resignation. Even though

Ibáñez's rule amounted to little more than a dictatorship, he continued with a number of Alessandri's proposals for economic nationalism.[51]

By far the most explosive example of economic nationalism in Latin America during the early twentieth century occurred in Mexico. The story of the Mexican Revolution has been told by many scholars, and there is no need to go into all of the details here. Two aspects of that revolution, however, explain its relationship to the concept of economic nationalism.

The first aspect is the role of the middle sectors in the outbreak of revolution in Mexico. The long rule of Porfirio Díaz (1876–1910) had brought stability to Mexico, and that stability had encouraged increasingly large investments by foreign interests. Great ranches, mines, railroads, and other enterprises were established by foreign investors, mostly in northern Mexico. From those enterprises developed small, but steadily growing, middle and industrial classes in Mexico. While economic times were good, those classes generally supported Díaz. When, between 1900 and 1910, the economic climate in Mexico began to deteriorate, their support waned. As Friedrich Katz so aptly puts it, during that period "foreign investment began to show its ugly underside." Problems that began to hit Mexico hard included a rising inflation rate during peak investment years, onerous taxes during slow years, and "a heightened vulnerability to the business cycle of the United States." Along with their economic discontent, the middle class and the proletariat had to contend with political frustration, as the Mexican oligarchies in the various regions throughout the nation refused to allow their political power to be diluted by "outsiders."[52]

During those years the middle sectors began to turn their frustration on the United States and other foreign investors. Most manufacturing plants in Mexico were owned by foreigners, and by 1910 foreign interests held 25 percent of Mexico's land. As Shoshana Tancer notes, "The battle cry was 'Mexico for the Mexicans'; an aspect of antiforeign investment nationalism had pervaded all of Mexico by 1910."[53]

The second, and perhaps more important, aspect of the revolution that relates to economic nationalism is the Mexican constitution of 1917. This document, constructed during a convention at Querétaro from November 1916 to February 1917, was "the closest approximation to a Mexican consensus on the Revolution's goals."[54] The new constitution contained some very progressive notions concerning the role of the church and the protection of labor, but the heart of the document was in Article 27, which gave the state the right to expropriate private property for the public welfare and vested ownership of subsoil rights in the nation. This was deemed necessary by the men who met at Querétaro, as Frank Brandenburg has noted, because hopes for a true Mexican state would not be realized "with foreigners in possession of the subsoil, or with Mexico controlled by foreign capital, foreign ideas, or foreigners themselves."[55]

The goal of Article 27 seemed clear: to give Mexico greater participation in, direction of, and profit from the tremendous mining activities in the nation, particularly from the booming oil industry. In place of private (and largely foreign-owned) enterprises, Article 27 implied a system in which the public welfare would reign supreme over private profit. José Vasconcelos, who was head of the Mexican Ministry of Education from 1920 to 1925, defined the essential meaning of Article 27 and similar actions as a "safeguard for the future of Mexican prosperity and Mexican democracy."[56]

Most students of Mexican history would agree that the goals of Article 27, and the Mexican constitution of 1917 as a whole, have not been fulfilled. Yet the constitution was an important step for Mexico and, indeed, for Latin America. It marked the high point of economic nationalism in Latin America between 1900 and 1930, and it inspired the Mexican attacks on the foreign-owned oil fields that culminated in 1938 with their nationalization. It also marked the high point of a movement toward what some scholars have called "social constitutionalism." Herbert Klein has argued that, following the Mexican constitution, many economic nationalists and radicals in other Latin American republics "demanded that the state take a positive role in the education and welfare of all citizens even if it reduced the property rights of the individual." Other nations, including Uruguay later in 1917 and Chile in 1925, began to rewrite their constitutions to deal with "the social responsibility of capital, the economic rights of the worker, and the state responsibility for the protection and security . . . of all its citizens and classes."[57]

By the end of World War I economic nationalism had made a powerful impression in Latin America, and it continued to do so during the 1920s. A number of the more developed nations of that region, particularly in South America, declared their disenchantment with the world economic system and their place within it, and they put forward proposals to help themselves break free of their dependent status.[58] An important change in the Latin Americans' criticisms of foreign investors and traders occurred during and immediately after the war. As U.S. interests began to displace their European competitors in the markets to the south, the Latin Americans began to place a large share of the blame for their economic woes on the "Northern Colossus."

Diplomatic battles between the nations of that region and the United States erupted often during the 1920s. That was not surprising. During World War I the United States saw valuable opportunities for trade and investment develop in Latin America. These were not seen simply as easy ways to make money; they were deemed absolutely necessary for the survival of the world capitalist order. Economic nationalism, with its talk of expropriation and nationalization, could hardly be tolerated.

It was an ironic turn of events. In 1913, Woodrow Wilson had promised to "emancipate" Latin America from the "subordination to foreign enterprises." U.S. investors and traders did so by taking the places of those "foreign" enterprises. By 1920, however, at least one Latin American newspaper was asking, "who is to protect us from the United States?"[59] It was a realistic question.

Notes

1. Donald Baerresen, Martin Carnoy, and Joseph Grunwald, *Latin American Trade Patterns* (Washington, 1965), 20.

2. Refer to Chapter 1 for a more detailed report on the growth of U.S. trade and investment in Latin America.

3. Arthur P. Whitaker and David C. Jordan, *Nationalism in Contemporary Latin America* (New York, 1966), 3, 5.

4. Ibid., 14–15.

5. Tancer, *Economic Nationalism*, 1–16. See especially the definitions offered on page 12. It also should be noted that economic nationalism had developed earlier in other areas, and it would develop elsewhere after World War I. A good summary of its different manifestations can be found in Harry G. Johnson, ed., *Economic Nationalism in Old and New States* (Chicago, 1967). Separate articles discuss the impact of economic nationalism in Germany and Great Britain in the nineteenth century and in China, Mexico, Canada, and Mali in the twentieth century.

6. Celso Furtado, *Economic Development of Latin America: Historical Background and Contemporary Problems*, 2d ed., trans. Suzette Macedo (Cambridge, 1976), 47.

7. For more detailed analyses of the Latin American independence movements see John Lynch, *The Spanish American Revolutions, 1808–1826*, 2d ed. (New York, 1986); and Richard Graham, *Independence in Latin America* (New York, 1972).

8. Tancer, *Economic Nationalism*, 6.

9. Aníbal Pinto cited in Fernando Cardoso and Enzo Faletto, *Dependency and Development in Latin America*, trans. Marjory Mattingly Urquidi (Berkeley, 1979), 60. Claudio Velíz has called the mining-agricultural-trading entrepreneur establishment the "three legs of the national economic table" of Chile in the nineteenth century, although some scholars, such as André Gunder Frank, have applied the analogy to Latin America as a whole. Velíz cited in André Gunder Frank, *Capitalism and Underdevelopment in Latin America: Historical Studies of Chile and Brazil* (New York, 1969), 89.

10. For more detailed studies of the economic development of nineteenth-century Latin America see Cardoso and Faletto, *Dependency and Development*; Furtado, *Economic Development*; and Frank, *Capitalism and Underdevelopment*, which offer contrasting viewpoints of that development. Two works, Tulio Halperín-Donghi, *The Aftermath of Revolution in Latin America* (New York, 1973); and Stanley J. Stein and Barbara H. Stein, *The Colonial Heritage of Latin America* (New York, 1970), are insightful studies of Latin America's postrevolutionary economic development. The interaction between Latin America and Europe is covered well in Richard Graham, *Britain and the Onset of Modernization in Brazil, 1850–1914* (Cambridge, 1968), and Roberto Cortés

Conde, *The First Stages of Modernization in Spanish America*, trans. Tony Talbot (New York, 1974).

11. An excellent summary of this position is found in Frederick Stirton Weaver, *Class, State, and Industrial Structure: The Historical Process of South American Industrial Growth* (Westport, CT, 1980), 79–96. Also see Furtado, *Economic Development*, 42–47; and Gerhard Masur, *Nationalism in Latin America: Diversity and Unity* (New York, 1966), 64–65.

12. Furtado, *Economic Development*, 42–47; Frank, *Capitalism and Underdevelopment*, 3–14.

13. For the effects in Chile see Frank, *Capitalism and Underdevelopment*, 66–85; for Argentina consult Miron Burgin, *The Economic Aspects of Argentine Federalism, 1820–1852* (Cambridge, 1946), 90; and for Colombia see William McGreevey, *An Economic History of Colombia, 1845–1930* (Cambridge, 1971), 105ff. For a more general discussion see Halperín-Donghi, *Aftermath*.

14. Colombia's reliance on coffee during the nineteenth century provides an excellent example of the effects of fluctuations in demand on a monoculture nation. See McGreevey, *Economic History of Colombia*; and Charles Bergquist, *Coffee and Conflict in Colombia, 1886–1910* (Durham, 1978). For fuller explanations of the causes and consequences of monoculture "dependent" economies see the previously cited works by Frank, Cardoso and Faletto, Halperín-Donghi, and Stein and Stein. An excellent summary of the pros and cons of the dependency theory is found in C. Richard Bath and Dilmus D. James, "Dependency Analysis of Latin America: Some Criticisms, Some Suggestions," *Latin American Research Review* 11 (Fall 1976): 3–54.

15. Tancer, *Economic Nationalism*, 129.

16. Masur, *Nationalism*, 63–64.

17. As Samuel Baily has pointed out, while the word "nationalism" is frequently applied to Latin America, no one has "been able to provide us with a precise, universally accepted definition of the term nor . . . tell us very much about nationalism" (Samuel L. Baily, ed., *Nationalism in Latin America* [New York, 1971], 3). It is not the purpose of this work to investigate the entire concept of nationalism, let alone attempt to solve Baily's challenge. The term will be used here in its "negative" fashion to denote not so much a concept of love and devotion to one's own nation as a hatred or fear of what the nationalist perceives as foreign enemies.

18. Cited in José Luis Romero, *A History of Argentine Political Thought*, trans. Thomas McGann (Stanford, 1963), 193.

19. Cited in Frank, *Capitalism and Underdevelopment*, 87.

20. Cited in W. Raymond Duncan and James Nelson Goodsell, eds., *The Quest for Change in Latin America: Sources for a Twentieth-Century Analysis* (New York, 1970), 9–10.

21. José Enrique Rodó, *Ariel*, trans. F. J. Stimson (Boston, 1922), 91–92.

22. Bill Albert, *South America and the First World War: The Impact of War on Brazil, Argentina, Peru and Chile* (Cambridge, 1988), 307.

23. Cardoso and Faletto, *Dependency and Development*, 74.

24. Albert, *South America*, 180-305; Frank, *Capitalism and Underdevelopment*, 297; Weaver, *Industrial Structure*, 109–15. In discussing the "middle class" I am relying on the definition provided by Weaver: "white collar workers . . . including schoolteachers, bookkeepers, administrators, managers, journalists, clerks in shops and offices, and the whole panoply of salaried employees in the public and private sectors" (109). He notes, however, that "independent professionals and even some small entrepreneurs" sometimes

worked with the white-collar workers in pursuing the goals of economic nationalism.

25. Masur, *Nationalism*, 71.

26. Weaver, *Industrial Structure*, 107–15, notes that, although the working class and the new middle class both supported economic nationalism, the two groups did not share the same political-economic outlook. Both gave their support, and sometimes worked together, because economic nationalism served their particular group's interests. In addition, as Whitaker and Jordan, *Nationalism in Contemporary Latin America*, 14–15, point out, even within the groups (especially within the middle class) there were divisions.

27. Tancer, *Economic Nationalism*, 12; Masur, *Nationalism*, 70–72; Baily, *Nationalism in Latin America*, 19–20; Louis L. Snyder, *The New Nationalism* (Ithaca, 1968), 222–29.

28. It may be just as easily suggested that the United States had gone through its own rather lengthy period of economic nationalism, especially if one considers the nation's tariff policies prior to 1913. For the standard history of the tariff see F. W. Taussig, *The Tariff History of the United States*, 6th ed. (New York, 1914).

29. Snyder, *New Nationalism*, 225, 234–35.

30. Cardoso and Faletto, *Dependency and Development*, 75.

31. Poppino, *International Communism*, 27–28.

32. Three brief sketches of Batlle and his influence in Uruguay are found in Cardoso and Faletto, *Dependency and Development*, 94–96; Harold E. Davis, *Makers of Democracy in Latin America* (New York, 1968), 90–92; and Hubert Herring, *A History of Latin America: From the Beginnings to the Present* (New York, 1961), 702–6. For more detailed descriptions see Russell H. Fitzgibbon, *Uruguay: Portrait of a Democracy* (New Brunswick, 1954), 122–36; and Martin Weinstein's brief *Uruguay: The Politics of Failure* (Westport, CT, 1975), 20–49. Milton I. Vanger has written what is now the standard biography of Batlle: *José Batlle y Ordóñez of Uruguay: The Creator of His Times, 1902–1907* (Cambridge, MA, 1963).

33. Cardoso and Faletto, *Dependency and Development*, 95.

34. Weinstein, *Uruguay*, 21.

35. Quoted in Herring, *A History of Latin America*, 704.

36. Weinstein, *Uruguay*, 24–25.

37. For Argentina during the years 1900 to 1930 consult James R. Scobie, *Argentina: A City and a Nation* (New York, 1964), 200–14; George Pendle, *Argentina*, 3d ed. (New York, 1963), 65–72; Harry Bernstein, *Modern and Contemporary Latin America* (New York, 1965), 253–74; Cardoso and Faletto, *Dependency and Development*, 82–89; and David Rock, *Politics in Argentina, 1890–1930: The Rise and Fall of Radicalism* (London, 1975).

38. Rock, *Politics in Argentina*, is the definitive study of the rise to power of the Radical party.

39. Bernstein, *Contemporary Latin America*, 259–61.

40. Cardoso and Faletto, *Dependency and Development*, 86–87.

41. Benjamin Keen and Mark Wasserman, *A Short History of Latin America* (Boston, 1980), 307.

42. Cardoso and Faletto, *Dependency and Development*, 88.

43. A good discussion of the establishment of the YPF is found in George Philip, *Oil and Politics in Latin America: Nationalist Movements and State Companies* (Cambridge, 1982), 162–81.

44. *La Unión* editorial is found in Craig Wadsworth to Bainbridge Colby, 1 October 1920, 835.00/213, RG 59; *La Nación* editorial is enclosed in Frederic J. Stimson to acting secretary of state, 8 December 1920, 835.00/217, RG 59.

45. For some background works on Chilean history from 1890 to 1930 and on Alessandri himself consult Jay Kinsbruner, *Chile: A Historical Interpretation* (New York, 1973), 119–32; Bernstein, *Contemporary Latin America*, 516–33; and Cardoso and Faletto, *Dependency and Development*, 112–16. Ernst Halperin, *Nationalism and Communism in Chile* (Cambridge, MA 1965), has some general background to the Alessandri period but is rather short on the period itself. Frederick M. Nunn, *Chilean Politics, 1920–1931: The Honorable Mission of the Armed Forces* (Albuquerque, 1970), is very good on the Alessandri period. On Alessandri, Robert J. Alexander has written a lengthy biography, which is one of the few works in English dealing with the Chilean leader: *Arturo Alessandri: A Biography*, 2 vols. (Ann Arbor, 1977). Frank, *Capitalism and Underdevelopment*, 1–120, has a very good discussion of the economic development of Chile from the colonial period to the 1960s.

46. Kinsbruner, *Chile*, 120.

47. Albert, *South America*, 37ff, contains a wealth of information concerning the impact of the war on Chile.

48. Joseph Shea to Robert Lansing, 28 February 1919, 825.50/3, RG 59.

49. For the calls for nationalization of the nitrate fields see Shea to Charles Evans Hughes, 1 April 1921, and John F. Martin to Hughes, 13 May 1921, 825.00/195, /198, RG 59. Collier's reports are found in Collier to Hughes, 13 December 1921, 24 January, 14 February 1922, 825.00/213, /217, /219, RG 59.

50. Kinsbruner, *Chile*, 129.

51. For a more complete discussion of the military's role in Chile see Nunn, *Chilean Politics*.

52. Friedrich Katz, *The Secret War in Mexico: Europe, the United States and the Mexican Revolution* (Chicago, 1981), 3–49.

53. Tancer, *Economic Nationalism*, 129.

54. James Cockroft, *Intellectual Precursors of the Mexican Revolution, 1900–1913* (Austin, 1968), 5.

55. For a translated copy of Article 27 see Baily, *Nationalism in Latin America*, 98–110; Frank Brandenburg, *The Making of Modern Mexico* (Englewood Cliffs, 1964), 55.

56. For a discussion of the meaning of the Mexican constitution and Article 27 see Donald Hodges and Ross Gandy, *Mexico, 1910–1976: Reform or Revolution?* (London, 1979), 24–26; and James Fred Rippy, José Vasconcelos, and Guy Stevens, *American Policies Abroad: Mexico* (Chicago, 1928), 138.

57. Herbert Klein, *Bolivia: The Evolution of a Multi-Ethnic Society* (New York, 1982), 205–6; idem, "Social Constitutionalism in Latin America: The Bolivian Experience of 1938," *The Americas* 22 (January 1966): 258.

58. While economic nationalism was a more potent force in the more developed nations of Latin America, it also found its way into some less developed countries. For an example see Brenda Gayle Plummer, *Haiti and the Great Powers, 1902–1915* (Baton Rouge, 1988).

59. Woodrow Wilson, "Address on Latin American Policy in Mobile, Alabama, 27 Oct. 1913," *The Papers of Woodrow Wilson*, 36 vols., ed. Arthur Link (Princeton, 1966–1982), 28:450; *El Mercurio* editorial enclosed in Shea to Colby, 18 May 1920, 825.00/132, RG 59.

Chapter Three

"Lions in the Woods": The U.S. Response to Economic Nationalism

In March 1923, Stanley K. Hornbeck of the State Department's Office of the Economic Adviser sent a letter to several other department officials asking their opinions on a matter that had recently come to his attention. A representative of Edward Doheny, president of the American-owned Mexican Petroleum Company, had inquired about the oil industry in Venezuela. The representative was especially interested in whether foreign oil companies operating there had run into any of the difficulties that had "been encountered in Mexico, difficulties arising from official attitude and from character or tendencies of legislation." Mexican Petroleum actually expected no problems in Venezuela; in Hornbeck's words, the company merely wished to be assured "that the woods are not full of lions."[1]

In many ways, Hornbeck's analogy summed up U.S.-Latin American relations from 1917 to 1929. The "woods" of Latin America, which had appeared so inviting to U.S. investment and trade during and immediately after World War I, had taken on some menacing aspects: The "lions" of economic nationalism now prowled the region. While economic nationalism, particularly in the more developed nations of South America, was never clearly understood by American officials and businessmen, it nevertheless came to be seen as a serious threat. The confrontation between that philosophy and the interests and goals of the United States in Latin America was the key element determining U.S. policy toward that region from 1917 to 1929.

With the passage of the 1917 constitution in Mexico, especially the promulgation of Article 27, the United States for the first time came face to face with the full implications of economic nationalism. Understanding how the United States perceived and reacted to the Mexican challenge is necessary to understanding the larger issue of American relations with Latin America as a whole.

That Mexico, even before 1917, was the focus for a vague but ominous anti-U.S. feeling in Latin America was acknowledged in a June 1916 letter from John Barrett, director general of the PAU, to Leo Rowe (who would succeed Barrett a few years later). Commenting on President Woodrow Wilson's plan for a Pan American pact, Barrett concluded that "we are unfortunately up against a kind of agitation in Latin America by friends of Mexico and other anti-Americans."[2] The collapse of Wilson's plan indicated that Barrett was correct.[3] That debacle, especially Argentina's refusal to become involved until Mexican-American differences were settled, clearly upset Wilson's adviser Edward House, who wrote to the president in June 1916: "Heaven knows, you have done all that you could to help the people there [in Mexico] and the fact that they are not able to follow your kindly lead is no fault of yours." In July House wrote to the U.S. ambassador in Mexico, Henry Fletcher, concerning the situation: "I cannot understand the viewpoint of the A.B.C. [Argentina, Brazil, and Chile] powers. The President is looking to the larger good and to having America lead the way to a better understanding among the nations of the world." Yet House did not give up all hope. Later in 1916 he wrote to Robert Lansing about the appointment of Hugh Wallace to the London embassy. Wallace, House stated, should "cultivate" the Latin American representatives in that nation and "let the American Embassy be the rallying ground in London for the Americas."[4] This view reduced the "problem" of Mexico to one of politics and diplomacy: If only the United States could "cultivate" Mexico and the other nations of Latin America and have them follow its "kindly lead," the problem would go away.

Other U.S. policymakers decided that economics was at the heart of the matter, that Mexico's poor internal financial structure and its correspondingly poor performance in meeting its external debt were the sources of its turmoil. In July 1916, State Department Counselor Frank Polk, writing to House about the situation in Mexico, stated that "it is an economic question, rather than political, and if they could only be put into some shape financially, many of the evils could be cured." House was not entirely convinced, but he responded: "Is there any prospect of doing something for Mexico in an economic way? . . . It may be that nothing can be done and yet it is the only quick solution."[5]

Mexico's own solutions to its economic difficulties were laid out in early 1917 with the passage of the new constitution, and they came as nasty surprises to U.S. observers. Article 27 was perhaps the nastiest of all. Expropriation of subsoil deposits, and the land under which they lay, seemed to be at stake. Secretary of State Lansing, upon hearing of the proposed Article 27 in January 1917, immediately wrote that it implied "a proposed policy toward foreigners which is fraught with possible grave consequences" for Mexico's relations with other nations.[6] Although the imminent entry of the United States into World

War I prevented Lansing and other officials from considering Article 27 deeply, they did mull over possible responses to Mexico's actions.

One of the first responses considered was withholding diplomatic recognition. After the passage of Mexico's new constitution, the State Department debated how recognition could be used to secure changes in that document. Chandler Anderson, formerly with the department but by then serving as a lobbyist for American oil companies, recorded the progress of the debate in his diary. On 8 March he met with representatives of several oil companies and put forward the suggestion that the American government should "make recognition of the new government [in Mexico] dependent upon the conclusion of a treaty with this government satisfactorily protecting American rights and property in Mexico." Two days later, Anderson met with Lansing and Polk to discuss his suggestion. Lansing believed that it was an "advisable" plan, while Polk, who also agreed that it was a good idea, feared that President Wilson would extend recognition just to keep Mexico out of the German sphere of influence. A little over two weeks passed before Anderson again met with Polk and Lansing. He now thought, and the others agreed, that a treaty would be problematic; perhaps a simple exchange of notes or a declaration by Mexico renouncing retroactive applications of Article 27 would be sufficient.[7] Anderson's proposal was put into effect in a limited way in August 1917 when, on the basis of Mexican president Venustiano Carranza's vague promises concerning the application of Article 27, de jure recognition was granted. Anderson was unhappy that a stronger statement had not been secured.[8]

A much more promising approach to the Mexican problem was to use America's tremendous financial power to induce, or if need be to coerce, changes in Mexico's policies. Anderson was in the forefront of those counseling that path of action. In an April 1917 meeting with Lansing, he argued that any loans to Mexico should be tied to concessions on the land issue. "Bert [Lansing] said that the question of a loan was under consideration," Anderson wrote after the meeting, "and perhaps the simplest solution of our present difficulties might be to buy our peace with Carranza and make a loan conditional upon securing from him the various assurances and guarantees which we desired."[9]

Between 1918 and 1921 the Wilson presidency came to grips with the problem of Mexico and formed basic premises concerning Article 27 and economic nationalism. Although the Warren Harding and Calvin Coolidge administrations elaborated certain of those premises and stressed some more than others, the fundamental assumptions governing how the United States perceived and responded to economic nationalism were formed during those three years.

The most basic of these premises was that a proposal such as Article 27 seriously threatened American economic interests, on both a Latin American and a global scale. C. E. McGuire, assistant secretary-general of the IAHC, laid out the U.S.-Latin American relationship in no uncertain terms: "The establishment of markets in South America for the goods produced in the United States carries with it an increasing obligation to establish dependable and expanding markets in the United States for the raw products of Central and South America." McGuire was confident that the United States could meet its part of the bargain with "entire satisfaction."[10] But Mexican actions threatened this arrangement in several ways.

The concept of economic nationalism embodied in measures such as Article 27 was vastly different from, and in conflict with, the U.S. path toward political, social, and economic development during the postwar years. World War I had raised serious questions about the place of the state in the economy and society of the nation, questions involving the entire concept of private property. Although during the war years involvement of government in the direction and management of business had grown, the postwar consensus among U.S. policymakers and businessmen was that this involvement was ultimately dangerous. Charles McChord of the Interstate Commerce Commission spoke for many others in 1919 when he wrote that "a protecting government hand in time of war is quite apt to become a restraining government hand in time of peace." Government ownership of private industry particularly was to be avoided, because that would mean "shifting the burden from the owners, where it belongs, to the general public, where it does not belong." George E. Roberts, vice president of the National City Bank, in that same year wrote that plans for government control of industry were "foreign to our system of government" and that such plans "constitute an encroachment upon individual rights, upon the individual freedom and initiative which has been the chief factor in the wonderful progress of industry in this country."[11]

Article 27 contained two intertwined threats to such beliefs: economic nationalism, with its demand for state participation in and direction of the economy (particularly of natural resource development), and social constitutionalism, which demanded that private property be subordinated to the general welfare. These could only be perceived as shots across the bow of the American system. As Lansing put it in 1918, in reference to Mexico's oil policies, "The United States can not acquiesce in any procedure ostensibly or nominally in the form of taxation or the exercise of eminent domain, but really resulting in confiscation of private property and arbitrary deprivation of vested rights."[12] Oil company lawyer Frederic Kellogg went a step further, issuing the ominous warning in 1919 that "the success of such a program as this in Mexico is bound to be followed by strong reactions in this country, where many people are giving thought to questions involving" nationalization of railroads, mines, utilities, and other resources.[13]

Of more immediate concern, however, was the effect of Mexico's new political-economic direction on its economic relationship with the United States. American officials agreed that the results would be disastrous. First, Mexico's actions seemed to indicate that it no longer desired the presence of foreign investors and capitalists. The most powerful statements of this perception are in the letters of Ambassador Fletcher. In June 1918 he wrote to Frank Polk that he believed he understood Carranza's goals quite well: "economic, financial, diplomatic—every sort of independence of the United States." The Mexican president thought that he had America "in the nine hole and the only way out will be to abandon the property rights of American citizens in Mexico to the tender mercies of the Mexican Gov't and Article 27 of the new Constitution."[14]

Second, the ultimate outcome of such independence would be that Mexico would be left to its own devices for economic development and resource exploitation. American observers, however, were as one in the opinion that foreign (preferably U.S.) investment and guidance were necessary for the proper development of Mexican resources. Writing in early 1918, Lansing expressed confusion about Mexico's new oil and land policy; after all, Mexico was "at a stage in its progress when the development of its resources so greatly depends on its maintaining good faith with investors and operators."[15] Frederic Kellogg pointed out the results of Mexico's oil policies to banker Thomas Lamont in 1919, noting that such policies would reduce oil exports from Mexico. Such an occurrence would "result not merely in increases of price of fuel petroleum and petroleum products" but in the inability to procure oil needed for America's merchant marine, railroads, and armed forces.[16]

Furthermore, American policymakers were convinced that Article 27 not only threatened their concepts of economic development and the U.S.-Mexican trade relationship but also posed a direct danger to the entire world capitalist order. As William Appleman Williams has put it, American capitalists and statesmen

> saw specific issues of property—say a railroad or a loan in China, a factory in Russia, or oil wells or silver mines or farm land in Mexico—as part of a global system of capitalism. The system— even specific entrepreneurs—could tolerate the loss of this, that, or the other investment or loan, but it could not survive countries taking themselves out of the system. . . . any contracting out of the global marketplace threatened both the theory and the practice of capitalism.[17]

Such beliefs, in part, prompted Ambassador Fletcher's declaration in 1918 that his work in Mexico was grounded in "a real desire to see this country return to the ranks of production. The world will need it."[18] While it was engaged in revolutionary activities and radical economic policies, Mexico to a large degree had taken itself "out of the system."

Instead of playing its proper role within that system, it had taken the path of economic nationalism, a direct threat to the "global marketplace." It was not so much Mexico's dollars-and-cents value in that marketplace as its role in the huge and interdependent machinery of the world capitalist order that really mattered.

During the last years of the Wilson presidency, Mexico's actions conflicted with widely held U.S. beliefs concerning economic development. The direct threat to private property combined with the implicit threat of state control of that property to make what American officials saw as a catastrophically inefficient experiment. The Mexicans' lack of knowledge and ability to develop their economy would send their nation spinning out of the world capitalist orbit.

These impressions influenced the formation of U.S. responses to Mexico. Just as in 1917, the uses of financial and diplomatic means to counteract economic nationalism were preferred. Policymakers in Washington were still quite willing to use America's economic might in their diplomacy with Mexico, but they, together with many prominent businessmen, favored a more "positive" approach. This was built upon the notions that economic ills were at the core of Mexico's problems (and so they were, but hardly in the way the United States perceived the matter) and that American financial power and expertise could be used to "reconstruct" the Mexican economy, which had fallen into chaos due to the Mexicans' mishandling.

Officials such as House and Polk were convinced that the solution to U.S.-Mexican problems was fundamentally economic. In July 1918, House wrote Polk that "if some plan can be thought out by which this Government can safely finance Mexico the trouble will cease, and it will not cease until this is done." Polk agreed and wrote to President Wilson in August concerning the "financial reconstruction" of Mexico. What was needed, he argued, was to prod American bankers into loan negotiations, which would serve three purposes: to show Mexico that "we earnestly desire to assist them"; to undercut German influences in Mexico; and, most important, to "relieve the present oil situation by diverting attention of the Government [of Mexico] from that source of revenue to the offers of our bankers."[19]

By early 1919, Polk was in contact with a number of bankers and businessmen in an attempt to resolve the Mexican problem. During a March meeting with J. P. Morgan, Jr., he explained that "it would be obviously money in our pocket to put Mexico on its feet and prevent trouble." Another banking representative, writing to Polk one month later, demonstrated that he agreed with that assessment: "The State Department knows that the banking and currency reform the mercantile group has done in Latin America has proved to be the only practical way of solving the problem of the countries in question."[20]

The United States also moved on the diplomatic front to negate the effects of economic nationalism in Mexico. The question of recognition, seemingly settled during the presidency of Carranza, was raised anew with the rise of Alvaro Obregón to power in 1920. Writing to Wilson, Secretary of State Bainbridge Colby (Lansing's successor) asserted in 1920 that Mexico "should give convincing proof of her ability as well as her disposition to sustain her international obligations" before recognition would be granted.[21]

U.S. policymakers also perceived the need for a spirited effort to cultivate intrahemispheric goodwill and a sense of Pan Americanism led, of course, by the United States. This need had been made clear in a long letter from Ambassador Fletcher to Edward House in 1918. Fletcher declared that Mexico hoped to "destroy its [the U.S] influence in this hemisphere." Referring to the travels of Carranza's representative Luis Cabrera in South America, the ambassador reported that "he is preparing the ground and sounding those governments in regard to the 'showdown' which Carranza may have with the United States over the retroactive enforcement of Article 27." He concluded:

> I am unwaveringly of the opinion that this issue will sooner or later have to be met, and that only by standing firm on the principles which the Department has already laid down, can we hope to avoid endless trouble and difficulty, and in this connection, I have no apprehension as to the effect which a firm stand in support of justice and fair dealing will have on our relations with the South American nations.[22]

Acting on Fletcher's analysis of the situation, Jordan Stabler, a former chief of the State Department's Latin American Division, attended the Paris Peace Conference with the idea of promoting goodwill among the Latin American participants. His success was less than notable.[23]

For American policymakers during the years 1918 to 1921, it was difficult to comprehend Mexico's and, increasingly, the rest of Latin America's reluctance to follow the "kindly lead" of the United States. The nations to the south seemed intent on exercising their political and economic independence, most frighteningly through their programs of economic nationalism. This had been powerfully demonstrated by Mexico's Article 27 and the resulting disputes with the United States over property rights and oil fields during the last years of the Wilson administration. The years of the Harding and Coolidge administrations witnessed even greater efforts to understand and respond to the threat of economic nationalism.

Neither Charles Evans Hughes, secretary of state under Warren G. Harding and Calvin Coolidge until 1925, nor Frank B. Kellogg, Hughes's successor from 1925 to 1929, could conceal his frustration and anger over the situation in Mexico. Hughes, in a 1922 speech dealing with Mexico's land policies, insisted that "an essential condition of international intercourse" was that there would be "no recourse to confiscation and repudiation." Later that year, he vented his anger in a conversation with Thomas Lamont. According to notes taken by

Lamont's secretary, the secretary of state said that "the situation could not be settled too quickly to please him" and closed the discussion by stating that "we do not want promises from Mexico; we want '*things*.' "[24] Frank Kellogg went even further, declaring in a 1925 speech that Mexico's property policies had put that nation "on trial before the world." In a 1925 interview with the *New York Times*, Kellogg remarked that "alien land and petroleum laws" in Mexico had "created a serious situation" for American interests.[25]

Just as during the Wilson period, officials during the Harding-Coolidge years wrestled with the problem of the role of the state in a national economy. But by that time it was obvious that some sort of compromise was needed in the business-government relationship. The solution that a number of public figures viewed as the best hope for America's economic future, as historian Ellis Hawley has described it, "lay neither in antitrust action nor governmental direction but rather in a 'new individualism' developed and disciplined in private associations and guided through scientific inquiries and coordinating councils." Such a system would witness the "consignment of social duties to properly enlightened social orders, in the creation of machinery through which those orders could act together for the common good." In that scheme of things the state would "serve as the agent or 'midwife' for bringing such arrangements into being."[26]

The embodiment of this "new individualism" was Herbert Hoover who, while serving as secretary of commerce, made clear that at the core of this philosophy was the concept of private property. In 1922 he wrote:

> Our development of individualism shows an increasing tendency to regard right of property not as an object in itself, but in the light of a useful and necessary instrument in stimulation of initiative to the individual; not only stimulation to him that he may gain personal comfort, security in life, protection to his family, but also because individual accumulation and ownership is a basis of selection to leadership in administration of the tools of industry and commerce. It is where dominant private property is assembled in the hands of the groups who control the state that the individual begins to feel capital as an oppressor.[27]

Officials such as Assistant Director of the BFDC Thomas Taylor added that "every business man and every business paper should share in the campaign against governmental controls."[28]

As the decade progressed, a number of American policymakers grew especially concerned about government interference in the development or control of natural resources. In a 1925 speech Hoover complained that foreign controls over the production and prices of certain resources "amount practically to trade war." Foreign governments, he noted, had helped their businessmen to establish monopolies in "coffee, silk, nitrates, potash, rubber, quinine, iodine, tin, sisal," and a number of other products. As Hoover pointed out, however,

> The problem which faces the world, and possibly the more serious problem, is not alone the commodities that are now controlled but the spread of these ideas. There are many other raw materials whose sources are so situated that they could also be controlled by the action of a single government. The price of wool could be controlled by governmental action within the British Empire. The prices of oil, cotton and copper could be controlled for many years by similar governmental action in the United States. Tea and jute could be controlled by India; antimony and tungsten by China; nickel and asbestos by Canada.[29]

Grosvenor Jones, chief of the Finance and Investment Division of the BFDC, agreed: "If only our leaders understood that the control and fostering by foreign governments of monopolies of essential raw materials is a virulent and contagious disease that is liable to spread here and wreak havoc everywhere, more of them would look at this question with more far-seeing intelligence."[30]

The new ambassador to Mexico, James Sheffield, put the question in more dramatic terms in 1927. "Property rights are human rights," he wrote. "Oil companies are merely an aggregation of many human beings owning stock, and many of those people are clerks, school-teachers, and others of very limited means." In his unpublished autobiography, Sheffield concluded that "nothing but actual experience in trying to change the law of economics by statute would alter" Mexico's view "and that meanwhile Mexico would suffer in her economic and industrial life."[31]

Sheffield's belief notwithstanding, both the Harding and Coolidge administrations also considered other methods of educating the Mexicans about the "law of economics." Both administrations preferred to use the economic weight of the United States to try to convert Mexico to the proper mode of economic development. The debate continued, however, about whether that weight should be used as an incentive or as a punishment.

Thomas Lamont, in a letter to Secretary of State Hughes in December 1923, made the case for the former approach, explaining that the Mexicans "need financial advice very solely" and that if such advice could be given them it would set Mexico "on the real path for generations to come."[32] The opposing viewpoint was expressed, as it had been in earlier years, by Chandler Anderson, who continued his lobbying efforts during Frank Kellogg's tenure as secretary of state. He suggested that it be pointed out to Mexico that, although the United States had loaned over $1 billion to Latin America, none would be forthcoming for Mexico "so long as the menace of confiscation of foreign property under the Mexican Constitution continued."[33] As

Robert Freeman Smith has explained in greater detail, the years from 1925 to 1932 saw the "triumph" of Lamont's brand of "finance diplomacy," a "triumph" lasting until 1938. That must have been of great satisfaction to those like the former first secretary of the American embassy in Mexico City, Arthur Bliss Lane, who wrote that "it seems obvious that the economic and financial rehabilitation of Mexico is essential before the vexatious agrarian problem can be satisfactorily disposed of."[34]

Other solutions to the Mexican problem were bandied about from 1921 to 1929. Military intervention had an emotional appeal, but it never gained sufficient support, either from the American public or from leading government officials. The severance of diplomatic relations was often called for, but it never gained much acceptance as a realistic or effective solution. For most U.S. officials and businessmen those solutions, while not totally discarded (they were, in fact, sometimes used elsewhere in Latin America to deal with economic nationalism), were not the preferred answers. The answers that were preferred—using the diplomatic and especially the economic power of the United States to effect the changes it desired—should have come as no great surprise. World War I, after all, had made the United States the predominant diplomatic and economic power in the region, and its power was used to protect American interests in Mexico.

American policymakers at the time understood that economic nationalism was not a problem of simply protecting oil companies in Mexico. Indeed those officials, during both the Democratic and Republican administrations, were often skeptical about the plight of particular American oil companies in Mexico. In 1919, for example, Polk expressed his dissatisfaction: "I have been having rather a time with the Mexican oil people," he wrote. "They have been diging [sic] out some publicity and at the same time swearing they were not doing it." Edward Doheny, head of Huasteca Petroleum in Mexico, came in for special attack for telling reporters that he was traveling to the Paris Peace Conference to present claims for the oil companies, after having assured Polk that he would not present them. "I am going to stop Doheny's passport when he gets to London and make him sweat a little," Polk wrote gleefully, and he warned his correspondent to "look out for Doheny."[35]

By 1927, Assistant Secretary of State Robert Olds was claiming that the seizure of American-owned land, excluding oil lands, was the most serious problem in Mexico. The oil companies had not really been affected: "Not a square foot of their land has been taken," Olds stated, and he sarcastically remarked that "they [the oil companies] have been coming to us with the same story for a decade."[36] Obviously, for observers such as Polk, Olds, and others, the "oil question" was secondary to more important considerations raised by Mexico's policies.

Furthermore, the fear among American policymakers of Mexico's Article 27, and of the economic nationalism embodied within it, was compounded by their belief that the "Mexican problem" would not always be confined to Mexico. Article 27 came to be seen as merely the first of many such challenges that American interests would face in Latin America, and as such it also came to be viewed as a test case for U.S. policy.

This was plainly laid out in a meeting between Frank Polk, Thomas Lamont, and other State Department officials and businessmen in 1919. Polk recalled in his diary that "they all felt that unless we could protect the capital in Mexico, there was no chance of getting Americans to invest in foreign countries."[37] In a December 1927 meeting between Lamont and Palmer Pierce of Standard Oil, Pierce pointed out that the oil companies were involved in a number of other Latin American nations, and that "the companies must remember that if they gave way in a matter of principle in the Mexican dispute, they would be forced to do likewise in these other countries." That was exactly the point James Sheffield had tried to make in 1926. Officials in Washington, he argued, "must realize that the principle of protection of American property in Mexico is involved in the protection of American property throughout Latin America." "As we deal with Mexico," he continued, "so we will eventually have to deal with every other Latin American republic on this continent." This had been put in a blunter fashion in an April 1927 meeting between Chandler Anderson, a number of oil company representatives, and a sprinkling of State Department officials: "We also pointed out that this situation was being watched keenly by all Latin-America, and if Mexico could get away with it the same thing would be done elsewhere."[38]

Several points concerning the U.S. perception of and response to economic nationalism in Mexico seem clear: First, economic nationalism was perceived as a very serious threat, not only to the American interests operating in Mexico but also to the entire concept of a world capitalist system based on a distinct division of labor that U.S. policymakers were formulating from 1917 to 1929.

Second, Mexico's Article 27 seemed to attack two of the basic assumptions behind that emerging world capitalist view: the sanctity and importance of private property, and the limited role of the government in directing economic development.

Third, American officials were convinced that if Mexico pursued economic nationalism, the results would be an unmitigated disaster. Demonstrating a remarkable lack of insight into what was prompting Mexico's actions, they assumed that Mexico could be rehabilitated—but only with U.S. money and expertise.

Fourth, a number of responses to Mexico's actions were discussed and often used by the United States. The two most prevalent were (1) the use of diplomatic pressure, either by directly cutting off diplomatic ties or by indirectly isolating Mexico through "cultivating" American friends in the hemisphere, and (2) the use of America's dominant financial power to either coerce or induce Mexico into taking the proper path to development.

Finally, and perhaps most important, U.S. officials were aware that Mexico could be just the tip of the iceberg. Economic nationalism had the potential to threaten all sorts of U.S. interests anywhere and everywhere in Latin America.

Notes

1. Stanley K. Hornbeck to Henry P. Starrett, Richard W. Flourney, and Charles Boyd Curtis, 7 March 1923, 831.6363/233, RG 59.

2. John Barrett to Leo S. Rowe, 21 June 1916, Box 25, RG 43, Records of the IAHC.

3. For a more detailed discussion of the defeat of Wilson's Pan American treaty see Gilderhus, *Pan American Visions*, 49–77.

4. Edward House to Woodrow Wilson, 25 June 1916, Box 121, Folder 265; House to Henry Fletcher, 13 or 14 July 1916, Box 44, Folder 411; House to Robert Lansing, 18 December 1916, Box 69, Folder 273, House Papers.

5. Frank Polk to House, 15 July 1916; House to Polk, 28 July 1916, Box 8, Folder 167, Polk Papers.

6. Lansing to Mr. Parker, representing American interests, 22 January 1917, U.S. Department of State, *Papers Relating to the Foreign Relations of the United States, 1917* (Washington, 1926), 947–49 (hereafter cited as *FRUS*, with date).

7. Chandler Anderson diary, 8, 10, 29 March 1917, Papers of Chandler P. Anderson, Manuscripts Division, Library of Congress, Washington (hereafter cited as Anderson Papers).

8. Smith, *Revolutionary Nationalism*, 109.

9. Anderson diary, 30 April 1917, Anderson Papers.

10. C. E. McGuire, "The Value of the Inter-American High Commission as a Bond of International Peace," 12 September 1917, Box 25, RG 43, Records of the IAHC.

11. Charles McChord to Newton D. Baker, 17 May 1919, Baker Papers; George Roberts, "Unrest and Lessened Production Threaten America's Prosperity," *The Americas* 5 (August 1919): 3.

12. Lansing to embassy in Mexico, 19 March 1919, Box 29, Folder 487, Polk Papers.

13. Frederic Kellogg to Thomas Lamont, 22 December 1919, Box 195, Folder 1, Lamont Papers.

14. Fletcher to Polk, 26 June 1918, Box 5, Folder 179, Polk Papers.

15. Lansing to embassy in Mexico, 19 March 1919, Box 29, Folder 487, Polk Papers. See Chapter 4 for a discussion of the role that racism played in the U.S. belief that Mexico and other nations in Latin America could not develop on their own.

16. Kellogg to Lamont, 22 December 1919, Box 195, Folder 1, Lamont Papers.

17. William Appleman Williams, *Empire as a Way of Life: An Essay on the Causes and Character of America's Present Predicament along with a Few Thoughts about an Alternative* (New York, 1980), 148.

18. Fletcher to Polk, 3 December 1918, Box 5, Folder 180, Polk Papers.

19. House to Polk, 10 July 1918, Box 8, Folder 267; Polk to Wilson, 1 August 1918, Box 14, Folder 503, Polk Papers.

20. Polk diary, 19 March 1919; Gavin McNab to Polk, 12 April 1919, Box 10, Folder 344, Polk Papers.

21. Bainbridge Colby to Wilson, 25 September 1920, Box 4, Papers of Bainbridge Colby, Manuscript Division, Library of Congress, Washington, DC (hereafter cited as Colby Papers).

22. Fletcher to House, 17 July 1918, Box 44, Folder 412, House Papers.

23. See Chapter 4 for a more detailed discussion of Stabler's activities at the conference.

24. Hughes's speech contained in Hughes to George W. Oakes, 29 March 1922, 710.11/588, RG 59; "Memorandum of a conversation with Secretary Hughes, Mr. Hanna [Matthew Hanna, chief of the Division of Mexican Affairs] at State Department, Washington, October 16th and October 20th, 1922," 21 October 1922, Box 197, Folder 19, Lamont Papers (emphasis in original). See Grieb, *Latin American Policy*, 129–55, for an analysis of Harding's role in negotiations with Mexico during 1921–1923. Grieb asserts that Harding had a substantial impact on those negotiations through informal, personal contacts with Mexican President Alvaro Obregón.

25. *New York Times*, 13 June 1925; ibid., 1 January 1925.

26. Ellis Hawley, *The Great War and the Search for a Modern Order: A History of the American People and Their Institutions, 1917–1933* (New York, 1979), 10–11.

27. Herbert Hoover, *American Individualism* (New York, 1979), 37–38.

28. Thomas Taylor to Dr. Harrison Howe, 25 March [?] 1926, 060.0-General, RG 151.

29. Hoover, "Foreign Combinations Now Fixing Prices of Raw Materials Imported into the United States," address delivered before Chamber of Commerce, Erie, PA, 31 October 1925, 060.0-General, RG 151.

30. Grosvenor Jones to James Clark, 11 March 1926, 060.0-General, RG 151.

31. James Sheffield to Arthur Schoenfeld, 1 February 1927, Box 8; "Autobiography," p. 26, Box 11, Papers of James R. Sheffield, Yale University Library, New Haven, Connecticut (hereafter cited as Sheffield Papers).

32. Draft letter, Lamont to Hughes, 31 December 1923, Box 208, Folder 7, Lamont Papers.

33. Anderson diary, 29 April 1927, Anderson Papers.

34. Smith, *Revolutionary Nationalism*, 229–65; Arthur Bliss Lane to Delbert Haff, 6 February 1928, Box 56a, Folder 918, Papers of Arthur Bliss Lane, Yale University Library, New Haven, Connecticut (hereafter cited as Lane Papers).

35. Polk to Gordon Auchincloss, 4 February 1919, Box 1, Folder 20, Polk Papers.

36. Robert Olds, "Mexico," 22 June 1927, Box 1, Folder 10, Lane Papers. As Smith has noted, "it is impossible to make an accurate estimate of all these [U.S] losses." He cites a 1931 estimate ("an exaggerated index") of $759,852,662 (Smith, *Revolutionary Nationalism*, 91).

37. Polk diary, 9 July 1919, Polk Papers.

38. Memorandum for Lamont by Vernon Monroe, secretary, International Committee of Bankers on Mexico, 13 December 1927, Box 208, Folder 12, Lamont Papers; Sheffield to Col. Henry W. Anderson, 7 April 1926, Box 8, Sheffield Papers; Anderson diary, 21 April 1927, Anderson Papers.

Chapter Four

Bolsheviks and Half-breeds: Anticommunism, Racism, and U.S. Policy

The U.S. response to economic nationalism in Latin America involved not only economic issues but also political and even cultural factors. Two of these factors—anticommunism and racism—had tremendous influence on both the perceptions of U.S. policymakers and their responses to economic nationalism. This was hardly surprising; after all, the Russian Revolution began in the same year as the promulgation of Mexico's new and ominous constitution and could hardly have failed to have some impact on U.S. perceptions of the goings on in Mexico. Furthermore, as noted in Chapter 2, those same observers were already convinced that economic nationalism in Latin America represented the intrusion of some strange and alien economic philosophy into the world system—and what could be stranger or more alien than communism? Perhaps there was a connection. Racism's role is even more understandable, since, in one form or another, racism had been a fairly consistent element in earlier U.S. policies toward Latin America. Under the influence of the negative U.S. attitude toward economic nationalism, however, racism's role underwent yet another revision.

I

Less than one year after the promulgation of Mexico's radical constitution, the United States and the entire capitalist order faced a much more spectacular challenge: the Russian Revolution. American policymakers believed that, like Mexico, Russia was not content simply to withdraw from the system (which was bad enough) but that it desired to spread its ideology elsewhere. That notion had been at the crux of the DeWitt Poole memorandum prepared in 1919 cited in

Chapter 1: "It is the essence of the Bolshevik movement that it is *international and not national in character*." The Bolsheviks "aim directly at the subversion of all Governments."[1]

As America's policy toward Latin America was not formulated in a vacuum, problems with Russia, coupled with a belief in that nation's subversive goals, had a powerful impact on the U.S. reaction to events in Latin America. After 1917 there was a strong suspicion that Mexico and Bolshevik Russia were proceeding along parallel pathways. In addition, particularly during Frank Kellogg's service as secretary of state, there was a growing uneasiness about the role Russia might have in Mexico and elsewhere in Latin America.[2]

"Socialistic," "Bolshevistic," and "Communistic" were terms commonly applied to Mexico by American policymakers following the promulgation of the 1917 constitution; economic nationalism was lumped together with those radical philosophies in the American mindset. Writing to Frank Polk in December 1918, Henry Fletcher declared "state socialism complete—legitimatizing strikes and if strikers' demands not acceded to the Government will step in and run the plants." Late in 1919, during a confrontation with Colombia over its oil laws, Robert Lansing reminded the American ambassador to Bogotá that "a serious condition is confronting this Government through legislation in Mexico of a socialistic tendency." That same year Chandler Anderson, writing about unrest in Central America, expressed concern over the "Bolshevik tendencies which the Mexican influences are producing in Salvador."[3]

During the first few years after the Russian Revolution, however, there seemed to be little concern among American officials that Mexico was becoming a Russian satellite. Although its 1917 constitution was uncomfortably akin to some of the ideas being heralded in Bolshevik Russia, only a few American observers would go so far as to link the two revolutionary governments in any other way. By 1921 to 1929, however, suspicion was growing among U.S. policymakers and businessmen that Mexico was not simply emulating the Russian experiment, which was unsettling enough, but was serving as an agent for the spread of bolshevism into the Western Hemisphere.

Concern over the matter was already surfacing during Charles Evans Hughes's tenure as secretary of state. A memorandum of a conversation between Hughes and Thomas Lamont in 1921 shows that Hughes firmly believed that Mexico was involved in a "socialistic experiment." Whether Hughes believed that Moscow was behind this "experiment" is not clear, but it is evident that the secretary was convinced of the worldwide nature of the Bolshevik threat. In a letter to labor leader Samuel Gompers in 1923, Hughes exclaimed that "what is most serious is that there is conclusive evidence that those in control at Moscow have not given up their original purpose of destroying existing governments wherever they can do so throughout the world." Lamont's appraisal of the political-economic direction of the Mexican Revolution, found in a memorandum prepared in 1923 or 1924, included the fear that if President Alvaro Obregón fell from power, "a chaotic condition will follow . . . developing along the same lines of Soviet Russia."[4]

The high point of American fears of Soviet involvement in Mexico, and by extension in all of Latin America, was reached during the years 1925–1929, while Frank Kellogg served as secretary of state, and climaxed with his revelation in January 1927 that the Soviet Union was actively encouraging and aiding bolshevism in Latin America. Kellogg's chief biographer, L. Ethan Ellis, has declared that this issue was simply a "red herring" designed to garner congressional support for a stronger stance against Mexico's increasingly adamant stand on the land issue.[5]

It is true that some members of the State Department, notably Assistant Secretary of State Robert Olds, were not above using the specter of bolshevism to achieve this end. Yet Kellogg and many of his close advisers shared a belief that, just as the Bolsheviks had taken Russia out of the "civilized" world system, they were now plotting to do the same in Latin America using Mexico as their base of operations.

Kellogg's personal fear of bolshevism, and especially of its spread beyond Russia, was constant and long-standing.[6] As a senator in 1919, Kellogg enunciated his concern over the spread of radicalism in the United States, declaring that "it is the I.W.W.—the escaped nihilists, who come to this country from Russia, the scum of Europe comprised of men who call themselves socialists but who are mere anarchists. They try to incite the dissatisfied elements of this country to a class warfare." After the 1924 election Kellogg wrote to Frank Polk that "the one thing that pleased me most in the election was the defeat of [Robert] LaFollette, of [Burton] Wheeler, and of the Socialists, the Communists and the I.W.W.'s." He was happy to see that both the Democratic and Republican parties were "going to throw them out, as you say,—way out."[7]

As secretary of state, Kellogg's distaste for radicalism did not disappear. Commenting on his barring Shapurji Saklatvala, a Communist spokesman from India, from entry into the United States in 1925, the secretary bluntly concluded: "I believe that this is the only way to treat these revolutionists." The next year, Kellogg asked Secretary of Labor James Davis for some "ideas for campaign speeches" on the labor situation. Kellogg wanted to "touch upon the question of admitting Communists into this country who are trying to bore into the labor unions."[8]

Kellogg increasingly became convinced that Russia was serving as a center for radicalism and revolution. In a letter to the American ambassador to England, he outlined the three conditions upon which American recognition of Russia depended: first, Russia must settle its debts to the United States; second, it must either return or make compensation for property taken; and third, the Russians "must cease their propaganda in the United States." By 1927, Kellogg had concluded that recognition of Russia was not likely in the foreseeable future. "I am confident," he wrote to author James Beck, "that the recent events have convinced the people of this country of the futility of attempting to establish relations, on the basis usual between friendly nations, with a regime dedicated to the promotion of world revolution."[9]

Nor was Kellogg a voice crying in the wilderness. Chandler Anderson, for example, recounted that Secretary of Commerce Herbert Hoover had told him that "he had made a careful investigation" in the Commerce Department "for the purpose of eliminating all sympathizers with Bolshevism and LaFolletteism, and he thought he had gotten rid of all disloyal elements." And in response to Kellogg's request for data on the labor situation in the United States in 1926, A. E. Cook of the Department of Labor wrote that during 1920–21 it was "natural" that "red radical agents should be particularly active." Since then restricted immigration had allowed America to "sift out more carefully foreign anarchists and communists." Some had been "found insidiously at work" and deported.[10]

Kellogg found support both in and out of government. When, in mid-1925, the secretary launched some scathing attacks on Mexico, culminating in a speech in June proclaiming that Mexico was "on trial before the world," a number of newspapers carried stories and editorials praising his action. The *New York City Herald Tribune* ran a story on 28 May 1925 that stated that "Bolshevism has gained a grip in Mexico," that it was "being encouraged, it is alleged, by Russian agents," and that labor and agrarian forces in Mexico "are Bolshevist and recognize no rights of property." The *Philadelphia Morning Public Ledger*, two days after Kellogg's "trial" speech, hailed the secretary and proclaimed that "Bolshevism and capitalism will get along no better together in Mexico than they do in Russia."[11]

Kellogg's advisers supported the view that bolshevism was the primary problem in Mexico. Ambassador James Sheffield wrote in late 1925 that the Mexican government was "shot through with bolshevism, but without any real comprehension of what it wants or what it will do when it gets it." Sheffield recounted in his unpublished autobiography that he had been shocked when he arrived in Veracruz during a rent strike: "A thousand houses were occupied by those who refused to pay rent to the owners and they were supported in this position by the City and State authorities." The city, he concluded, was "completely dominated by radical labor leaders." In a lighter vein the *New York Times* reported in January 1926 that the ambassador had personally felt the sting of the labor forces in Mexico. After a round of golf, Sheffield had returned to find the clubhouse empty, since the workers had gone on strike, and for a time he was detained because strikers had locked the gate leading from the course. All ended well, however, when the "weary representative" was allowed to return to the embassy, "where warm water and a hot luncheon awaited America's golfing Ambassador."[12]

Chandler Anderson, after his early 1926 trip to Mexico, concluded that "the present situation in Mexico is very similar to that in Russia." Following his return to Washington, Anderson met with Kellogg to discuss Mexico and other problems in Central America. He explained to the secretary that a "menacing" situation existed in Nicaragua, and that the Liberals in that nation "were being encouraged by bolshevistic influences in Mexico." Just prior to that meeting, Anderson had written to Sheffield that, although he felt that Kellogg did not share all of Sheffield's views on bolshevism in Mexico, nevertheless Sheffield should release to the press his information on Communist influences in Mexico.[13]

That Kellogg also found support in Congress was revealed in the *New York Times* on 5 March 1925, which reported Representative John Baylor's (Democrat from New York) strongly worded speech concerning Mexico and the Soviet Union:

> "The two nations are on a par so far as their attitude toward fundamental rights of humanity are concerned," he [Baylor] continued. "It is time our official attitude toward Mexico became that which has characterized our relations with the Soviet. We do not deal with Russia because we look upon the Trotsky-Lenin regime as an international outlaw, in fact and law; yet, at the same time, we have maintained diplomatic relations with Mexico, although its Constitution of 1917 places it in the same category with Russia."[14]

Based on a philosophy of devout antibolshevism, on alleged evidence of Russian involvement in Mexico, and on demands for action from several quarters, Kellogg and the State Department went on the attack. Just a week after Representative Baylor's statement to Congress, Chandler Anderson wrote to Sheffield about a resolution adopted by the Emergency Foreign Policy Conference, a group critical of the Coolidge administration's Mexican policy. It was, Anderson stated, "identical word for word with the form of a resolution which was prepared in Mexico City by some Russian Bolshevistic representative there." He had already informed Assistant Secretary of State Olds, and he had received a phone call from Kellogg, who wanted to "confer with him about giving this information to the press." Anderson did not think that that was "advisable" at the moment, but the wheels were set in motion.[15]

At a June 1926 meeting between Olds and Arthur Schoenfeld, counselor of the American embassy in Mexico, Olds outlined two options open to the United States: a policy of "laissez-faire" toward Mexico, or a policy that contemplated the "use of force." The assistant secretary favored the latter course, but he believed that "public support . . . could not be had on an issue of property rights only but that some sensational and emotional appeal must first be presented like the sinking of the Maine in '98." Sometime later in 1926, Olds prepared a "Confidential Memorandum" which asserted that "the Soviet Government in Moscow indisputably regards Mexico as the appropriate base from which to spread its peculiar doctrines in the Western Hemisphere" and went on to outline the evidence for this. Then, in November, department official Robert F. Kelley, in a note initialed by Olds to the American legation in Riga, asked for "exact translations of short extracts from proceedings of Soviet governmental bodies or of organs of Communist International and auxiliary organizations which relate to Soviet or Communist activities in Mexico and Latin America."[16]

Whether or not the memorandum and the request for information about Soviet statements dealing with Latin America were products of Olds's cynical desire for a "sensational" issue to use against Mexico, Kellogg clearly was impressed by it all. On 12 January 1927 he left a lengthy paper with the Senate Committee on Foreign Relations entitled "Bolshevik Aims and Policies in Mexico and Latin America," which asserted that "the Bolshevik leaders have had very definite ideas with respect to the role which Mexico and Latin America are to play in their general program of world revolution. . . . Latin America and Mexico are conceived as a base for activity against the United States."[17]

The reaction to what Kellogg apparently considered a "bombshell" was less than he had hoped. A month later Schoenfeld wrote to Sheffield about a dinner he had had with Senator Walter Edge of the Senate committee. Edge "deplored the statement given out by the Secretary in January regarding alleged Bolshevik inspiration of Mexican policy." The senator believed that "the Mexicans required no inspiration" and that, without proof of "this bogey," Kellogg's intentions were "futile" and would hamper the "understanding of the real situation which was quite worthy of denunciation in itself."[18]

Other sources reveal that Kellogg's action did not meet with universal disapproval. Writing to former President William Howard Taft ten days after the secretary's appearance before the Senate committee, Ambassador Sheffield stated that "the firmness now being displayed by the President and the Secretary of State is having a most beneficial effect." And, near the end of Kellogg's term as secretary, Sheffield congratulated him for his stand on Mexico, particularly for his June 1925 statement that Mexico was "on trial," which "did much to halt the Bolshevik tendencies of the group of men then in control of the Government of Mexico."[19]

As for the press reaction to Kellogg's revelation, the *New York City American* of 13 January 1927 congratulated the secretary and asserted that his appearance in Congress had "firmly forged" a positive sentiment for his policies. The memorandum on bolshevism had not caused a great sensation, the paper said, but it had helped swing congressional support to Kellogg's side. A 17 May 1927 article from the *Chicago Tribune* supported Kellogg's position entirely and stated that the Soviet Union was undoubtedly fomenting unrest in Latin America. Correspondent George Seldes concluded that "this is Red Russia's revenge for the American refusal to recognize the Soviet government."[20]

Some important businessmen also supported Kellogg's stand. Henry Stimson, in a memorandum of a conference with Palmer Pierce of Standard Oil, recounted that the company believed that the problems in Latin America were "organized by Mexico and think they have traced some of the money and activities to Russian sources." In November 1927, Pierce wrote to Sheffield that "Mexico is only the stalking horse for Soviet ideas on the complete nationalization of property."[21]

Kellogg was not, as Robert Freeman Smith suggests, a "convert" to the "red scare" tactics of people such as Chandler Anderson and James Sheffield.[22] His antipathy toward radicalism, and especially toward bolshevism, was long-standing and did not evaporate when his January 1927 evidence did not spark as strong a reaction as he desired. In July of that year, Kellogg wrote to Henry Fletcher concerning troubles in Latin America. One of the primary problems, he stated, was "the propaganda which has been going on in South and Central America by Mexico, by Russian propagandists and by some organizations in our own country which are unpatriotic and always against the government." There were, he went on, "liable to be elements going to the next [Pan American] Conference purely for the purpose of making trouble for the United States."[23]

The State Department's instructions for the U.S. delegation to the Sixth International Conference of American States, held in 1928, reflected Kellogg's concern, albeit without direct references to Russian machinations. "The past year," the instructions read, "has seen the development of a vigorous anti-American propaganda throughout Latin America based on charges of 'imperialism' and characterized by violent criticism of the relations existing between the United States and Mexico and the American policy in Nicaragua." Any discussion of this at the conference was to be avoided.[24]

The role of antibolshevism in the U.S. reaction to economic nationalism in Latin America cannot be easily or precisely defined. As indicated in Chapter 3, American denunciations of Mexico's actions concerning property rights were first formed around ideological (government-state relations to economic development) and material (loss of the Mexican market and its effect on U.S. and world capitalism) considerations. Yet the Russian Revolution, coming hard on the heels of the Mexican constitution of 1917, prompted American officials to consider the similarities between the two. By 1927–28 important elements of the U.S. government had become convinced that Mexico had become an agent state seeking to spread bolshevism throughout the Western Hemisphere. Economic nationalism (the roots of which had never been completely examined or understood by American observers) became synonymous with communism until, by the latter years of the 1920s, Mexico's policies and actions were believed to lack an indigenous base; they were simply manifestations of that nation's increasingly Bolshevistic alignment. By the end of the 1920s it had become common practice for U.S. officials and businessmen, whether out of cynical desires to goad the American people to take action against Mexico or based on sincere beliefs in the expansive nature of Russian bolshevism, to smear the Mexican Revolution, and especially the 1917 constitution, with the label of communism.[25]

II

In March 1926 the American ambassador to Mexico, James Sheffield, wrote to Senator James Wadsworth, Jr., describing his exasperation with the outstanding differences between the United States and Mexico. Blustering with indignation, Sheffield decried "the futility of attempting to treat with a Latin-Indian mind, filled with hatred of the United States and thirsty for vengeance, on the same basis that our government would treat with a civilized and orderly government in Europe." Calming himself a bit, the ambassador suggested that "the United States with its power and its wealth and its well ordered civilization owes to Mexico as well as to itself from a moral point of view all the help it can render to uplift and set on its feet this backward people."[26]

Sheffield's remarks, blunt as they are, should not surprise those who study U.S.-Latin American relations. Racism, in forms both virulent and paternalistic (the ambassador's letter is a good example of how these forms can be joined), has always been a factor in U.S. policy concerning its neighbors to the south. Yet, during the Progressive period, the advent of "scientific" racism dramatically affected U.S. domestic and foreign policy. And the racist component of U.S. Latin American policy must be viewed in the context of Jim Crow, Asian exclusion, and restrictive immigration legislation. Furthermore, racism was not a vice peculiar to the United States. Many Latin American countries had racial tensions as serious as those of the United States, and many members of the Latin American elite viewed the United States as culturally if not racially inferior.

Prior to 1917 racism played a relatively small role in the determination of U.S. policy toward Latin America.[27] This was hardly surprising, because U.S. officials rarely gave much in-depth thought to the actual inhabitants of that region. From the Monroe Doctrine, through its various corollaries, to Woodrow Wilson's Mobile speech in

1913, the aim of U.S. policy had been to incorporate Latin America into the American economic empire.[28] The primary challenge to that policy had always come from the European imperial powers—Great Britain especially—with their economic and political holds on various nations in that area. U.S. declarations of policy, therefore, were aimed at teaching the Europeans that Latin America was to be considered a U.S. sphere of influence. After 1917, however, a new challenge—economic nationalism—arose to confront U.S. economic and political goals in Latin America. This challenge produced a new and vital role for racism.[29]

In both public and private assessments of economic nationalism in Mexico and elsewhere in Latin America by U.S. officials, racism remained a constant, and important, ingredient. Just how important is revealed by a close examination of a letter from the U.S. ambassador to Mexico, Henry Fletcher, to Woodrow Wilson in 1919. Article 27, he claimed, "practically closes the door to future foreign investments and threatens those already made in the country." This "would be of little importance if Mexico and the Mexicans were able to keep themselves going," but Fletcher did "not see that they can. They have not the genius of industrial development, nor have they had the training required."[30] This indicates that the real fear among American policymakers was not that programs of economic nationalism would work in Latin America; indeed, the thought rarely occurred to them. Belief in the ultimate failure of these programs inspired U.S. denigration of them as well as efforts to contain and thwart them. This belief was founded on the notion that Latin Americans were racially incapable of determining their own economic and political futures.

During and immediately after World War I, it became exasperatingly apparent to U.S. policymakers that a number of Latin American nations (with the example of the Mexican Revolution and the 1917 constitution before them) were determined nonetheless to chart their own courses in the world. Ambassador Fletcher put the issue in perspective in June 1918, laying out what he believed to be the goals of Mexico's President Venustiano Carranza: "The least connection possible between Mexico and the United States is his ideal. His official newspaper is preaching economic, financial, diplomatic—every sort of independence of the United States. The so-called Carranza doctrine is to replace the Monroe Doctrine [and] the hegemony of the United States on this Continent is to pass away."[31]

Earlier that month, Fletcher had claimed that the time was fast approaching when the United States and Mexico would have to have a "show down" over those issues. While some Americans in Mexico were optimistic, he did not believe that such a feeling was warranted. "I know these birds—a bit," he concluded, thereby reducing the situation to the United States figuring out the mysterious thinking processes of the Mexicans. The United States, he suggested, had to put a plan for resolving the issues before Carranza "firmly but kindly," a stance one might take toward a mischievous child. If the plan was not accepted, Fletcher sadly concluded, he could "see nothing ahead here."[32]

The fear that the Latin Americans might destroy the "hegemony of the United States" in the Western Hemisphere became stronger when U.S. officials stopped to consider the role of the Latin Americans in the proposed League of Nations. As Edward House, Wilson's trusted aide, explained in July 1918, if equal votes were granted to all members of the new league "Mexico and the Central American States" could outvote the world powers, but they "would not only be impotent but unwilling to share the responsibilities."[33]

It obviously would be necessary to secure the backing of the nations of Latin America in the proposed world organization. Reporting from the Paris Peace Conference in early 1919, former chief of the State Department's Latin American Division Jordan Stabler commented on his efforts in that direction. He stated that he had "all my Latins carded and tabulated and have started to see them." He was appalled to discover that "they have been left alone too much and have been having Latin American conferences among themselves." Stabler vowed to "try to get them to give us their entire support." A few weeks later, however, Stabler confided that he was having a "very difficult time with the Latin Americans" over the question of their representation on the conference commissions. Latin American representation on the important Financial and Economic Commission was very limited, and this caused "a storm against the Great Powers," the United States included. The best that Stabler had to offer in return was to host a dinner for the Latin Americans. "A tempest in a teapot, you may say," he concluded, "but I for one think tea leaves are rather bitter and do not want the U.S. to have to drink any."[34]

In addition to that bitter brew, U.S. officials also had to contend with the plans by various Latin American nations to control and develop their own natural resources. It was in commenting on these efforts that their racism came through most clearly. Almost as one, U.S. officials branded those plans as hopelessly naive and pathetic. Fletcher's claim that the Mexicans lacked the "genius" necessary for such undertakings was echoed by American Minister Hoffman Philip and by Jordan Stabler when they spoke out against Colombia's postwar efforts to enforce stricter control over its oil resources.[35] Writing to the State Department in August 1919, Philip bemoaned the fact that the Colombians were "very ignorant" about how to protect their national interests, but he concluded that perhaps they would be "susceptible to advisory suggestions." The Colombians proved to be less "susceptible" than Philip had hoped, and in 1927 problems over the foreign oil interests in their nation arose anew. When Chile attempted to gain more direction over its nitrate resources, an American official described this as an "unwarranted interference of the State in an enterprise which it neither understands nor is capable of directing."[36]

U.S. officials often expressed their belief that the Latin Americans were racially inferior. During the latter years of the Wilson administration the notion had already developed that the Latin Americans were not to be "left alone too much." Following the Republican victory in 1920, American racism gradually took on a harder edge. American officials, businessmen, and other observers of the Latin American scene often expressed the idea that the people of that region, especially the Mexicans, were definitely in need of "guidance."

Secretary of State Hughes, in a speech to the Council on Foreign Relations in January 1924, summed up the problem between Mexico and the United States: "We had the friendliest feelings for the people of Mexico and were sensible of their desire for social and political betterment," Hughes claimed, "but revolutionary tendencies and chaotic conditions made it impossible to find a sound basis for intercourse."[37] Always the diplomat, Hughes had made the same point that other American officials had made, but in more tactful language. The implied assumption, of course, was that without that "intercourse," Mexico could not hope to achieve "social and political betterment" on its own. Once again, an American official found himself perplexed as to why Mexico would fail to bow to America's good intentions.

In a letter to Hughes's successor, Frank Kellogg, in January 1927, George Lockwood, editor of the *National Republic*, enclosed an editorial entitled "Stand by Your Government." In it, Lockwood claimed that people might attack the United States for "imperialism" or "capitalism" in its dealings with Mexico and Latin America, but nevertheless those nations needed U.S. help and money to develop. Banker Thomas Lamont took a more paternalistic stance in explaining the situation to Agustín Legorreta, head of the Banco Nacional in Mexico, in early 1927. If Mexico would only abandon its nationalistic policies, Lamont was sure that there would be an "almost immediate impetus to oil production." The tax burden on all Mexicans would lessen, debts could be paid, internal improvements could be made, and educational programs could be enhanced. Lamont concluded that it would "enable the Mexican Government to carry out those very principles of improved conditions for the Mexican people at large, which it has been enunciating for the last few years." These ideas were shared by Alexander Dye, a commercial attaché in Buenos Aires. "In striving to protect foreign investments in Mexico," Dye wrote in 1927, "we are striving not merely for the protection of material things but for the *only hope* which the indian has to take his place alongside educated labor of other countries with the opportunity to rise which the individual has in the United States."[38]

While such paternalistic racism continued during the years after 1920, there was also a perceptible rise in a more vicious racism that portrayed Mexicans and other Latin Americans as semihumans who were probably incapable of ever rising above their present state. Lamont, a frequent correspondent with Secretary Hughes, explained in a December 1923 letter that in dealing with the Mexicans one had to keep in mind that "ignorant as they are, unwise as they are, untrusty as they are, nevertheless, if you once take time and patience, one can handle them." In an undated memo that was probably prepared in 1923 or 1924, Lamont denigratingly referred to Plutarco Calles as "the dark man in the woodpile who will probably be the next trouble maker in Mexico."[39] This was certainly a far cry from Lamont's efforts in 1927 to explain to a Mexican official that the United States wished only to help Mexico help itself.

Others, especially during the Kellogg years, were even more outspoken about their perception of the racial inferiority of Latin Americans. Most vocal of all was Ambassador Sheffield. Soon after he arrived in Mexico in 1925, he summed up his view of the leaders of that nation: "The main factors are greed, a wholly Mexican view of nationalism, and an Indian, not Latin, hatred of all peoples not on the reservation. There is very little white blood in the Cabinet—that is it is very thin." He diplomatically concluded that "I expected to find corruption, ignorance, and cruelty. I have not been disappointed in my expectations."[40] Former State Department counselor Chandler Anderson, writing about his trip to Mexico in 1926, assessed the majority of that nation's population as "so ignorant and of such a low mental capacity that they are utterly unfitted for self-government." Such people were "easily dominated" by the "unscrupulous and selfish half-breed Mexicans who are in control of the Government today."[41] Later that year Anderson met with Assistant Secretary of State Olds, Secretary Kellogg, and oil company lobbyist Judge Delbert Haff. The latter's opinion on U.S.-Mexican relations was that "the situation was much like that of the relationship between a vicious animal and its trainer; if the trainer showed fear, the animal would attack him, but if he showed courage and force, the animal would submit."[42]

Mexico was not the only target of such racist assumptions. According to the American minister in Colombia, the real problem with nationalistic oil legislation was the "woeful ignorance" of Colombia's leaders. A 1928 report by the U.S. military attaché in Brazil dismissed out of hand most of the people of that nation as unimportant because 80 percent were illiterate. Fraud and apathy were pervasive in the Brazilian electoral system, and the nation's government was inefficient at best. Its leaders were contemptible, good only for giving dull speeches and carrying guns to debates. As for Venezuela, a lengthy report on conditions there in 1929 concluded that its people were "indolent" and suffered from "political immaturity" and "racial inferiority."[43]

All of these assessments demonstrated the U.S. belief that, due to their racial inferiority, Latin Americans would not be "able to keep themselves and their country going," as Ambassador Fletcher put it. The result would be that the production of oil from Mexico or Colombia, or nitrates from Chile, or other products, would collapse. Such an inevitability was not taken lightly by U.S. policymakers.

While some government spokesmen talked extensively about the postwar world economy in terms of a "well oiled machine" or a "Family of Nations," other observers made it clear that the various "cogs" and "relatives" had very different responsibilities.[44] A statement from an officer of the National City Bank of New York put this into perspective:

> For food and manufacturing material man had already developed the producing power of the Temperate Zones, especially the Northern Temperate, and now he is demanding that the Tropics shall perform their proper share of the task of supplying the food and manufacturing material required by the 1700 million people of the globe.[45]

In somewhat plainer language, the relation of Latin America to the United States within the world economy was not to be so much that of one "family member" to another as that of a day laborer to his or her employer. The racist assumptions of U.S. policymakers and businessmen deemed this the only constructive work that the "ignorant" Latin Americans were capable of doing.

U.S. policymakers gave little thought to the notion that the Latin Americans should have much say in intrahemispheric economic planning or management, which is not surprising considering the American reaction to the involvement of Latin America in the League of Nations. This was made painfully clear by the American officials and business representatives who commented on the IAHC, which was established to carry out some of the economic reforms suggested at the First Pan American Financial Conference in 1915. Secretary of the Treasury William Gibbs McAdoo, in a press release of 14 May 1915, stated that the purpose of the commission would be to develop financial cooperation between the United States and Latin America "of the most beneficial sort to our respective countries . . . based on common ideals and common interests." Almost as an afterthought, McAdoo listed several topics that he felt should be discussed, although the list was made "merely as a suggestion."[46] In a private letter to C. E. McGuire, the assistant secretary of the IAHC, McAdoo made clear his concept of cooperation. "What, to my mind," the secretary began, "is most important is to formulate practical and definite suggestions for prosecuting our work and sending them to the Finance Ministers of each of the Latin American countries." He concluded that "unless we tell each one of these Ministers exactly what ought to be done and urge them to go ahead and do it, we will get nowhere."[47]

Another example of what kind of input was expected from the Latin Americans came from Paul Warburg, who worked energetically on the IAHC's International Gold Clearance Fund Convention. Commenting on a proposed inter-American meeting at which former secretary of state Elihu Root would be speaking, Warburg opined that "I am afraid that he will make a very slow speech; but then they wont [*sic*] understand it anyhow and the slower it will be, the more learned it will appear to them."[48]

American businessmen, while sharing these racist assumptions concerning the Latin Americans' ability to comprehend or master complex economic matters, were quick to point out that the Latin Americans did have some qualities that made them exemplary unskilled laborers. They were, after all, the pool of cheap labor from which would be "demanded" the performance of their "proper share" of providing food, raw materials, and markets for the industrialized nations. Articles with titles such as "The Friendly Brazilian and His Country" and "The Amazing Argentine" attempted to portray the nations of Latin America as commercial gold mines filled with willing arms and legs to do the work.[49] One business bulletin carried an article simply entitled "Labor," which said of the workers of Uruguay that "the peons are mostly Italian and Spanish mixed with Indian blood and they make excellent workmen." Whereas in the United States the introduction of machinery had resulted in lower labor costs, this article noted a real difference in the workers to the south: "With coal at $30 to $40 a ton, trenching machines and the steam shovels found it hard work competing with this labor and did comparatively little. Six and one-half cubic yards of deep excavation in eight hours for one dollar is hard to beat." A picture on the article's first page prominently displayed a "Six Footer who dug 19 1/2 cubic yards in a day and who drove away 40 strike agitators."[50] The prevailing American view may have been that Latin Americans were "ignorant," "unwise," and "racially inferior"; nevertheless, they had their uses.

We can thus see the role of racism in U.S. perceptions of and responses to economic nationalism in Latin America. Because economic nationalism during the postwar years generally surfaced in the more developed nations of Latin America, the traditional U.S. responses to problems in that region—military intervention, nonrecognition, or economic pressure—could either not be brought to bear with the same effect as in U.S. dealings with less-developed nations in the Caribbean or Central America or else could not reasonably be used at all.

One new answer to this new challenge has had a long and devastating effect on U.S.-Latin American relations: the U.S. support for pro-American, antiradical dictators. During the 1920s the support of dictators such as General Juan Vicente Gómez in Venezuela (see Chapter 6) seemed to many to be an altogether logical response to anti-American economic nationalism. After all, if the ignorant masses of Latin America and the corrupt inefficient leaders who catered to them were incapable of understanding their proper economic roles, perhaps a right-thinking strongman could set them straight. Elihu Root stated in 1927 that the U.S. recognition of the independence of Latin America had been "probably premature," as the Latin Americans were "admittedly like children and unable to maintain the obligations which go with independence." A few months earlier, Root had suggested a possible solution to this dilemma. Speaking before the Council on Foreign Relations, he compared the Mexican attempt at democracy and self-government with the granting of voting rights to blacks after the American Civil War: "a dismal step, a terrible mistake, with most serious evils following." Mexico's solution, Root hinted, might be found in the example of postwar Italy, since the people there had also "undertaken to govern themselves without quite having learned the hang of it." Fortunately, under Benito Mussolini, Italy now had a "revival of prosperity, contentment and happiness under a dictator."[51] Dictatorship in place of disorder appeared to be the proper prescription for the Mexicans. The same reasoning guided U.S. relations with the dictatorial Gómez government in Venezuela during the entire postwar period.

By 1929 and the Great Depression, racism had assumed an important and sometimes decisive position in the U.S. attitudes and policies toward Latin America. Economic nationalism brought new importance to racist notions about the peoples of Latin America. While it is obvious that racism was not the only deciding factor in U.S. perceptions of and responses to economic nationalism, it was an important factor. Racism colored the U.S. belief that the Latin Americans could not successfully determine their own economic and political futures, and it also underlay the idea that dictatorships might check such dangerous thoughts among the ignorant masses.

To be sure, not all U.S. observers were entirely satisfied with such conclusions. Leo Rowe of the Pan American Union, writing to a friend in the State Department in 1917, conceded that many revolutions were "due entirely to personal ambition" but added: "I believe that we must also recognize circumstances in which a revolutionary movement represents in reality an attempt to bring the political system into closer touch with the needs of the country and the wishes of the people." That was "certainly true of the . . . Mexican Revolution of 1910."[52]

Due to their philosophy combining economic expansionism with racism, most American policymakers saw Rowe's statement as somewhat naive. The Mexican Revolution and the outbursts of economic nationalism which it spurred in other nations in Latin America were far too dangerous to trust to the wisdom of a "country" or "people" in that region. Since the Latin Americans were racially unable to chart their own paths, it would henceforth be necessary for the United States to determine for them the proper amount of "needs" and the desirable level of "wishes."

Notes

1. Poole's memorandum enclosed in Joseph Tumulty to Newton D. Baker, 23 October 1919, Baker Papers (emphasis in original).

2. The impact of antibolshevism on the formation of U.S. foreign policy, especially toward Mexico and Latin America, during the postwar period is a subject that has not received the scholarly attention it deserves. Those historians who have considered it (L. Ethan Ellis, Robert Freeman Smith) have generally disposed of antibolshevism as having little or no role. Douglas Little, "Antibolshevism and American Foreign Policy, 1919–1939: The Diplomacy of Self-Delusion," *American Quarterly* 35 (Fall 1983): 376–90, is a much-needed step in the right direction. Little claims that antibolshevism among American policymakers had become "institutionalized" by the end of the 1920s. Progressive principles (desire for free trade, free elections, and so on), the reorganization of the State Department during the mid-1920s which brought the Division of Eastern European Affairs under the control of Robert Kelley (a "zealous foe of the Soviet Union"), and the "professionalization" of the Foreign Service (through the active recruitment of generally well-to-do young men who "emulated" West European culture and denigrated the Soviet Union) were the major factors in this process.

3. Henry Fletcher to Frank Polk, 18 December 1918, Box 5, Folder 180, Polk Papers; Robert Lansing to Hoffman Philip, 25 November 1919, 821.6363/82, RG 59; Chandler Anderson diary, 13 October 1919, Anderson Papers.

4. Memorandum of conversation between Secretary Charles Evans Hughes and Thomas Lamont, 26 September 1921, Box 195, Folder 6, Lamont Papers; Hughes to Samuel Gompers, 19 July 1923, Box 5, Papers of Leland Harrison, Manuscript Division, Library of Congress, Washington (hereafter cited as Harrison Papers); Lamont [?], "Memo 1919–1924," Box 195, Folder 4, Lamont Papers.

5. L. Ethan Ellis, *Frank B. Kellogg and American Foreign Relations, 1925–1929* (New Brunswick, 1961), 70–71.

6. For a short summary of this thesis see Michael Krenn, John P. Rossi, and David Schmitz, "Under-Utilization of the Kellogg Papers," *SHAFR Newsletter* 14 (September 1983): 1–9.

7. "Notes on Congressional Record of Kellogg, Compiled under the Direction of Charles J. Moos, 1936–37. Based on *Congressional Record* for 65, 66, 67th Congresses, March 4, 1917-March 3, 1923," Papers of Frank B. Kellogg (microfilm edition), Minnesota State Historical Society, Minneapolis (hereafter cited as Kellogg Papers); Kellogg to Polk, 8 December 1924, Box 8, Folder 290, Polk Papers.

8. Kellogg to Fred C. Van Dusen, 5 October 1925; Kellogg to James Davis, 1 October 1925, Kellogg Papers.

9. Kellogg to Alanson B. Houghton, 11 October 1926; Kellogg to James Beck, 22 June 1927, Kellogg Papers.

10. Anderson diary, 11 April 1925, Anderson Papers; A. E. Cook to Kellogg, 6 October 1926, Kellogg Papers.

11. Both articles found in James Sheffield, "Scrapbooks," Box 23, Sheffield Papers.

12. Sheffield to Nicholas M. Butler, 17 November 1925, Box 8; Sheffield, "Autobiography," 19–20, Box 11; Sheffield, "Scrapbooks," Box 23, Sheffield Papers.

13. Anderson diary, "Mexican Trip. February 18 to March 14," 1926; Anderson diary, 28 April 1926, Anderson Papers; Anderson to Sheffield, 19 March 1926, Box 8, Sheffield Papers.

14. *New York Times*, 5 March 1926.

15. Anderson to Sheffield, 16 March 1925, Box 8, Sheffield Papers.
16. Arthur Schoenfeld to Sheffield, 18 June 1926, Box 8, Sheffield Papers; R. E. O. (Robert E. Olds), "Confidential Memorandum," c. 1926, Box 56a, Folder 986, Lane Papers (The reader may here note a difference of opinion between this author and Robert F. Smith as to the authorship of the 1926 memorandum. Smith concludes in *Revolutionary Nationalism*, 237, that Arthur Bliss Lane was the author. The typed notation at the bottom of the document, "A-O REO:HWC," indicates that Robert E. Olds was the likely author.); Kelley to American Legation in Riga, 22 November 1926, 810.00B/15a, RG 59.
17. "Bolshevik Aims and Policies in Mexico and Latin America," 12 January 1927, Kellogg Papers.
18. Schoenfeld to Sheffield, 28 February 1927, Box 8, Sheffield Papers.
19. Sheffield to William Howard Taft, 22 January 1927, Box 8, Sheffield Papers; Sheffield to Kellogg, 28 December 1928, Kellogg Papers.
20. *New York City American*, 13 January 1927, "Scrapbooks," Box 24, Sheffield Papers; *Chicago Tribune* article enclosed in George Seldes to Kellogg, 31 May 1927, Kellogg Papers.
21. Henry Stimson, "Memorandum of Conference with Palmer Pierce, June 24th, 1927," Papers of Henry Stimson (microfilm edition), Yale University Library, New Haven (hereafter cited as Stimson Papers); Pierce to Sheffield, 2 November 1927, Box 9, Sheffield Papers.
22. Smith, *Revolutionary Nationalism*, 238.
23. Kellogg to Fletcher, 26 July 1927, Kellogg Papers.
24. "Instructions to Delegates Sixth International Conference of American States, Havana, Cuba, 1928," 11, Box 17, Papers of Francis White, Record Group 59, General Records of the Department of State, National Archives, Washington (hereafter cited as box number, White Papers).
25. Little, "Antibolshevism," writes that the "psychological dimension of foreign policy" must also be considered when dealing with this issue. Comparing the responses of American policymakers to revolutionary activity in such diverse nations as Italy, Greece, Spain, Mexico, and El Salvador, he concludes that these diplomats found themselves in a "cognitive predicament." Facing an increasingly unstable and revolutionary world, they fell back on their "[i]nstitutionalized bolshevism," which "provided them with a framework for understanding revolutionary phenomena around the world." When the facts of a given situation did not lend themselves easily to the conclusion that bolshevism was the culprit, "policymakers have frequently responded by distorting their perceptions of the world around them." I would argue that much of the "psychological dimension" revolved around the economic dimension. Nevertheless, Little provides an interesting and provocative interpretation which may spur research on this neglected subject.
26. Sheffield to Senator James Wadsworth, Jr., 4 March 1926, Box 8, Sheffield Papers.
27. Three works that may be helpful in understanding the role of racism in American attitudes and policies toward Latin America are Reginald Horsman, *Race and Manifest Destiny: The Origins of American Racial Anglo-Saxonism* (New York, 1981); Rubin Frances Weston, *Racism in U.S. Imperialism* (Columbia, 1972); and Michael H. Hunt, *Ideology and U.S. Foreign Policy* (New Haven, 1987), especially Chapter 3, pp. 46–91. Horsman's study deals mainly with the mid-nineteenth century; its analysis of the development of racist sentiment in the United States is nonetheless fascinating. Weston's study concentrates on the years from the Spanish-American War through the early years of the first Wilson

administration. The American interventions in Cuba, Puerto Rico, Haiti, and the Dominican Republic are the main focus as far as Latin America is concerned. The drawback of the work is that it considers racism's impact only in terms of territorial expansion by the United States.

28. For more extensive analyses of pre-World War I U.S. economic interest in Latin America consult Richard Van Alstyne, *The Rising American Empire* (New York, 1960); Walter LaFeber, *The New Empire: An Interpretation of American Expansion, 1860–1898* (Ithaca, 1963); and William Appleman Williams, *The Roots of the Modern American Empire: A Study of the Growth and Shaping of Social Consciousness in a Marketplace Society* (New York, 1969).

29. The first author to more fully consider the role of racism in determining American reactions to economic nationalism was Robert Freeman Smith in his important work, *Revolutionary Nationalism.* His analysis of the problem of the "backward nation" for postwar U.S. policymakers and businessmen is insightful and revealing. Smith seems to undercut the significance of American racism, however, by stressing that more moderate voices among U.S. officials and business interests (Thomas Lamont and Dwight Morrow, for example) were ultimately more influential and that they sought a paternalistic approach to Mexico which would lead to "development." Whether Lamont can be categorized as a "moderate" racist is open to debate (see his comments later in this chapter). This present work disagrees most visibly with Smith's interpretations of the "paternalism" shown by the Americans and the type of development they sought for Latin America. What the United States desired most from Latin America were arms and legs to do the work of tending the fields and digging the mines; "development" beyond that rudimentary stage was discussed in vague and remote terms, if at all.

30. Fletcher to Woodrow Wilson, 1 March 1919, 821.00/23111a, RG 59.

31. Fletcher to Polk, 26 June 1918, Box 5, Folder 179, Polk Papers.

32. Fletcher to Polk, 5 June and 3 December 1918, Box 5, Folders 179 and 180, Polk Papers.

33. Edward House to Woodrow Wilson, 14 July 1918, Box 121, Folder 285, House Papers.

34. Jordan Stabler to Polk, 1 and 25 March 1919, Box 12, Folder 445, Polk Papers.

35. For a discussion of the U.S. reaction to Colombia's postwar oil legislation, see Chapter 5.

36. Philip to Lansing, 18 August 1919; John F. Martin to Hughes, 13 May 1921, 711.21/482, 825.00/198, RG 59.

37. "Address of Honorable Charles Evans Hughes," 23 January 1924, Records of Meetings, vol. 1, Archives of CFR.

38. George Lockwood to Kellogg, 11 January 1927, Kellogg Papers; Lamont to Agustín Legorreta, 14 January 1927, Box 192, Folder 10, Lamont Papers; Alexander Dye to the BFDC, 12 March 1927, 400-U.S.-Latin America, RG 151 (emphasis added).

39. Lamont to Hughes, 31 December 1923, Box 208, Folder 7; Lamont [?], "Memo 1919–1924," Box 195, Folder 4, Lamont Papers.

40. Sheffield to Nicholas Murray Butler, 17 November 1925, Box 8, Sheffield Papers.

41. Anderson diary, "Mexican Trip. Feb. 18 to March 14," 1926, Anderson Papers.

42. Anderson diary, 29 October 1926, Anderson Papers.

43. Minister Samuel Piles to Kellogg, 11 June 1928; report to Major Lester Baker, contained in William Manning to Dana Munro, 14 October 1929; C. Van H. Engert to Stimson, 23 December 1929, 821.6363/410, 832.00/649, 831.00/1449, RG 59.

44. See the comments by Norman Davis and Herbert Hoover cited in Chapter 1.

45. Austin, "Development of the Tropics," 25.

46. Press release, 14 May 1915, Box 544, Papers of William Gibbs McAdoo, Manuscripts Division, Library of Congress, Washington (hereafter cited as McAdoo Papers).

47. McAdoo to C. H. McGuire, 13 September 1916, Box 9, RG 43, Records of the IAHC.

48. Paul Warburg to John Bassett Moore, 29 December 1919, Box 42, Papers of John Bassett Moore, Manuscripts Division, Library of Congress, Washington (hereafter cited as the Moore Papers).

49. *The Americas* 1 (October 1914): 6; ibid. (November 1914): 11–13, 29–31.

50. *Bulletin of AIC* 1 (May 1918): 34.

51. Root's comments are found in Stimson, "Memorandum of Conference with Mr. Root, July 6, 1927. Re Nicaragua," Stimson Papers; Elihu Root, speech before a dinner meeting of the Council on Foreign Relations, 14 December 1926, Records of Meetings, vol. 2, Archives of CFR.

52. Leo Rowe to Polk, 27 March 1917, Box 12, Folder 422, Polk Papers.

Chapter Five

Progress, American Style: Colombia, 1919–1929

Between 1919 and 1929 the United States and Colombia confronted each other repeatedly over the issue of economic nationalism, particularly over Colombia's attempts to exert greater state control over its petroleum and other natural resources. Coming just a short time after the promulgation of the 1917 Mexican constitution, Article 27 of which threatened nationalization and expropriation, Colombian efforts to control more strictly its mineral resources alarmed American interests in Colombia and officials at home. Colombia was seen by many as a test case, for it was felt that if it were allowed to put such controls into effect other countries in South America might follow suit. To counteract this development the United States, in ways similar to its policies toward Mexico, used its economic might as both an incentive and a weapon to convince Colombia that its policies of economic nationalism were inimical to both nations' interests.

Nationalism in Colombia did not appear suddenly in the post-World War I years, nor was it simply a response to the U.S. and European presence. Indeed, the growth and development of economic nationalism in Colombia was intimately, and sometimes conflictingly, tied not only to economic conditions but also to political and social issues. The U.S. view, however, was that economic nationalism was merely misguided and mischievous anti-Americanism, dangerous to the United States as well as to Colombia.[1]

The first significant steps toward the establishment of a real political system in Colombia were taken during the 1840s. Following its war for independence from the Spanish empire in the early 1800s, caudillismo was the dominant force in Colombian government. Wealthy landowners controlled a highly stratified society in which they held most political and economic power.

By the 1840s, however, a number of issues began to divide the landowners into two opposing camps, the bases for the parties that have dominated Colombian politics to the present day: the

Conservatives and the Liberals. The Conservatives were fervently pro-church and worked for a closer connection between church and state. Liberals, on the other hand, saw such an arrangement as a vestige of Colombia's colonial past and sought to separate the two. The two parties also advocated different governmental structures for Colombia. The Conservatives favored a highly centralized form of rule; the Liberals, influenced by the example of the United States, sought a more federalist system.

Conservatives and Liberals were also divided on economic questions. Following Colombia's independence from Spain, the large landowners, still influenced by their colonial heritage, generally subscribed to a system of protectionism enforced by tariffs. This system created what Charles Bergquist has referred to as the " 'politics of scarcity' generally associated with a stagnant, closed domestic economy with limited social mobility."[2] Tariffs went hand in hand with the Conservatives' view of government; the revenues from such taxes would finance the powerful central government they desired. While some domestic industries found "protection" under the tariffs, Conservatives generally viewed the tariff as a revenue source, not a development tool. Indeed, Colombian "industry" during that period remained largely of the handicraft sort and had little effect on the influx of varied and superior consumer items imported from Europe and the United States by the planters.

Early Conservatives supported that static situation, but early Liberal elements decried it. These Liberals were clustered in the cities, which had most of the still-limited contact with foreign traders. Many Liberals, as J. León Helguera has characterized them, were "deeply imbued with British economic liberalism and French political libertarianism."[3] Belief in Britain's trade liberalism by the nascent merchant class was understandable: Their livings were determined by imports and exports.

As Fernando Cardoso and Enzo Faletto have concluded, however, "It would be a mistake to think that the struggle between Liberal and Conservative in the nineteenth century expressed a conflict between landed gentry and bourgeois capitalists."[4] By the 1840s both Liberal and Conservative elites had become convinced that a solid import-export trade was the solution to Colombia's economic problems. They were lured by the profits that they could reap by cultivating such products as tobacco and coffee (a crop which was just beginning to take hold). The Liberals saw that viable export crops would mean a viable import-export economy. Thus, the 1840s saw Colombia become one of what Celso Furtado has called Latin America's "economies exporting tropical agricultural commodities."[5]

The Liberal economic philosophy of free trade gained general acceptance in Colombia, and with only slight interruption the Liberals ruled from the late 1840s until 1880. Supported by a booming Colombian export trade dominated by coffee sales, the Liberals were able to enact much of their philosophy. Tariff rates were slashed or eliminated, antichurch laws took effect, and a very decentralized system of government was established. When the export boom stumbled in the 1870s, however, political violence between Liberals and Conservatives flared, and Liberal power waned. The 1880 election of the Liberal-turned-Conservative Rafael Núñez inaugurated fifty years of Conservative rule.

Conservative power brought many changes to Colombia. Much power was restored to the Catholic church. A strong central government was set up. New tariffs were established. The economy progressed quickly, led by another boom in coffee sales. Foreign money began to play a decisive role in Colombian development, especially in the field of transportation. Liberals, however, opposed Núñez's support of the church, his centralization program, and what they perceived as his near-despotic rule. Violence once again erupted, and the bloody One Thousand Day War (1899–1903) wreaked havoc in Colombia. Taking advantage of the chaos, the United States saw to it that Panama gained its "independence" from Colombia and then quickly sealed a deal with the new nation for an isthmian canal.[6]

Despite the internal conflict and external humiliation, the Conservatives were able to maintain control in Colombia. Under the extremely strong rule between 1904 and 1909 of Rafael Reyes, prosperity returned and what had been a steady flow of foreign investment from Europe and, increasingly, the United States became a near-flood. Transportation and communication attracted much of the foreign money, and the Conservatives were happy to encourage it. Through much effort, the regions of Colombia were drawn closer, and the central government was able to exert its control more effectively. Coffee still reigned as the king of Colombia's exports.

In sum, from the 1840s to the years before World War I, the Conservatives favored a relatively closed political and economic system. At first they attempted to achieve this through laws restricting popular participation in politics; next they used protectionist policies to solidify the economic position of the large landowners. The Liberals supported greater political and economic freedom through laws increasing suffrage rights and through a free-trade policy. It is important to note, however, that often the Liberals went no further than espousal of such actions. Elite elements among the Liberals were no more willing than their Conservative counterparts to relinquish their position. Their calls for free trade were based solidly on the merchants' desire for greater economic, and therefore political, power.

Both parties had seen their philosophies put into action. The Liberals, backed by a successful export economy during the mid-nineteenth century, had been able to institute liberal political and economic programs in Colombia. Conservatives, enjoying the prosperity, generally acquiesed. When the Liberals fell from power during a poor financial period, the Conservatives rose to assume control and presided over a period of growing trade and wealth. Again, the "out" party—this time the Liberals—while not giving in on issues of church power and governmental organization, found little to condemn in the "in" party's economic policy. This typifies what Benjamin Keen and Mark Wasserman have dubbed "The Politics of Acquisition."[7] At least in terms of economics, the Conservative-Liberal split was not as wide as one might imagine. Their means for economic growth were indeed different, designed to benefit the elites of their respective parties. Their goals, however, were largely the same: the construction of a strong import-export economy and, as the nineteenth century drew to a close, the encouragement of foreign investment in transportation, communication, public works, and extractive industries. The first goal solidified their position in the Colombian economy; the second was intended to solidify their position in the world economy by tying themselves more strongly to the developed nations.

World War I presented both parties with new problems, new demands, and new opportunities which forced them to reassess both their economic means and their goals. And, while the war presented a unique opportunity for a closer U.S.-Colombian economic relationship, the problems it raised and Colombia's answers to those problems led to tremendous friction between the two nations in the postwar period.

Trading and investment contacts between Colombia and the United States prior to World War I were not inconsequential, nor were they particularly striking.[8] In 1906, the American minister to Colombia, John Barrett, had written to the State Department concerning the immense possibilities for American capital in Colombia, which he emphatically concluded had "a latent capacity of development second only to that of Mexico." Barrett hoped that the department would see to it that an article he had written and sent along, "Colombia, A Land of Great Possibilities," would be published so as to inform American interests of the opportunities awaiting them. His appeals were met with a limited response. By 1913, American trade with Colombia totaled only $22 million, and the U.S. investment in that nation was a mere $2 million.[9]

World War I altered that situation tremendously. Isaac Manning, American consul to Colombia, wrote in August 1914 that the war had had a "very demoralizing effect on conditions in this country, and especially on its business." Money was scarce, and prices had skyrocketed.[10] The Colombians themselves quickly became aware that, as old sources of investment and trade had dried up during the war, new ones would have to be created. Thus, at the 1915 Pan American Financial Conference, and again at the Pan American Scientific Congress in 1915–16, Colombian representatives eagerly pointed out the investment opportunities for American capital, especially in public works and natural resource development.[11]

American oil companies heeded the calls for investment in Colombia. In 1914–15, Standard Oil became the first American company to become heavily involved in searching for oil in that nation, but it had little immediate luck in finding a profitable field. Another American firm, the Tropical Oil Company, drilling in another region of Colombia, found sizable deposits of high-grade oil in 1917–1919.[12]

Colombia's platinum deposits also attracted considerable attention from American investors. Earl Harding, chairman of the Colombian Commercial Corporation, laid out the aims of a group that was forming to exploit Colombian platinum in 1918. Guaranteeing a "steady delivery" of the mineral to the United States and its allies was one goal, but many other benefits would accrue from the establishment of the platinum industry. It could "form the basis from which to expand into shipping and general export and import trade." From there, Harding concluded, a monopoly on platinum production could be built, shipping lines could be taken over, and American financiers could be assured of the greater share of Colombia's financial transactions. "As Americans," he wrote, "we are reluctant to surrender the advantages which should come to the foreign commerce of our own country in this rich corner of South America, where our influence should predominate."[13]

The new opportunities for American interests in Colombia collided with an old diplomatic problem between the two countries stemming from the 1903 Panamanian revolution. Colombia's anger had never subsided over what it perceived as American collusion in the rapid sequence of Panama's declaration of independence from Colombia, its recognition as an independent nation by the United States, and its treaty with America for the construction of an isthmian canal. Colombian suspicions were hardly assuaged by Theodore Roosevelt's blustering statement in 1911 that he "took the Canal Zone and let Congress debate."[14]

In 1914 this problem seemed to be coming to a satisfactory conclusion. Under the direction of Woodrow Wilson and his secretary of state, William Jennings Bryan, the Thomson-Urrutia Treaty expressed "sincere regrets" for the enmity arising out of American actions concerning Panama. It also stipulated that Colombia be paid $25 million as an indemnity.[15] Wilson's desire to seek a solution to the rift was likely due to the Panamanian incident being widely used by Latin American critics of the United States as a prime example of U.S. imperialistic and expansionistic designs in Latin America. His professed desire for better relations with the nations to the south would have made the alleviation of this problem highly desirable.[16]

However, neither regrets nor remuneration sat well with Republican senators, and the treaty especially infuriated Roosevelt, who said in a letter to Senator William Stone that "I regard the proposed Treaty as a crime against the United States, an attack upon the honor of the United States."[17] His criticisms carried considerable weight. One of his closest friends, Henry Cabot Lodge, was a member of the Senate Foreign Relations Committee, and Roosevelt himself still exerted influence in Republican circles. Few Republicans could afford to offend the popular former president by coming out in favor of the treaty. All of this exacerbated the Senate's uneasiness over the American "apology" and the size of the indemnity, which led to its refusal to approve the treaty. By 1917 the treaty was still unratified. Bryan's replacement in the State Department, Robert Lansing, concluded that the treaty would receive Senate approval only with a number of amendments that he felt would leave the final document "confused" and "inartistic."[18] America's entry into World War I saved Lansing from having to confront that messy problem immediately. Following the end of the war, and, not coincidentally, Roosevelt's death in January 1919, the Wilson administration once again attempted to tie up some loose ends in Colombia.

The decision to seek a settlement of America's differences with Colombia cannot be explained by a simple desire for tidiness, however. By 1919 a number of American officials were convinced that foreign oil sources were necessary for the economic and strategic well-being of the nation. Colombia was a promising source. Unfortunately, as the American minister to Colombia, Hoffman Philip, wrote in May 1919, the "undeveloped riches" of that nation were a "difficult field for foreign enterprises at present." Much of the difficulty, he surmised, was due to Colombia's "fear and suspicion of outside domination." The passage of the five-year-old treaty would help matters immensely and "afford an opportunity for serious American investors."[19]

Such considerations were not lost on the American Senate, and in late July 1919 it was reported that discussions concerning the Versailles peace treaty would be suspended temporarily in order to bring the Colombian treaty to the floor. Lodge was quoted as saying that the treaty most likely would be ratified in the first week of August.[20] Instead, at that time the Senate angrily returned the treaty to committee because of a new and threatening petroleum law recently enacted in Colombia.

The problem first came to light in a decree issued by Colombia's President Marco F. Suárez on 20 June 1919. Executive Decree No. 1255 noted that the development of the petroleum industry in Colombia was a "most alluring" prospect. It made clear that subsoil rights in Colombia were owned by the government and went on to set the rules and regulations by which exploration and drillings would be conducted: Permits were required, information was to be provided on the specifics of the exploration, and time and area limits were set for drilling. A month later Suárez defended his position in a speech to Colombia's national congress. He stated that legislation was urgently needed to "fix clearly the right of the Nation" as well as the landowners and to "promote discreetly the influx of foreign capital." He then asked whether this legislation should be

> for the exclusive benefit of private parties or whether the State
> should participate in the proprietorship of the subsoil from motives

of public policy and as a right derived from eminent domain. The latter conclusion appears the more reasonable, not for the purpose of interfering with the exploitation of the subsoil or enhancing its value in an inequitable manner, but for that of facilitating and regulating its exploitation.[21]

American officials in Colombia were dismayed. Throughout late June and July, a number of notes were sent to the State Department concerning the decree. Philip declared that the act was of "great moment" to American interests in Colombia and would discourage American development of oil there. Consul Claude Guyant was even more emphatic that the decree was "causing much discontent" and was a "serious menace to Americans interested in petroleum development." By late July, however, Philip acknowledged that Colombia needed some sort of legislation regarding petroleum, but he concluded that "I foresee many difficulties for American operators in this field." In a happier mood Philip informed the department on 29 July that Suárez had suspended the decree pending action by the Colombian national congress.[22]

All of this information arrived back in the United States in early and mid-August, and it caused a much greater sensation there than it had in Colombia. On 7 August, Senator Lodge informed the Senate that the Colombian decree, which was "very similar to the Mexican decree," would probably lead to a "confiscation of private property in oil." Until the matter was cleared up, he urged that the treaty be sent back to committee. That was immediately done.[23]

Two days later, Lansing informed Philip that, after conferring with the Senate subcommittee to which the treaty had been sent, the decision had been reached about the "best way of safeguarding American interests in Colombia." An amendment should be attached to the 1914 treaty stating that neither nation would "nullify, or alter, or question, the rights of the citizens of the other signatory, to real estate, mines, petroleum deposits . . . acquired prior to the exchange of the ratifications of this treaty." The secretary urged Philip to make Colombia understand that the United States did not want to "interfere with the sovereign rights of Colombia in the disposition of her public lands."[24] Several days later Philip told Lansing that the Colombians were taken aback by the Senate's action. He also revealed some uneasiness about linking passage of the treaty to the oil decree. Such linkage, he believed, would "probably have a very different effect than that intended." Furthermore, he felt that a new petroleum law then under consideration in Colombia was in most respects "favorable to foreign interests."[25]

Lansing, however, was intent on using the unratified treaty to attempt to force guarantees of American property rights from Colombia. In a message to Philip on 13 August, Lansing bluntly concluded that "if Colombia enforces nationalization we must expect other Latin American countries to follow suit and this should be averted." On 21 August, Lansing sent a longer message to Philip explaining again why such action was necessary. Referring first to Mexico's actions concerning petroleum properties, Lansing called the problem "one of the most serious international questions that ever confronted this Government." Colombia now also had raised this question with its recent oil decree which was "made after studies in Mexico." Such a problem could not "pass unchallenged," for that would "establish a precedent embarrassing to this Government in relation to similar matters in Mexico and possibly other countries."[26] Colombia was thus regarded as a test case for American policy. If economic nationalism, with its threat of nationalization and expropriation, could gain a hold in that nation it might very well spread through all of South America. It must be stopped, and the pending treaty seemed to be a good tool for achieving that goal.

Colombia did not accept the American plan. In mid-August, Philip informed Lansing that Colombia was "disinclined" to make an amendment to the treaty concerning oil. It would, however, sign a separate protocol guaranteeing American property rights. The minister also pointed out that a great deal of anti-American sentiment had been stirred up over the issue and that the Colombian press was blasting the "imperialistic and coercive" action of the United States. He believed that the protocol was probably the best solution. Philip ascribed Colombia's stance on petroleum properties to the fact that it was "very ignorant" about how to protect its interests. He concluded that perhaps Colombia would be "susceptible to advisory suggestions." Later that month, however, Philip reported that neither the idea of amending the treaty nor that of signing a separate protocol was acceptable to the Colombian national congress. On 22 August he wired the department that the definitive reply of Colombia was that no protocol would be signed. The Colombian constitution guaranteed the rights of foreigners, and that would have to suffice.[27]

Philip's reports were mulled over by officials in the State Department. Boaz Long, attached to the Latin American Division, felt that it would indeed be a "happy circumstance" if Colombia were to accept American suggestions about an "ideal law" dealing with subsoil rights: "If this were accomplished, Colombia's lead might be followed by other Latin American Governments." In other words Colombia could become a showplace, an alternative to Mexico's destructive "lead." Long also believed that for the time being some sort of petroleum agreement with Colombia was needed. He had serious doubts about the efficacy of the proposed protocol, but he concluded that "the thought that they must do nothing to prevent the ratification of the treaty cannot influence them much longer." Furthermore, the absence of an agreement might lead other nations, such as Mexico, to believe that the United States "had no hold over another government."[28] Lansing shared those sentiments. On 28 August he wired Philip that the

United States desired a separate protocol and that the treaty would stay in committee until a "binding agreement" was made on the subject of nationalization.[29]

Although Lansing had concluded that Colombia's actions were merely part of the overall "Mexican problem," the real reasons for Suárez's decree were much more complicated. Suárez was no strident nationalist. Early in his administration he had pronounced the policy of the "Polar Star," the main goal of which was to ensure an ever closer relationship between the United States and Colombia by having the latter look to the former for economic direction.[30] In this, Suárez was merely stating what seemed to be the reality. World War I had destroyed Colombia's traditional trading lines. The United States had become its greatest trading partner (with coffee leading the way), and it had also taken the lead in foreign investments, with American money pouring into railroad building, public works, and the new Colombian oil industry. By 1919 the United States had $5 million invested in the mining of precious metals and stones (mostly platinum and emeralds), $8 million in sugar production, $10 million in fruit production, and $20 million in oil production in Colombia.[31]

Furthermore, it is evident that the only menacing aspect of the oil decree was that it came so soon after Mexico's Article 27. Despite Lansing's fears that Colombia was becoming another Mexico, Executive Decree No. 1255 was in reality a mild document. Suárez's goal was, as he stated in his speech to the national congress in July 1919, the "facilitating and regulating" of the oil industry by putting it under state control.[32] Coming from a member of the Conservative party, which had as its credo greater centralization of political and economic power in Colombia, his statement should have come as no surprise. Nothing in the State Department files indicates that American policymakers ever considered these issues in their analyses.

Those policymakers also did not clearly understand the pressures under which Suárez was working. The war had significantly altered Colombia's economic and social makeup. As the first postwar president, Suárez was the first to attempt to cope with changes such as the booming oil industry and the rise of new economic groups in his nation.[33]

American officials were oblivious to such concerns, and their harsh stance on the oil problem brought on an additional problem for Suárez. By linking the 1914 treaty to Colombia's oil policies, they unwittingly released new and stronger waves of nationalistic sentiment in Colombia. Suárez's and his party's philosophy dictated a strong economic relationship between Colombia and the United States, and he now found himself buffeted by nationalist criticism.

As Philip reported in mid-September, nationalist elements in Colombia were in an uproar over news that Suárez planned to retire after calling for the annulment of the petroleum decree and the encouragement and protection of foreign investment. That would be an "unfortunate" development for American interests, which would be "best served by an effort to strengthen the hand of the present executive." The State Department evidenced little sympathy for Suárez's plight. Assistant Secretary of State William Phillips expressed regrets over the situation, but he informed Philip that the "treaty situation" could be improved only if an "early agreement may be reached as to the protocol." In a follow-up letter Phillips referred to the minister's mention of Suárez's encouraging foreign capital in Colombia: "preferential consideration to American capital" perhaps could be "included in the proposed protocol." "This Government," he concluded, "would be pleased to see its nationals play a leading part in the development of Colombia."[34]

Philip, however, continued to voice concern over the rigid stance that the United States had adopted. In late September he wrote Lansing that America's insistence on the protocol was "particularly unfortunate," as it played into the hands of "active Mexican propaganda" circulating in Colombia. It was with some real hope for a solution, then, that he informed the department on 3 October that the Colombian senate had passed a resolution designed to make a protocol unnecessary. Philip conceded that it was not the best solution, because although it affirmed Colombia's stand to protect "the rights of all foreigners," the resolution also contained some indignant slaps at American policy. Still, he felt that it was a positive step toward a resolution of the problem.[35]

Events in the State Department precluded such a resolution. Senator Albert Fall, a staunch enemy of Mexico's property laws and Article 27, sent two letters to Boaz Long on 8 October documenting that the problem in Colombia was merely an extension of the older problem with Mexico. One letter enclosed two memorandums from unnamed sources: The first claimed that Colombia's oil decree had been copied from Mexico's decree, the second described the anti-American machinations of the Mexican embassy in Bogotá. Colombian students were supporters of Mexico, and the embassy was a propaganda outlet. It was a serious problem, because "the smaller South American countries look on Mexico as a leader." Fall's second letter to Long stated that the Foreign Relations Committee believed that Colombia's recent decree and Mexico's 1917 constitution were simply different aspects of the same problem. Both nations were wrongfully attempting to change their land laws, which had "existed from time immemorial."[36]

Lansing's response to Philip's report on the Colombian senate's resolution reflected such thinking. It tersely explained that the Colombian resolution was "not pleasing" and not acceptable. A protocol was the "appropriate way" to settle the problem. "It is the hope of the United States," the secretary continued, "that the new proposed agreement with Colombia may be so reasonable in its nature as to admit of its serving as a basis for similar agreements with other countries which would welcome the development of their natural resources."[37]

As Philip indicated in his next message, however, there were deep divisions within the Colombian government about just how "reasonable" the American proposal was. While Suárez and most of his cabinet favored the private ownership of subsoil rights, many others in the national congress were leaning toward nationalization. Compromise legislation being proposed at that time stated that oil lands would be acquired by contract, not condemnation, and that owners of private oil lands who developed them within twenty years after the passage of the law would own the lands in perpetuity; otherwise, the lands would revert to the nation. While Philip did not come out in favor of the new law, he did make clear his belief that the present American stance was doing more harm than good. The Colombian press was up in arms, and the nation as a whole "deeply resented" American ratification of the 1914 treaty being made contingent upon Colombia's oil legislation. Philip concluded that he could "see no advantage to be derived from the position we have taken which would not have been procured with better results through a settlement of the treaty as originally proposed."[38]

Secretary Lansing still insisted on a separate protocol, although he showed quite a bit of interest in the twenty-year option section of the proposed Colombian law. Unfortunately the final version of the law, passed by the Colombian house of representatives, led even Philip to conclude that it was a "somewhat veiled project for the nationalization of all oil lands." The issue was rendered moot in late November, when the Colombian supreme court ruled the law, and major portions of the June 1919 decree, unconstitutional. Philip was ecstatic. He wrote that the Colombian congress was hard at work on a new and, he hoped, fairer law. "By approving the treaty now," he stated, "we would be assisting Colombia in a pro-American policy."[39]

Once again, however, the minister and the secretary were at cross-purposes. It is evident from his correspondence that Philip strongly believed that the American holdup on the treaty was bringing on the problems in Colombia. Suárez's administration, which as he had already noted desired the input of foreign capital into Colombia, was eager to settle the issue but had to contend with the nationalist fervor stirred up by America's insulting attitude. The passage of the treaty would be a show of good faith and would give Suárez and his followers "much additional strength against their opponents and with that the required courage to openly advocate the seeking of American assistance." But Lansing believed that withholding the treaty to force the signing of a separate protocol was the only way in which the problem could be definitively solved. Furthermore, in a 25 November message to Philip, the secretary made it clear that he hoped "that the high intelligence of the Colombian statesmen will recognize the benefit of an agreement and that results will be so promptly apparent that other states will desire to follow Colombia's example." If not, and if Colombia were to follow the example of Mexico's oil legislation, then Lansing was equally clear about the consequences:

Such an unsettled tenure of property cannot fail to discourage the investment of capital, investment which is seriously needed in Colombia for the development of its potential riches, and which might be turned to other channels if American investors should be uneasy as to the permanence of their titles.[40]

A cartoon in a Colombian newspaper of the time, depicting Uncle Sam atop a "Colombian mule" dangling a carrot marked "Twenty-five Millions" tied to a stick just before the creature's nose, summed up the matter nicely. Philip wanted to use the "carrot" of the treaty and American economic input as a lure to induce Colombia to modify its stance on the oil issue. Lansing preferred the "stick": withholding of the treaty and threatening to withdraw American capital to coerce Colombia into signing a binding protocol which, he hoped, could be used as an example to other nations in South America considering the Mexican option. The two approaches were similar in one important respect: Neither doubted which nation would be in the saddle.[41]

Philip's approach eventually won out, but not without a fight. In early January 1920 he wired Lansing that Petroleum Law 120 had been passed in December. There seemed to be no threat of nationalization in the bill, and he concluded that, while some American oil interests would protest its provisions (particularly those dealing with higher taxes), the law "would not discourage foreign capital." There was "no reason why it should be considered just cause for the further postponement of action on the Treaty of 1914." Frank Polk at the State Department agreed and wrote to Philip that "as long as we keep the treaty held up the more we are going to do to encourage pro-Mexican feeling, and in fact any kind of anti-American feeling."[42]

There the matter stood through February while the department was reshuffled following the departure of Robert Lansing, whose increasing policy differences with President Wilson had resulted in Wilson asking for his resignation. His replacement, Bainbridge Colby, seemed content to follow his predecessor's policy toward Colombia. Advised on 12 April by Hallett Johnson of the department's Latin American Division that Petroleum Law 120 was part of a "carefully thought-of plan to interest American concerns with a view to eventually taking over American oil enterprises," Colby was impressed enough to write to Wilson the next day. The law, he averred, was a sign that Colombia was "seeking indirectly by oppressive regulations to accomplish, at least measurably, the objects aimed at by the Executive decree" issued in June 1919.[43]

As he had done with Lansing, Philip now attempted to convert Colby to his point of view. On 26 April he urged Colby to see that the treaty was ratified. There were "valuable opportunities" in Colombia, and the passage of the 1914 treaty could serve "as the necessary means of assuring predominance of American interests." By now Philip had support from a number of American concerns that viewed the unratified treaty as an obstacle to their economic pursuits in Colombia. This support was enough to convince the Senate to report the treaty out of committee in June 1920, but a vote on the treaty had to be postponed as time ran out in the congressional session.[44]

Opposition to the treaty still existed. A number of oil companies, while certainly desirous of cordial relations between the United States and Colombia, still expressed serious doubts about the December 1919 oil legislation. Representatives of Henry L. Doherty and Company, Prudential Oil, Standard Oil, and Sinclair Consolidated Oil were unanimous in their condemnation. Such considerations affected the treaty debate, and, as the matter dragged on into October 1920, Philip once again went on the attack for a quick settlement. In an angry letter to Colby on 28 October, the minister claimed that the reason that the new petroleum law was not very good was that the treaty was being held up. As for the complaints of the American oil companies, Philip recommended that they make a "concerted effort" in Colombia to secure revisions in the law.[45]

Other opposition to ratification of the treaty came from the defenders of Theodore Roosevelt. As the final push for ratification came in January 1921, Senator Frank Kellogg leapt to the defense of Roosevelt's actions in 1903. His purchase of the Panama Canal Zone had been "one of the great acts of a great president in a great era of American history."[46] The tide was running strongly against such obstacles, however. The belief was growing more powerful that the treaty issue was damaging America's economic position in Colombia and, indeed, in all of Latin America. From Colombia, Philip wrote that American gold and platinum interests, bankers, and other businessmen were almost as one in support for a settlement of the treaty question. Even Dr. Frederick Miller of the Rockefeller Institute complained that the withholding of the treaty was hampering his efforts to effect humanitarian reforms in Colombia. Colby had also come around to that conclusion. In a February 1921 speech to the Pan American Advertising Association, the secretary asserted that "from the single standpoint of our commercial progress in South America, the delayed ratification of the treaty is not only an unmixed calamity, but an immeasurable one." The delay had already cost the United States "friends, confidence and commercial opportunity."[47]

The election of Warren Harding in 1920, and the naming of Charles Evans Hughes as the new secretary of state, brought Philip even more support for his plans for an early ratification of the treaty. An episode that occurred just weeks after Hughes had taken office was indicative of that new support. Writing to Third Assistant Secretary of State Robert Bliss on 23 March 1921, Philip warned that the impending treaty could not be used as a weapon to obtain a better petroleum law in Colombia and that quick passage of the treaty was the best solution to the problem. When, three days later, Secretary of the Navy Edwin Denby made the suggestion to Hughes that the 1914 treaty be used as a "lever" to force changes in Colombia's oil legislation, Hughes answered with a letter that was nearly a carbon copy of Philip's earlier message.[48]

By the time a final vote on the ratification was approaching, even the oil companies favored passage of the treaty. Reports from Colombia that British oil interests were becoming actively involved there probably catalyzed the American companies' change of heart. Evidence from the congressional debate on the matter shows that, like so many other American interests in Colombia, the oil companies had concluded that withholding the treaty was causing more problems than it was worth.[49] Ironically, Henry Cabot Lodge was the chief spokesman for passage of the treaty when it came to a vote in April 1921. Concentrating his arguments on the economic advantages America would accrue through friendly relations with Colombia, Lodge also attempted to lay to rest the ghost of Theodore Roosevelt that continued to haunt any discussion of the Panamanian incident by stating that, if Roosevelt were alive, he would support the treaty. Demonstrating uncharacteristic restraint, the deceased leader did not leap from the grave to attack his old friend. The treaty was passed by a comfortable margin on 20 April.[50]

American officials now turned their attention to actively developing the Colombian market. The intense interest manifested in the matter was revealed in June 1921, when the Harding administration was considering the replacement of Hoffman Philip as minister to Colombia, which Hughes argued against. The proposed replacement was a competent man, the secretary conceded, but he had no "special acquaintance with Latin America," nor did he speak Spanish. Because America's "affairs at Colombia are likely to assume special importance," and a "new and important commercial treaty should be negotiated," Hughes was convinced that only a top-ranking diplomat should be there. With the treaty ratified "there is a special opportunity in Colombia and a situation requiring particular attention."[51] Philip remained at his post until mid-1922, when he was replaced by Samuel Piles.

Piles, perhaps even more so than Philip, was very excited about the possibilities for American capital and trade in Colombia. In a long letter to President Harding in September 1922, Piles described how Colombia was "wonderfully rich in undeveloped resources" and concluded that "this is the country in South America in which we should make our stand." If America could become the "dominant force in Colombia's future development," he wrote, ". . . we shall have a striking example here of the very great help and prosperity we are capable of bringing to other countries; thus showing what our real intentions are in South America." Becoming the "dominant force" in Colombia would also mean developing "trade and commerce that will be worth many years of devoted effort." Colombia had been "asleep for more than a hundred years"; with U.S. help, however, "it looks to me as though a new West were in the making here."[52] This was the example the United States was seeking to counteract the pernicious influence of the Mexican example.

Harding's reply to Piles made it clear that he shared the minister's enthusiasm. He, too, believed that Colombia offered "exceptional possibilities" for American capital; such considerations had led him to send Piles there. "The opportunities for American capital will undoubtedly be promptly responded to if the way is suitably pointed out."[53]

While Colombia did not exactly become a "new West," American capital did play an extensive role there during the 1920s. Investments in gold, platinum, and emerald mining were the most glamorous activities, but American money also played an important part in many agricultural enterprises in Colombia, and in oil development the investments reached truly great heights. A corollary of that substantial investment was a good growth in Colombian-U.S. trade. Little wonder that the era was referred to as the "Dance of the Millions" in Colombia.[54]

The period following the ratification of the 1914 treaty was not without problems. The massive influx of American money into Colombia, especially into the development and exploitation of natural resources, fueled a resurgent nationalism based on, as historian Stephen Randall has put it, "a fear of loss of sovereignty; the belief that the society would not reap the rewards of direct foreign investment; and an ambiguous popular anti-Americanism."[55]

It soon became clear that the primary trouble spot was, once again, the oil lands. As early as January 1923, Piles reported that the Colombian house of representatives was again showing an interest in Mexico's oil laws, "laws which have safeguarded the immense Mexican national wealth," as one Colombian report put it.[56] In October, Piles informed the department of the adverse reaction in Colombia to concessions granted to an American oil company, Andian Oil. The criticisms centered around the popular belief that "Colombian interests have been sold out without the sanction of the representatives of the people." It was somewhat ironic that the minister could not understand the Colombians' suspicions about American rapaciousness: In the same letter, Piles discussed his idea for "rediverting to the United States . . . a large share of the present and future Treaty payments" by encouraging Colombia's purchase of railroad equipment in America.[57]

Throughout 1924 and 1925 sporadic attempts were made in Colombia to enact new and, as perceived by the United States, harsher oil legislation. Late 1925 and 1926, however, witnessed a rapidly growing demand in Colombia for action to protect the nation's natural resources from foreign exploitation. An article in the Colombian newspaper *El Tiempo* in December 1925 charged that petroleum was shipped out of the nation "without giving any benefit to the country of its origin." What was needed was a "national crusade to save the country's wealth." In January 1926, *El Espectador* commented on statements by Herbert Hoover concerning the adverse effects of imposing restrictions on the flow of commodities and resources. The article noted that Colombia would not be able to separate itself from the "commercial war" that would be "inevitable should the countries which produce commodities of necessary consumption by American people not resign themselves to accept those prices which the consumer may arbitrarily impose."[58]

From 1919 to 1922 the United States attempted to use its newfound economic and diplomatic muscle to coerce Colombia into accepting the American definition of proper economic development and behavior. Using the 1914 treaty as both a carrot and a stick, American policymakers had alternately enticed Colombia with promises of economic prizes and threatened it with economic reprisals. U.S. officials hoped that forcing Colombia to back down on the oil legislation issue would provide an example to other South American nations that might be considering the same sort of legislation. With Colombia back on the straight and narrow path of economic development, American money and technology could transform that sleeping nation into an exemplary dynamo of growth and progress. But by 1925 it was clear that Colombia was again intent on bucking Uncle Sam.

The rumblings of nationalist discontent in Colombia during 1924–25 were disconcerting to American policymakers who had assumed that such matters had been settled by the ratification of the Thomson-Urrutia Treaty in 1921. The news from Colombia early in 1926 was the first definitive warning that the battle over oil concessions was not over. In February, Minister Piles reported that Colombian President Pedro Nel Ospina had issued a decree canceling the Colombian Petroleum Company's (an affiliate of Standard Oil) contract for the Barco concession, which had been held by the company for nearly seven years. Piles said that the reason given by the Colombians for the cancellation was the company's noncompliance with its contract. The decree had been met with general jubilation in Colombia, and the government had been much praised for its decisive action.[59]

While it initially disdained forceful diplomatic tactics in hope of avoiding another incident such as the unpleasantness of 1919–1921, the State Department did make known its desire that American interests in Colombia be afforded due process of law. This merely intensified the Colombian reaction against the American oil companies. Even the fairly conservative newspaper *Diario Nacional* warned that "we live resolved to sign no indenture of slavery with any power in the world, no matter how powerful its appearance." *Mundo Al Dia*, on 16 September 1926, advised Colombia to "follow very closely the evolution in Mexico . . . because from a study of the Mexican legislation we may derive great benefit for the organization of the exploitation of oil and minerals." Colombian papers also began to decry the Latin American policy of the United States as a whole, especially American involvement in Nicaragua.[60]

By 1927 relations between the United States and Colombia were becoming increasingly uneasy. Piles reported in August that a new law had been proposed for government development of iron and copper deposits. He noted that "this tendency in favor of governmental ventures into the field of industry appears to be gaining popular favor." Most railroads were government owned, and a number of Colombians were demanding that the government also take control of the oil deposits. Piles noted that such a trend was unfortunate, because the "enormous benefits" that private development of those industries had brought to Colombia were "apparently lost sight of." Jordan Stabler, a former chief of the department's Latin American Division, echoed Piles when he wrote in September that "the Colombians seem to have gone mad on the subject of petroleum and as they know nothing about the industry or the science of geology" their nationalistic aims were sadly mistaken.[61]

Despite American doubts about the feasibility of greater Colombian participation in the development of its natural resources, it was evident by late 1927 that Colombia was determined to embark on this path. In October, Piles reported that the Colombian house of representatives was considering legislation which "to a great extent 'nationalizes' the petroleum industry." If passed, it would be "a serious blow to American oil interests." Francis Loomis, representing Gulf Oil, wrote to Secretary of State Kellogg that the situation in Colombia was "delicate" and "menacing." Asked to provide more information, Piles reported early in November that the new oil legislation would probably not be passed in this congressional session. However, Minister of Industries José Antonio Montalvo had called for an emergency petroleum act to be in effect until congress could reconvene.[62]

Piles noted that the act that was finally passed, Law 84, was "not as devastating as in its original form" but would tend to hold oil operations in limbo. The minister cautiously concluded that this action indicated that Colombia had "tendencies to look to Mexico" for its lead in oil legislation. In a later message to Kellogg, he added that the oil companies were upset about the law, especially about its high tax rates.[63] Nonetheless, Colombia put Law 84 into effect in January 1928 under the auspices of Decree 150.

Decree 150 was difficult for foreign oil companies to accept. They were given thirty days to produce hard evidence demonstrating their ownership of their lands. New, higher taxes were set up. Furthermore, the minister of industries and not the courts was to determine whether the land titles were indeed legal. The State Department responded quickly. After receiving complaints from the oil companies, Kellogg directed Piles to point out to the Colombian government the "unfortunate" effects that the law would have. Piles agreed that the law was "extremely burdensome," but he advised the secretary that he did not think it wise to act at the moment.[64]

Kellogg obviously preferred more direct action, and on 18 February he ordered Piles to meet with Colombia's President Miguel Abadía Méndez and impress upon him the wrongfulness of Decree 150 and the good intentions and prospective results of American involvement in Colombian oil development. Piles agreed reluctantly to the meeting, as some American businessmen had advised against such a move. After the conference, however, he informed Kellogg that he felt "encouraged" about the matter.[65]

Others were not so encouraged. At a 6 March meeting between Robert Olds, Stokeley Morgan, and Arthur Young of the State Department and representatives of Gulf Oil, the oilmen suggested that, at least until Colombia changed its present policies, the State Department should withhold its blessing from further loans to that nation. Olds replied that this device might lead to further difficulties for American oil interests because of the anti-Americanism it would foment. In Colombia, Piles was coming around to the same idea. Noting that Colombia was "badly" in need of funds, he also suggested linking the questions of loans and oil decrees. The withholding of loans might work to America's advantage, because otherwise "the Government might not feel so inclined to remedy present conditions."[66] For the moment nothing came of these suggestions, but later events would revive them.

The first clear indication that Piles's earlier feeling of encouragement had indeed been premature came in May 1928. On the 14th, Piles informed the department that a new bill was being debated in the Colombian congress calling for the deportation of foreigners who brought diplomatic pressure on Colombia or incited armed revolt. It was, he noted, "apparently aimed primarily at foreign petroleum interests."[67] Three days later Piles disclosed that enforcement of Decree 150 had been ordered, the results of which would be the "probable subsequent seizure of millions of dollars of American property." Kellogg immediately and forcefully responded. Piles was to make a "vigorous" oral protest and give the Colombian president a memorandum stating that the decree was unfair to foreign interests. America wanted the decree suspended until the Colombian supreme court ruled on its constitutionality.[68]

When Piles reported that he had met with Abadía Méndez, had received assurances that the decree would be suspended, and had accepted the return of the memorandum, Kellogg's anger flared. He fired off a heated message directing the minister to return the memo and not to withdraw it unless authorized by the department.[69]

Such impatience on Kellogg's part had only a limited effect on Colombian policy. On 2 June he was informed that Colombia had suspended Decree 150, but Law 84 was left in place until a court ruling on its constitutionality could be reached. The oil men would still need to go through the complicated process of proving ownership of their lands. A few days later Piles noted that a new bill had been introduced in the Colombian congress calling for the organization of a government-administered and government-financed company to exploit petroleum. This was but another sign of the "absurd" course Colombia was pursuing and a demonstration of its "woeful ignorance."[70]

In July and August 1928 the long-standing Barco concession issue came to a head. Piles claimed that Minister Montalvo was playing politics with the problem and suggested that a message be sent directly to the Colombian president to try and solve the conflict. Instead, the State Department directed Piles to tell the Colombians that the U.S. government wished to see the nullification of the Barco concession revoked. After doing so, Piles wired Kellogg that his message had not had exactly the desired result: A presidential decree had been released confirming the forfeiture of the oil lands.[71]

By late August matters had gone from bad to worse, and Piles was becoming more discouraged. On 24 August he announced that the Colombian house of representatives had appointed a committee to study the oil laws of the United States in order to discover whether Colombians had reciprocal rights to exploit petroleum there. More important, the committee also had been directed to find some basis for the forfeiture of both the Tropical Oil and Andian Oil concessions. While Piles did not expect any definite action by Colombia on the oil question in the near future, he also did not foresee any "favorable developments" taking place. It was obvious that Colombia had "aligned" against a friendly policy and was instead taking a course of "blind nationalism."[72]

Throughout September and early October the passage of a new Colombian oil law and the growing problems of the Andian and Tropical oil companies did little to convince American officials that Colombia was not on a path of "blind nationalism." The new Colombian oil law first came to the attention of the State Department on 10 September when Piles enclosed the first ninety-two articles of the law with a promise to send the rest as it was translated. Over two weeks later Chargé H. Freeman Matthews, who had been left in charge upon Piles's departure to the United States, wired Kellogg that a Colombian senate committee had approved Article 2 of the new law with the following addition: "Therefore, the competent authority may decree on petition of a legitimately interested party the expropriations necessary for the exercise and development of said industry." Matthews explained in a later message that such an addition might be used against "private property rights."[73]

Concerning the oil companies, Matthews informed Kellogg on 26 September that a Colombian congressman had told him that a committee report would be issued recommending the cancellation of Tropical Oil's concession. A few days later Matthews reported that a secret bill calling for the expropriation of both companies was soon to be released. On 1 October, the congressional committee recommended that Tropical Oil's concession be cancelled. Matthews believed that the attacks on Tropical Oil and Andian Oil were due to Colombia's " 'getting away with' the Barco forfeiture" without any reprisal from the United States.[74]

As in 1919, American diplomats now looked for a lever to use against Colombia to halt its march toward "blind nationalism." Having no outstanding treaty handy with which to force Colombia's hand, American policymakers quickly found another area where Colombia was vulnerable: its need for loans. Piles had informed the department in July 1928 that Colombia's foreign debt was a staggering $200 million. American interests there urged that "our bankers should insist upon not only fair treatment for American interests . . . but a great supervision of expenditures of the various loan proceeds." At the State Department, Stokeley Morgan asked Arthur Young, the economic adviser, whether Piles's note should be released to the public. It seemed to him that "the Department of Commerce ought to get the situation out before the American investing public." Young replied that he had forwarded the note to Commerce, which had recently published a circular on the financial situation in Colombia. He understood that the Colombian minister to the United States had asked that the circular not be released and that the information be discreetly disseminated instead. Morgan answered that, nonetheless, the circular should go out to protect American investors. This, of course, was separate from "the question of Colombian oil legislation and the possible injustices to American interests in Colombia."[75]

The circular was released late in September 1928, and the effects in Colombia were immediate. On 11 October, Matthews reported to Kellogg that he had heard that the Colombian minister in Washington had warned his government that "economic 'reprisals' " might take place as a result of the Tropical Oil dispute. The Colombian government was decidedly uneasy over this development, and one week later Matthews wrote that the Colombian president would issue a report stating that he considered the Tropical Oil contract valid.[76]

Matthews now became quite interested in the circular, which he at first called the "note of Mr. Hoover." The Colombian minister of finance had declared that the information in the document would mean the end of the "era of foreign loans." After discovering that "Mr. Hoover's note" was in reality Department of Commerce Circular No. 305, Matthews proceeded to bombard Kellogg with his analysis of the beneficial effects of the report. On 27 October he announced that Colombia had decided to reopen discussion of the Barco concession. In another cable later that day Matthews stressed that if Colombia should decide that "there is no danger of the stoppage of foreign loans it would probably resume its former policy of hostility." Matthews wrote on 30 October that "the importance attached to and beneficial effects of circular cannot be overemphasized." Claiming that Colombia was becoming very anxious over the issue, he concluded on 31 October that "if this anxiety is not dispelled it may result in favorable change of attitude toward United States and American interests."[77]

Secretary Kellogg had a number of ways to approach this matter. He could relay to Colombia assurances that the circular was not a definitive statement of U.S. policy. That, however, would destroy the bargaining leverage about which Matthews had been so ebullient. On the other hand he could take a hard line with Colombia, using the circular as a threat to that nation's finances. The drawback of that approach was that it would almost certainly result in an intensely nationalistic and anti-American outburst throughout Colombia that would further endanger American interests. Kellogg also could do what he eventually did—nothing. In answer to the many telegrams Matthews had sent about the circular, Kellogg wrote back on 31 October. The most important section of the message stated that "if Colombian Government should . . . refer to this circular as a note or intimate that it was a communication from the United States Government to the Government of Colombia, you will see that this impression is corrected." Before the message was sent, however, Kellogg crossed that passage out.[78] Apparently the secretary was not ready to dispel Colombia's anxiety. Since Matthews had informed him that the Colombian government *thought* that the circular was an official note condemning Colombia's finances, why let it think otherwise?

Meanwhile, Matthews continued to keep Kellogg apprised of the circular's effect. His first dispatch following Kellogg's 31 October telegram reported that he had come across a United Press item stating that the State Department had denied that the circular was an official note sent to Colombia. This had the unfortunate effect of detracting from the circular's importance "and consequently from its high beneficial effects." He concluded that "the time is most opportune for obtaining fairer treatment of American interests."[79]

Matthews seemed assuaged by the fact that the department did not officially confirm the press release, and a short while later he was once again hammering away on the importance of the circular, calling it a "valuable opportunity" to make Colombia understand that unless it rectified its financial mess and the "unfair" attacks on American interests, no loans would be forthcoming. Already, Matthews claimed in a later note, the Colombian government was softening its position on the Barco decision due to the circular. It had sent a note to its minister in the United States telling him to assure the State Department that the decision had not been a "hostility" but had been made in the "public interest."[80]

Matthews noted a decided change of attitude in Colombia concerning its petroleum legislation and its attacks on American interests. The circular had "enormously helped this healthy reaction," and he advised the department that "the continuance and growth of this reaction lies largely in Washington." According to Matthews the "healthy reaction" was due to "a better realization of Colombia's financial and economic dependence upon the United States and consequently the necessity for better relations."[81]

It soon became apparent that the circular also was having the desired effect of discouraging foreign loans to Colombia. Allen Dulles, of the law firm of Sullivan and Cromwell, wrote to Stokeley Morgan on 14 November that loan negotiations had broken down between Colombia and Lazard Brothers of London. The Colombians were despondent and had no confidence of securing a loan abroad. Dulles was encouraged, because this meant that Colombia's "present attitude indicates a desire to lessen the existing friction with American interests."[82]

The effects on Colombia's oil policy were indeed gratifying for American policymakers. Jefferson Caffrey, who had replaced Piles as American minister in November 1928, wired Kellogg in early December concerning a meeting with the Colombian president, who had assured him that everything would be done to restore the Barco concession and eliminate the burdensome oil legislation. Like Matthews, Caffrey believed that the major reason for Colombia's changed attitude was Circular No. 305, which had created a "vivid realization of Colombia's economic and financial dependence on the United States." The settlement of the problems with the Barco concession and the Tropical Oil Company were "two concrete results" of such a realization. Colombia had developed a "feeling that this is not the time to indulge in any 'nationalistic' acts or expressions which might be unfavorably regarded in the United States." In February 1929 another "concrete result" came about when the minister informed Kellogg that the Colombian government had settled its differences with the Andian Oil Company.[83]

Grosvenor Jones of the BFDC aptly reflected the new American optimism over the turn in U.S.-Colombian relations. In April 1929 he wrote to Assistant Commercial Attaché Frederic Lee in London, reviewing recent oil land problems. He pointed out that "during the last five months" Colombia had "passed new legislation doing practically everything we suggested in the circular," which had been a "timely warning." Jones concluded:

> Confidentially, I may say that all reports both from our own office and from the legation at Bogotá believe the circular was one of the leading factors in the recent abatement of the anti-American feeling which had prevailed previous thereto, and are inclined to believe that it will prove to be of great value in effecting a change in the attitude of Colombia toward American business and American citizens in general.[84]

Later that month, Jones prepared a memorandum in which he stated that "we here in Washington are fully aware of the advantage we have gained in issuing the previous circular and shall take every care to see that it is not counteracted by any precipitate action." He did not see the need for another circular, since "things have moved along splendidly since our last circular and we are entirely satisfied with the results."[85]

Perhaps most satisfying was the Colombian announcement in early 1929 that it was seeking foreign help in writing some new oil legislation. Of the six specialists finally enlisted to revise the petroleum laws, three were Americans. By mid-May they had produced a new bill. Caffrey gave it high praise and added that the minister of industry had given up on his "nationalization schemes." The new bill was introduced into the Colombian congress where it faced stiff opposition, mostly for strictly political reasons. The bill never passed.[86] Nonetheless, Caffrey was well pleased. In November 1929 he wired Secretary of State Henry Stimson that, after talks with the Colombian president, he had found that the president "had initiated a change in Colombian oil policy and desired cooperation of American capital for the development of Colombian oil resources."[87] Certainly it must have come as a relief to U.S. oil interests, who by 1929 had $136 million invested in the Colombian oil fields.[88]

A month earlier Caffrey had summed up the prevailing American view of the situation in Colombia. Writing to Francis White, he commented on the "better atmosphere" in Colombia. Prior to the circular's release Minister Montalvo had "adopted the former Mexican oil policy," but that had all changed now. In the last few days Montalvo had "reproached Mexico . . . , spoken bitterly of bolshevism, etc., etc." That last point had become important to Caffrey, since just recently Colombian workers of the United Fruit Company had gone on a strike which he characterized as "the recent communistic uprisings." He was happy to note that the Colombian government "took most prompt and energetic action, for which the[y] have been bitterly attacked, for the protection of the United Fruit Company during the recent strike." Caffrey concluded on a cautious but upbeat note: "However, I'll repeat again that 'all is not for the best' as yet: not by a long shot, in fact: all I can report is: progress."[89]

Conflict between the United States and Colombia over oil policies did not end in 1929. Colombia did not totally abandon its "schemes," nor did the United States give up its opposition to those plans.[90] The two major conflicts, over the 1919 decree and over the crises of 1926–1929, did not end with either side "winning." In the fight over the 1919 decree Colombia revoked the decree, but it steadfastly refused to amend the 1914 treaty or to sign a separate protocol guaranteeing American rights. During the late 1920s the Colombians seemed to back down on the petroleum issue and to give in on the Barco, Andian Oil, and Tropical Oil questions. Yet, when all had been said and done, and when the oil bill prepared by the foreign specialists had failed to pass, the oil companies were still operating under Law 84.

To a great extent the United States had itself created the "crises" it faced in Colombia. Its policymakers had failed to perceive that Colombia's oil legislation during the postwar years was not an anti-American plot for expropriation but simply the result of new demands generated by the new social, political, and economic situations created in Colombia during the preceding years. America's unbending resistance to the legislation had only succeeded in forcing Conservatives such as Suárez, who strongly favored U.S. participation in the Colombian economy, into taking a steadily more nationalist stance to maintain their power and position.

In Colombia's attempts to secure greater state control over its subsoil minerals, American officials had seen danger. These attempts were "madness"; they were "absurd." The Colombians, viewed as "woefully ignorant," were perceived as incapable of playing a fuller role in the exploitation and use of their own resources. Under Colombian control the oil industry would collapse and, with it, so would the Colombian economy. American capital, fearful of more nationalizations and expropriations, would find "other channels," and Colombia, desperately in need of capital, would founder in underdevelopment and stagnation. America would lose a valuable market and a supplier of a necessary resource.

America used its tremendous postwar financial power to make sure that Colombia veered away from such a course and remained "receptive" to U.S. economic leadership. That power, as can be seen in both the 1919–1921 and 1926–1929 episodes, could be used as both a carrot and a stick.

Minister Piles went to the crux of the question facing the United States in his 1927 statement that Colombia had "tendencies to look to Mexico rather than Venezuela."[91] Mexico represented nationalization, expropriation, and a breakdown of the entire capitalist order. Venezuela, as we shall see in the next chapter, represented a viable alternative that was very much in line with the American perception of what the U.S.-Latin American political and economic relationship should be.

Notes

1. Only a handful of works deal with the political and economic development of Colombia, although some superior work has appeared in the last few years. Frank Safford, *The Ideal of the Practical: Colombia's Struggle to Form a Technical Elite* (Austin, 1976), discusses Colombian efforts during the nineteenth century to develop a strong "technical elite" (engineers, scientists, and so forth) to meet the growing needs of the Colombian economy. Bergquist, *Coffee and Conflict*, emphasizes the strong ties between Colombia's coffee economy and its political

developments. A brief survey of Colombian history is provided in Harvey F. Kline, *Colombia: Portrait of Unity and Diversity* (Boulder, 1983). A good synthesis of the nation's history can be found in Bernstein, *Contemporary Latin America* and *Venezuela and Colombia* (Englewood Cliffs, NJ, 1964).

2. Bergquist, *Coffee and Conflict*, 8.

3. J. León Helguera, "The Problem of Liberalism versus Conservatism in Colombia: 1849–85," in *Latin American History: Select Problems: Identity, Integration, and Nationhood*, ed. Frederick Pike (New York, 1969), 227.

4. Cardoso and Faletto, *Dependency and Development,* 96.

5. Furtado, *Economic Development*, 47–48.

6. A good discussion of the U.S. involvement in the Panamanian revolution is found in Walter LaFeber, *The Panama Canal: The Crisis in Historical Perspective* (New York, 1978). A more recent analysis, Lael, *Arrogant Diplomacy*, 1–24, paints a somewhat more sympathetic picture of U.S. actions, although it chides policymakers for being insensitive to Colombia's position.

7. Keen and Wasserman, *Short History of Latin America*, 203–4.

8. Little work has been done on pre-World War I contacts between Colombia and the United States. The two best works, Parks, *Colombia and the United States*, and Rippy, *Capitalists*, are now considerably out of date, yet they still contain plenty of good information.

9. John Barrett to Elihu Root, 14 April 1906, *FRUS, 1906–1907* (Washington, 1934), 443–50; Winkler, *Investments in Latin America*, 274–75.

10. Isaac Manning to William J. Bryan, 8 August 1914, 821.00/386, RG 59.

11. U.S. Department of the Treasury, *Proceedings of the First Pan American Financial Conference* (Washington, 1915), 359; Rippy, *Capitalists*, 113–15.

12. U.S. Department of Commerce, Bureau of Foreign and Domestic Commerce, *Colombia: A Commercial and Industrial Handbook*, by P. L. Bell, Special Agents Series, no. 206 (Washington, 1921), 126–31.

13. Earl Harding document is found in Box 24, Folder 205, Polk Papers. While there is no date or identifying name on the document, it seems reasonable to assume that the paper was produced by Harding or an associate. On 7 June 1918, Harding had conferred with Chandler Anderson about setting up an Anglo-American platinum company. In his description of the meeting, Anderson noted that Harding had already notified the State Department, which had referred him to Anderson. Polk and Anderson were close acquaintances, and the fact that the document is found in Polk's papers gives added credence to the conclusion that Harding was the prime author (Anderson diary, 7 June 1918, Anderson Papers). Lael, *Arrogant Diplomacy*, 131–44, has an excellent discussion of U.S. efforts to obtain platinum concessions in Colombia.

14. *New York Times*, 25 March 1911. See Lael, *Arrogant Diplomacy*, Chapters 2 and 3, for an examination of the attempts to settle the issue during the Roosevelt and Taft administrations.

15. For a copy of the treaty see *FRUS, 1914* (Washington, 1922), 163.

16. Lael, *Arrogant Diplomacy*, 85–87, has a good discussion of Wilson's reasons for an amicable settlement.

17. Cited in William Harbaugh, *The Life and Times of Theodore Roosevelt* (New York, 1975), 437.

18. Robert Lansing to Woodrow Wilson, 23 March 1917, 711.21/640a, RG 59. Lael, *Arrogant Diplomacy*, Chapter 5 covers the problems faced by the Wilson administration in securing ratification for the treaty. Lael puts as much blame on Wilson, citing his lack of savvy in maneuvering the treaty through the Senate, as he does on Henry Cabot Lodge for his obstinance.

19. Hoffman Philip to Lansing, 24 May 1919, 821.00/446, RG 59.

20. *New York Times*, 26 July 1919.

21. Philip to Lansing, 28 June 1919, 821.6363/51, RG 59; "Extracts from the Message of President Suárez to the National Congress, July 20, 1919," *FRUS, 1919* (Washington, 1934), 724–25.

22. Philip to Lansing, 28 June 1919; Claude Guyant to Lansing, 7 July 1919; Philip to Lansing, 26, 29 July 1919, 821.6363/50, /51, /54, /55, RG 59.

23. *Congressional Record*, 65th Cong., 3d sess., 1919, 57:4:3668–69.

24. Lansing to Philip, 9 August 1919, 711.21/478b, RG 59. Lael, *Arrogant Diplomacy*, 141–51, downplays the impact of Article 27 and related events in Mexico on the U.S. attitude toward the Colombian legislation and does not address opposition to economic nationalism as a component of U.S. policy. Instead, he focuses on the strategic concerns of U.S. policymakers (especially the concern about securing oil for the U.S. Navy) as the basis for their antipathy to the oil decree.

25. Philip to Lansing, 12, 13 August 1919, 711.21/479, /481, RG 59.

26. Lansing to Philip, 13, 21 August 1919, 821.6363/58, 711.21/481, RG 59.

27. Philip to Lansing, 15, 18, 21, 22 August 1919, 711.21/480, /482, /484, /485, /497, RG 59.

28. Boaz Long to Joseph Richardson, 21, 27 August 1919, 711.21/482, /485, RG 59.

29. Lansing to Philip, 28 August 1919, 711.21/482, RG 59.

30. Bergquist, *Coffee and Conflict*, 257; Kline, *Colombia*, 124.

31. Lewis, *America's Stake*, 583, 588, 590.

32. "Extracts from the Message of President Suárez to the National Congress, July 20, 1919," *FRUS, 1919*, 724–25.

33. For more detailed discussions of Suárez's programs see the previously cited works by Bernstein, Kline, and McGreevey.

34. Philip to Lansing, 16 September 1919; William Phillips to Philip, 19, 25 September 1919, 711.21/494, /491, RG 59.

35. Philip to Lansing, 26 September, 3 October 1919, 711.21/509, /507, RG 59.

36. Albert Fall to Long, 8 October 1919, 821.6363/74, /75, RG 59.

37. Lansing to Philip, 13 October 1919, 711.21/507, RG 59.

38. Philip to Lansing, 29 October, 5 November 1919, 711.21/512, /515, RG 59.

39. Lansing to Philip, 8 November 1919; Philip to Lansing, 8, 22, 24 November 1919, 711.21/514, 821.6363/86, /85, 711.21/519, RG 59.

40. Philip to Lansing, 24 November 1919, 711.21/519, RG 59; Philip to Frank Polk, 19 December 1919, Box 11, Folder 393, Polk Papers; Lansing to Philip, 25 November 1919, 821.6363/82, RG 59.

41. Cartoon is found in Isaac Cox, " 'Yankee Imperialism' and Spanish American Solidarity: A Colombian Interpretation," *Hispanic American Historical Review* 4 (May 1921): 263.

42. Philip to Lansing, 3, 7 January 1920, 821.6363/100, /104, RG 59; Polk to Philip, 27 January 1920, Box 11, Folder 393, Polk Papers. Philip's optimistic view of the legislation was only partly correct. Law 120 simply limited the scope of the state's subsoil mineral rights: Landowners who had secured title to their property prior to 1873 retained subsoil rights; subsoil rights of property

purchased after that date would revert to the state. See Randall, *Diplomacy of Modernization*, 94–95, for more on the law.

43. Hallett Johnson to Bainbridge Colby, 12 April 1920; Colby to Wilson, 13 April 1920, Box 2, Colby Papers.

44. Philip to Colby, 26 April 1920; Colby to Philip, 4 June 1920, 711.21/533, /537b, RG 59.

45. F. G. Cottrell, director of the Bureau of Mines, to Wesley Frost, acting foreign trade adviser, 27 July 1920; Philip to Colby, 28 October 1920, 821.6363/116, /128, RG 59.

46. *Congressional Record*, 63rd Cong., 3d sess., 60:887.

47. Philip to Colby, 10 January 1921, 711.21/582, RG 59; "Extract from the Speech of Secretary of State Bainbridge Colby at the Dinner of the Pan-American Advertising Association, Hotel Astor, 28 February 1921," Box 8, Colby Papers.

48. Philip to Robert Bliss, 23 March 1921; Edwin Denby to Charles Evans Hughes, 26 March 1921; Hughes to Denby, 26 March 1921, 821.6363/137, RG 59.

49. For the reports on British activity in Colombia see E. C. Soule, American consul in Cartagena, to Hughes, 7, 16 April 1921, 821.6363/140, /144, RG 59. Good coverage of the final debates in Congress over the treaty can be found in Rippy, *Capitalists*, 115–17, and Parks, *Colombia and the United States*, 451–57.

50. *Congressional Record*, 67th Cong., 1st sess., 61:1:158–59, 161–66, 487.

51. Hughes to Warren Harding, 22 June 1921, Papers of Warren G. Harding (microfilm edition), Ohio State Historical Society, Cincinnati (hereafter cited as Harding Papers).

52. Samuel Piles to Harding, 18 September 1922, Harding Papers.

53. Harding to Piles, 12 October 1922, Harding Papers.

54. Parks, *Colombia and the United States*, 461–73; Rippy, *Capitalists*, 123–76.

55. Randall, *Diplomacy of Modernization*, 95.

56. Piles to Hughes, 8 January 1923, 821.00/514, RG 59.

57. Piles to Hughes, 15 October 1923, 821.00/525, RG 59.

58. For some of the Colombian attempts to impose stricter oil laws see Piles to Hughes, 20 February 1924; Piles to Kellogg, 1 December 1925, 821.6363/273, /284, RG 59. *El Tiempo* article contained in Piles to Kellogg, 11 December 1925; *El Espectador* item contained in Piles to Kellogg, 9 January 1926, 821.00/590, /591, RG 59.

59. Piles to Hughes, 6 February 1926, 821.00/593, RG 59.

60. *Diario Nacional* article contained in Piles to Kellogg, 26 February 1926; *Mundo Al Dia* article is found in Piles to Kellogg, 30 September 1926; Piles to Kellogg, 19 February 1927, 821.00/595, /614, /619, RG 59.

61. Piles to Kellogg, 25 August 1927; Jordan Stabler to Kellogg, 22 September 1927, 821.00/625, 831.00/1337 1/2, RG 59.

62. Piles to Kellogg, 17 October 1927; Francis Loomis to Kellogg, 22 October 1927; Robert Olds to Piles, 29 October 1927; Piles to Kellogg, 3 November 1927, 821.6363/339, /334, /337, RG 59.

63. Piles to Kellogg, 9, 28 November 1927, 821.6363/345, /348, RG 59.

64. Randall, *Diplomacy of Modernization*, 95; Kellogg to Piles, 13 February 1928; Piles to Kellogg, 14 February 1928, 821.6363/359a, /360, RG 59.

65. Kellogg to Piles, 18 February 1928; Piles to Kellogg, 20, 23 February 1928, 821.6363/360, /362, /363, /365, RG 59.
66. Memorandum of conversation, 6 March 1928; Piles to Kellogg, 10 March 1928, 821.6363/371, /376, RG 59.
67. Piles to Kellogg, 14 May 1928, 821.6363/399, RG 59.
68. Piles to Kellogg, 17 May 1928; Kellogg to Piles, 17 May 1928, 821.6363/392, RG 59.
69. Piles to Kellogg, 19 May 1928; Kellogg to Piles, 25 May 1928, 821.6363/393, RG 59.
70. Piles to Kellogg, 2, 11 June 1928, 821.6363/401, /410, RG 59.
71. Piles to Kellogg, 2 July, 6 August 1928, 821.6363/411, /436, RG 59.
72. Piles to Kellogg, 24 August 1928, 821.6363/443, /460, RG 59.
73. Piles to Kellogg, 10 September 1928; H. Freeman Matthews to Kellogg, 28 September, 5 October 1928, 821.6363/464, /478, /517, RG 59.
74. Matthews to Kellogg, 26, 29 September, 1, 2 October 1928, 821.6363/477, /482, /486, /488, RG 59.
75. Piles to Kellogg, 20 July 1928; Stokeley Morgan to Arthur Young, 29 August 1928; Young to Morgan, 12 September 1928; Morgan to Young and Francis White, 15 September 1928, 821.51/415, /419, RG 59.
76. Matthews to Kellogg, 11, 18 October 1928, 821.6363/498, /507, RG 59.
77. Matthews to Kellogg, 26, 27, 30, 31 October 1928, 821.51/422, /423, /425, /441, /429, RG 59.
78. Kellogg to Matthews, 31 October 1928, 821.51/428, RG 59.
79. Matthews to Kellogg, 1 November 1928, 821.51/430, RG 59.
80. Matthews to Kellogg, 6 November 1928, 821.51/433, /434, RG 59.
81. Matthews to Kellogg, 8 November 1928, 821.51/453, RG 59; Matthews to Kellogg, 15 November 1928, 821.00 General Conditions/8, RG 59.
82. Allen Dulles to Morgan, 14 November 1928, 821.51/444, RG 59.
83. Jefferson Caffrey to Kellogg, 7 December 1928, 4 February 1929, 821.6363/556, /572, RG 59; Caffrey to Kellogg, 27 December 1928, 821.00 General Conditions/9, RG 59.
84. Grosvenor Jones to Frederic Lee, 6 April 1929, 600-Colombia, RG 151.
85. Jones to O. P. Hopkins, asst. director of the BFDC, 12 April 1929, 600-Colombia, RG 151.
86. Charles Wilson to Kellogg, 28 February 1929; Caffrey to Henry Stimson, 17 April, 18 May, 15, 16 November 1929, 821.6363/587, /610, /615, /742, RG 59; Randall, *Diplomacy of Modernization*, 106–8.
87. Caffrey to Stimson, 28 November 1929, 821.6363/751, RG 59.
88. Lewis, *America's Stake*, 588.
89. Caffrey to White, 10 October 1929, Box 9, White Papers.
90. See Randall, *Diplomacy of Modernization*, 106–27, for more on the post-1929 period.
91. Piles to Kellogg, 9 November 1927, 821.6363/345, RG 59.

Chapter Six

"Everything but Democracy": Venezuela, 1917–1929

In 1917 relations between the United States and the despotic ruler of Venezuela, General Juan Vicente Gómez, bordered on outright hostility. However, faced with the growing threat of economic nationalism, first in Mexico and then elsewhere in South America, and the specter of Communist involvement in the hemisphere, the United States completely reversed its attitude toward Gómez during the postwar years.

In 1908 the ultimate personification of caudillismo took power in Venezuela when the nation's ruler, Cipriano Castro, left for Europe to recover from a lingering illness. Seizing the opportunity, Castro's right-hand man, Juan Vicente Gómez, took control. Thus began what historian Guillermo Morón has called "the most absolute despotism" in Venezuelan history. Gómez ruled in name during the years 1908–1914, 1915–1921, 1922–1929, and 1931–1935. In the interims he governed through puppets while maintaining control of the armed forces.[1] Whereas previous strong-arm rulers of Venezuela had come into office with at least the semblance of some political philosophy, Gómez seemed to understand only personal power. Harry Bernstein has written that "Gómez brought in an era of fascism, but he had no program or blueprint for fascism, no theory of society or class. . . . Money, rather than any philosophy about mass movements, modern nationalism or the nation-State, talked for Gómez."[2]

Writing on the political effects of Gómez's long and brutal rule, Daniel Levine has concluded that the dictator managed to crush the "regional military power" of the provincial caudillos, and at the same time eliminated the "traditional political parties—Liberals and Conservatives. . . . Indeed, a famous motto of the Gómez regime was *Gómez único* (Gómez alone, nothing but Gómez). *Gómez único* was more than a slogan; it was a social reality as well."[3]

As Morón explains, however, Gómez's rule exacted a terrible price from the nation of Venezuela:

> His period produced social loosening and moral deformation in the generations who had to live it through. The ideas of political liberty and civic integrity lacked all meaning since public feeling was blunted. Any voice which made a criticism was silenced; the gaol or exile were Gómez's "peace." In the Libertador castle of Puerto Cabello, the castle of San Carlos in Maracaibo and La Rotunda in Caracas about 38,000 political prisoners were kept—men who had committed no crime, but were opposed to the iron regime which lasted so long.[4]

Despite his unsavory approach to governing, relations with the United States prior to the U.S. entry into World War I were cordial. Gómez, in fact, went out of his way to resolve Venezuela's problems with foreign powers, problems that had been very much in evidence during the reign of Castro. He openly invited foreign participation in the Venezuelan economy. Historian Sheldon Liss has noted that "Gómez saw the 'splendid' job of luring and holding foreign capital done by Porfirio Díaz in Mexico and tried to emulate it. Above all, he strove to assure foreigners a fair deal in Venezuela."[5]

During the years before the election of Woodrow Wilson in 1912, Gómez worked to clear up Venezuela's international disputes and obligations and to make his nation a haven for foreign investors. He was remarkably successful, especially in the latter goal. For example, the exploitation of Venezuela's oil reserves had just begun in 1910. By 1912, as Luis Vallenilla explains, "A large area of Venezuela's territory already belonged to foreign companies through the transfer of long-term contracts, subject to low taxation and with hardly any participation by Venezuela in profits derived from exploitation." U.S. oil interests were actively involved in the Venezuelan oil industry, investing $5 million by 1914.[6]

With Wilson's coming to power in 1913, however, relations between the United States and Venezuela noticeably cooled. Wilson's professed disgust toward governments in Latin America that had not been legally elected was the initial stumbling block, but it was not the only one. Reports such as the State Department memorandum in November 1913 that stated that "it is apparent that Gómez is trying to terrorize Venezuela into continuing him in his dictatorship" probably did little to endear him to the Democratic president.[7]

The State Department was undecided about what to do about the Venezuelan dictator during the Wilson years. One member of the department summed up the matter in a colorful fashion: "It is an open question to my mind as to whether Gómez with all his faults may not be better than some weak creature without any stamina . . . or with a Bunny-Rabbit mind as old Guzman Blanco [General Antonio Guzman Blanco, who had ruled Venezuela from 1870 to 1888] had in his last days. The only thing that can do any good in Venezuela is a moderate soft-shell despotism."[8] Rutherford Bingham of the department's Latin American Division agreed, albeit in a much more staid manner. Gómez, he wrote in July 1914, was the "strongest man in Venezuelan politics." He had fostered "peace" and commercial activity, and he "also regards it to his advantage to be particularly friendly to the United States."[9] The slogan *Gómez único* obviously had meaning for American diplomats as well; although they viewed Gómez as personally distasteful, there seemed to be no viable alternative. Too rigid a stance with the dictator might bring on troubles like those in Mexico that were still plaguing American policymakers. Since U.S.-Venezuelan trade and commerce were increasing, it seemed the better part of valor to wait for a more suitable moment to consider the problem.

World War I seemed to offer such a moment. In September 1914 the American minister to Venezuela, Preston McGoodwin, wrote that the war had caused massive economic difficulties for that nation, especially for its dominant coffee industry. Early in 1916, McGoodwin noted that Gómez had "just received first-hand information regarding American business methods, which impressed him most favorably." Although others in the Venezuelan government had shown "favoritism" toward European nations, McGoodwin was sure that the situation would change with the "forthcoming return of General Gómez to the Constitutional Presidency," concerning which there could "be no doubt of the vast advantage which will accrue to American commerce and American interests in general."[10] The minister seemed to be implying that Gómez, under the spell of America's economic power, might be willing to loosen his dictatorial hold on the nation. After all, McGoodwin emphasized, Gómez was to become the "Constitutional President" of Venezuela. "American interests in general" would be well served.

As the war progressed, however, it became evident that Gómez was not changing his style of rule, nor did he seem to be an extraordinary friend of the United States. Throughout 1917, McGoodwin disgustedly reported on Gómez's tyrannical, pro-German rule. In May 1917, for example, he wrote a long report on the personal life of Gómez and his associates, including tales of "disgraceful orgies," "lewd women . . . who pranced about the premises in various stages of undress," and Gómez's "concubines" and "illegitimate children." All of that was a bit much for the old State Department veteran Alvey Adee, who warned McGoodwin that "gossip of such nature" should not be included in diplomatic reports.[11]

Other dispatches from McGoodwin were less titillating, but they were just as harsh on Gómez. In June 1917 he reported that the "government of Venezuela is deteriorating and growing constantly less amenable to the ordinary dictates of human conscience." The dictator himself had "made no noticeable effort to conceal his preference for Germany in the present War for the Rights of Humanity." In July the minister noted that "dissension is spreading in every section and Gómez is a pliant, pitiful tool of German interests." McGoodwin reported in August that Gómez had jailed a number of priests, and in September he complained about government control of the nation's press.[12]

The Wilson administration now began to take a keener interest in Gómez. In August 1917, Secretary of State Robert Lansing asked Jordan Stabler, chief of the Latin American Division, to prepare a memorandum on Gómez and the situation in Venezuela. A damning account of the Gómez regime was sent to Lansing two months later. Characterizing his rule as "extra-constitutional," the memo also argued that Gómez "shows little sympathy for the U.S." The dictator's rule was "severe and purely selfish," a government by "terrorism."[13] The memo was essentially correct: Gómez's rule was harsh and repressive, and, while the general maintained Venezuelan neutrality, he personally favored Germany in the war.

For Secretary Lansing that latter point seemed especially ominous. His fears were not assuaged by two other memos on the Venezuelan situation which crossed his desk in early 1918. The first, prepared by Glenn Stewart of the Latin American Division, was a strongly moralistic attack on Gómez, whose rule was "founded on corruption, fear and force. . . . Personal liberty and security do not exist, present conditions are only comparable to the worst days of the Inquisition." Furthermore, Venezuela under Gómez had "become steadily more and more pro-German." Stewart concluded that "there is only one way to guarantee good Government and Christian civilized conditions. Eliminate Gómez root and branch!" The second memo, written in February by another member of the Latin American Division, Ferdinand Lathrop Mayer, made the same points: "Actual living conditions in Venezuela are disgraceful beyond expression," he reported, "and the insecurity of civil liberty is analogous to that of times of medieval despotism." The pro-German stance of Gómez had become so bad that the War Trade Board had embargoed the shipment of paper to Venezuela because its newspapers were so blatantly in favor of Germany. Mayer concluded that "if this condition is permitted to persist until after the war it is considered that Venezuela will be a probable arena of friction between the United States and Germany in connection with the Monroe Doctrine and the hegemony of the United States in this hemisphere."[14]

Lansing's anxiety prompted him to forward Stewart's memo to Wilson. The president replied that he had read the document with the "greatest concern." He then exploded: "This scoundrel ought to be put out. Can you think of any way in which we can do it that would not upset the peace of Latin America more than letting him alone will?"[15]

Aside from the embargo on paper, however, nothing was done to put the "scoundrel" Gómez out of office. America's inaction was explained in an April 1918 letter from Mayer to department counselor Frank Polk. Mayer stated that, unless the United States was willing to give "real assistance" to a revolution against Gómez and to support his successors, it would be best to adopt a "conciliatory, friendly attitude" which would be more "profitable."[16] Of course, in early 1918 the United States had more pressing problems to cope with in Europe.

In the postwar decade the United States would go far beyond a "conciliatory, friendly attitude" toward Gómez. By 1929 the American perception of the dictator had changed from reluctantly accepting an unsavory situation to viewing the despot as a positive and necessary fixture in Venezuela.

The decision to work with Gómez, instead of against him, became official government policy in early 1921. From January to March this policy was debated in both the BFDC and the State Department. This debate had been sparked by a report from Trade Commissioner P. L. Bell describing the investment and trade opportunities in Venezuela. Although he was aware of Gómez's reputation, Bell nonetheless concluded that U.S. businessmen should work with him: "Leaving all considerations of ethics aside, and viewing the proposition from a purely commercial point of view—I am more and more inclined to recommend such an association."[17]

A BFDC memorandum prepared on 22 January 1921 revealed the differences of opinion within the bureau concerning Bell's report. James A. Robertson, chief of the bureau's Near Eastern Division, stated that "this is one of the most interesting reports I have seen for a long time. It is basic." He asked Thomas Taylor, assistant director of the BFDC, what should be done with it. Taylor contacted John K. Towles of the Division of Finance and Investment. Towles's stance was unequivocal:

> I cannot see my way to advise that this Bureau actively support cooperation with the Gómez regime. The Gómez group is admittedly a band of selfish exploiters. . . . I am unalterably opposed to any such basis of action. Unless we are thorough-going charlatans and falsifiers, this Government has always taken the position that our capital in foreign fields should place emphasis upon real service to the peoples of the countries concerned. We cannot with decency as men and as United States representatives present a proposal to our financial houses which requires that consideration of international and personal ethics be put aside.
> . . . There is now great and urgent demand in many lands for our spare capital; let us place it in decent enterprises in association with decent men. This is the best policy in the long run.[18]

Towles was in the minority. In February C. H. Herring, assistant director of the BFDC, sent Bell's report to the State Department for its opinion. Wesley Frost, the department's acting foreign trade adviser, sent the report along to Sumner Welles in the Latin American Division on 11 March, commenting in a cover letter, "I am disposed to believe with Mr. Bell that we cannot reconstitute conditions in Latin America, and should take advantage of favorable opportunities there even when it involves cooperation with groups whose ascendancy is more or less autocratic in character." Besides, Frost concluded, the government could hardly "actively influence American investors for or against" working with Gómez. Welles succinctly ended the debate with a two-word response: "I concur." So did U.S. oil interests: By 1919 they had $18 million invested in the Venezuelan oil fields.[19] The issues had been clearly laid out and the choice plainly made. America would henceforth embark on a new and closer relationship with Gómez, despite his "more or less autocratic" nature.

The new attitude toward Gómez was fully in evidence by April 1921. A statue of the great South American liberator Simón Bolívar was to be unveiled in New York City. For the new secretary of state, Charles Evans Hughes, this event offered a good opportunity for a warmer relationship with Venezuela. He drafted a message for President Warren Harding to send to Gómez assuring him that "this Government will do all in its power in cementing the traditional friendship and good understanding existing between the two countries." Undersecretary of State Henry Fletcher, upon learning that the Venezuelan representatives attending the unveiling were going to place a wreath on George Washington's tomb, promptly asked the secretary of the navy to provide naval transport for the group.[20]

A friendly attitude toward Gómez and Venezuela was also evident in a memo sent to Sumner Welles by Leo S. Rowe of the Pan American Union in May 1921. While the memo suggested that the United States should encourage a more democratic government in Venezuela, it also warned that America should not push too hard. If a revolution were to occur, it would destroy "all the substantial good that has been done during the last twelve years," in other words, since Gómez took power. Welles obviously agreed. In August he had a meeting with Dr. Ortega Martínez, a representative of a group of Venezuelan revolutionaries intent on overthrowing Gómez. Martínez informed Welles that the Royal Dutch Shell Company had promised his group support in a revolution in return for a large oil concession. He hoped that the United States would also help, since it had protested so adamantly against the harsh rule of Manuel Estrada Cabrera in Guatemala. Welles commented that Venezuela was quite different, since the United States "was on friendly and official terms with [the] Venezuelan Government."[21]

At the end of 1921, Chargé John C. Martin summed up the situation from Venezuela. Admitting that Gómez's rule was repressive, Martin quickly added that this was "characteristic of military rule in

Latin American countries and unfortunately may be said to form part of the political tradition of Venezuela." Gómez had maintained order and stimulated material progress, and he had "shown himself favorable to foreigners and foreign capital—since the war to America in particular." The chargé was satisfied that "as a generalization it would not be too much to say that he [Gómez] has made Venezuela safe for everything but democracy."[22]

Willis Cook, who had replaced McGoodwin as minister to Venezuela, echoed those sentiments in early 1922. Enclosing a letter from Venezuelans protesting against Gómez's dictatorial regime, Cook acknowledged that this reflected a considerable portion of opinion in that nation. Yet, like Martin, Cook believed that the situation was relative: "General Gómez is in control, he is aggressive and experienced in the handling of those people." The dictator had provided a "strong and stable government, one which maintains order," and one with which American businessmen had "friendly relations." A State Department paper prepared in January 1923 sheepishly admitted that Venezuela had maintained a "somewhat pro-German neutrality" during World War I but reminded the reader that "relations with the United States are good at all times."[23]

Cook readily pointed out that other nations were equally impressed with Gómez's Venezuela. For example the Dutch minister, in June 1923, spoke enthusiastically about the future of Venezuela "under the progressive government of General Gómez," which offered many "possibilities for the investment of foreign capital."[24]

The praise of the "new" Gómez had several common themes. True, his rule was severe. Yet American observers had come to believe that this was "characteristic"; Gómez, after all, was more "experienced in the handling of those people." In addition, Gómez had brought benefits to Venezuela: stable government, order, and "progressive" notions of encouraging and aiding foreign businessmen. Indeed, by the late 1920s, Gómez was viewed as an almost invaluable asset for Venezuela.

In 1917 the American government had been looking for ways to put Gómez out of power, but by the late 1920s a major concern of the United States was how long Gómez could sustain his rule. As Cook put it in January 1926, Venezuela was prosperous and had no "serious internal disaffection." However, "everything at present depends upon the maintenance of his [Gómez's] health. If that should seriously fail, it is impossible to foretell what would happen." Former department official Jordan Stabler voiced similar concerns in February 1927, writing to Assistant Secretary of State Francis White. "None of us here are too happy over the situation," Stabler stated, referring to recent political unrest in Venezuela. If Gómez were overthrown, he concluded, "this may mean chaos for some time." Later that year, in a letter to Secretary Frank Kellogg, he reported that the general had "everything so well organized and the people generally have become accustomed to the regime," so that the only question was what would happen when he died. Claiming that age, perhaps, had "mellowed" Gómez and that his people generally liked him, Stabler concluded that the death of the old caudillo might lead to serious troubles.[25] White, responding to Stabler in early 1928, agreed with his assessment by stating that "this recent outbreak I am afraid is symptomatic of what we may expect when anything happens to Gómez."[26]

American praise for Gómez's style of rule continued into 1929. Halbert Watkins, American commercial attaché in Caracas, wrote in April 1929 that "there are conditions when a one man Government is a good thing for the development of a country. It looks now as though General Gómez will continue to be President for some time to come." Indeed, America's position toward Gómez took on a protective aspect. In July 1929, Julius Klein, chief of the BFDC, wrote to Henry Luce, the publisher of *Time*, concerning some unflattering stories about Gómez that had recently appeared in the magazine. Certain "business contacts" had complained to Klein. He suggested to Luce that "you might want to check up on your correspondent to be sure that hereafter the Venezuelan column in that Department of the Magazine is a bit less tainted with anti-Gómez vitriol."[27]

An excellent synopsis of the new American view of Gómez was produced in December 1929 by the American chargé in Venezuela, C. Van H. Engert. In a lengthy and detailed report Engert sketched out the problems in Venezuela, the country's history, Gómez's rule, and the benefits that his rule had brought to that nation.

Engert began his report with some observations on the political history of Venezuela. The nation, he claimed, was an heir to Spanish misrule, and the people were therefore "accustomed" to inefficient and corrupt government. The "government had always been synonimous [sic] with tyranny." Much of the blame for this rested with the Venezuelans themselves. The masses had been unprepared for independence, and "democracy existed on paper only." While the laws of the nation had been copied from those of the United States and Great Britain, they "were far too advanced for the primitive communities they were intended to serve. . . . It would have been much more sensible to give the Indian peon a simple and paternalistic form of government which he could have understood and appreciated." The Venezuelan people were not much concerned with the political process, and they were "too indolent to insist upon their rights." This backwardness was due to "political immaturity" and "racial inferiority."

Those conditions led to a system of caudillismo and, Engert claimed, "General Juan Vicente Gómez is the typical and inevitable product of the conditions just described, except that his personality and character put him far above the average dictator Venezuela, or any other Latin American country has produced." In fact, the chargé declared, "he compares very favorably . . . with Porfirio Díaz." Willpower and physical courage had allowed Gómez to exert a "bold and sagacious leadership." The general could hardly be blamed for the lack of democracy in Venezuela, because "democratic institutions cannot be tried in this country for many years to come. Gómez has too much common sense not to realize this." As Engert explained:

He wisely decided that a benevolent despotism was preferable to an anarchical democracy, and with the example of Mexico since 1911 before him he felt that any premature attempt to introduce too liberal doctrines among a people of whom 80% were illiterates would only end in disaster.

According to Engert, the dictator was aware that in a "relatively primitive country the form of government was really of secondary importance." All the Venezuelan people needed was security and "a little material prosperity," which Gómez had provided through a firm rule and through showing a real interest in the "economic life and industrial development" of the nation.

Unfortunately, the chargé concluded, "Gómez cannot live forever" (although to some observers it appeared that he might). None of his possible successors "inspire one with the confidence which an absolute ruler should command who can dispose almost at will of the destinies of the State." After Gómez, there was a fear "of turmoil, if not civil war, until a firm and masterful hand once more takes hold with a tight grip."[28] The reclamation was complete: The "scoundrel" had become a savior.

Why did the United States come to view Gómez as a good example of proper and responsible government in South America? One possible answer is that Venezuela's oil wealth was the determining factor in America's policy. Historian Stephen Rabe argues that the United States, faced with what it perceived as a national shortage of oil, came to accept and work with Gómez in return for American participation in the development of petroleum reserves in Venezuela. Rabe points out that the United States faced a strong competitor for Venezuela's oil— Great Britain—and needed the goodwill of the general to gain the upper hand.[29]

There is no denying either that American policymakers were concerned with postwar oil reserves or that Venezuela was looked upon as a promising field for American development. From $5 million in 1914, the U.S. investment in Venezuelan oil production had grown to $100 million by 1924.[30] And Great Britain was very much on the minds of American diplomats interested in the petroleum riches of Venezuela. Yet Rabe's analysis fails, for several reasons, to explain the sustained and growing American admiration for Gómez during the postwar years.

First, it is evident that Gómez needed little coaxing from American officials to encourage U.S. investment in his nation. Almost immediately after the end of the war, Gómez let it be known that he very much desired U.S. participation in the development of the Venezuelan economy. This was probably not based on his repentance of his pro-German ways; more likely, it represented his awareness that the United States was now the nation from which the money would come. Nevertheless, in May 1919, State Department official Stewart Johnson wrote to Lansing that Venezuela's Minister of Foreign Affairs Dr. Gil Borges had let it be known that "General Gómez is equally friendly and desirous of encouraging trade with the United States and the investment of United States capital in Venezuela." Johnson felt that the "very progressive" attitude of that nation toward foreign trade boded well for the future. From Caracas, Minister McGoodwin reported that "General Gómez told me that he would welcome American capital to Venezuela" and wanted to "frankly" advise the United States that "he would offer 'absolutely every assurance of protection to American lives and property.' "[31] It appears that the United States did not need to go to any great lengths to secure the support of Gómez for its economic activities in Venezuela.

Second, although it is clear that American interests did indeed compete for Venezuela's oil with Great Britain, it is apparent that Gómez preferred to work with American companies, that much of the British success in Venezuela during the postwar years was due to American bungling, and that regardless of that ineptitude U.S. oil interests were on their way to dominance by 1922. Gómez had by 1920 indicated that he was dissatisfied with the pace of British development of his nation's oil fields and that he was looking for new developers. The troubles for one of the largest British oil companies began, as McGoodwin reported in April 1920, when Gómez threatened to annul the Colon Development Company's concession for nearly two million hectares of land. This did not deeply disturb the minister, since he understood that American interests had offered $1 million for a year's exploration rights on the land to be taken from the British. Furthermore, he had also been informed that, due to its precarious position, the Colon company had sold one fourth of itself to an American firm.[32]

Things were definitely looking up for U.S. oil interests in Venezuela, but diplomatic missteps almost led to catastrophe. Carib Syndicate, Limited, the American company that had purchased the quarter interest in the Colon firm, asked the State Department for assistance in precluding Gómez's threatened annulment. The department concluded, however, that since the Colon company was not an American concern, and the Carib interest was only a minority holding, no action should be taken.[33] McGoodwin happily reported in June 1920 that the Colon contract had been annulled and that two other British companies faced "similar action." American oil companies were "confident" that they could secure those lands.[34]

At that point, however, State directed McGoodwin to see that the "equitable rights" of the Carib Syndicate were "recognized and protected." That decision likely was based on a desire to quiet the complaints of the Carib interest and to offer assistance to what was, after all, an American firm. But it was not evident how the minister was to protect the interests of the Carib Syndicate without simultaneously arguing for the protection of the Colon company, as the former was merely a minority holder in the latter. McGoodwin himself was apparently unable to make this distinction, and so in March 1921 he informed the department that Venezuela, "actuated by its desire to protect the one-fourth American interest" in the Colon company, had agreed to extend its contract. The State Department was flabbergasted. J. H. Murray, a special assistant in the department, writing to Sumner Welles, could hardly contain his disbelief and dismay: "It is a particularly unfortunate piece of business that this tremendous British concession should come to life again through the efforts of our own Minister," since the "particular aim" of the United States had been to see that it remained dead.[35]

Despite that incredible faux pas America's oil interests in Venezuela continued to gain power, while Great Britain, for a number of reasons, lost its initial advantage.[36] By May 1922 the American consul general in London reported that Standard Oil of New Jersey and British Controlled Oilfields, Limited, had reached an important agreement regarding the development of Venezuelan oil resources. The British interests had "invited Standard Oil to share in development." This marked the "abandonment of the 'All British' idea" and "the beginning of a decidedly new alignment of oil interests in Great Britain and the United States." The consul was essentially correct, and his assessment was reflected in department policy. In July 1923, Willis Cook advised the State Department that Standard, which had contracted for one third of British Controlled Oilfields' concession and desired another third, was facing some problems. Venezuela hinted that it was going to cancel the entire concession, and Standard Oil "desires assistance." Cook, undoubtedly hoping to avoid another Colon-Carib fiasco, made it clear that "this will be in the name of British Controlled Oilfields, and will affect the entire concession." In 1920, American officials had been aghast that one of their diplomats would aid a concession in which U.S. interests had but a minority concern. But times had changed, and so had the balance of power in Venezuela. Cook was directed to give assistance to Standard Oil *and* the British company. Obviously, Cook's message that Standard Oil was on the verge of taking majority control of the British interest had made the difference.[37]

The British took a realistic view of the situation in Latin America. A report issued by the Department of Overseas Trade in 1923 stated that it had been "inevitable" that Great Britain would fall behind the United States in its trade with Latin America. Furthermore, America would do all it could "to ensure its success" in that region. All the British could do was hope that they could "possibly regain ground and check further encroachment."[38]

A third reason why Venezuela's oil wealth could not have been the sole determinant of U.S. policy is that, if U.S. support for Gómez and his policies during the 1920s had been based on America's desperate need to obtain Venezuela's oil, then that desperate need ought to have continued unabated until the Great Depression; certainly the unabashed American admiration for the dictator continued up to that time. But the State Department's interest in foreign oil lagged considerably after 1923, especially after the development of gigantic oil fields in Oklahoma and Texas.[39] Although the oil issue did not simply fade away, the period of crucial importance had ended by 1924. Yet American diplomats continued to praise Gómez.

The question remains, then: Why did the United States find so many praiseworthy qualities in the Gómez regime? American policymakers did not view Gómez as a bitter pill that had to be swallowed in order to gain a greater hold on Venezuela's petroleum resources. On the contrary, the Gómez government came to be seen as a model system, and Gómez was viewed as an astute leader bringing his nation into the twentieth century. How, and why, had a government once likened to the Inquisition, and a man once characterized as a merciless despot, come to be seen this way?

America's new relationship with Gómez during the postwar years was not based simply on favoring the dictator in exchange for economic gain. The Gómez regime came to be seen in a much better light by American officials during the 1920s because of what it was as well as what it was not. Faced with a Latin America in which the forces of economic nationalism, radicalism, and even communism seemed to threaten vital American interests, policymakers in the United States came to view Gómez's type of rule as a bulwark against such forces and an example from which other Latin American nations could profitably learn.

Gómez's attitude toward economic nationalism could hardly have been more pleasing. In stark contrast to the troubling policies adopted by Mexico and Colombia during and after the war, Gómez seemed eager to please American policymakers and investors. In fact the Venezuelan government went so far as to join in the American criticism of Colombia's nationalist legislation in 1919. Dr. Gil Borges told McGoodwin that he had no confidence in Colombia's promises to suspend its threatening oil decrees. The two nations also agreed about the real villain of the whole problem, Mexico. As Willis Cook summed it up in 1923, as far as Venezuela and Gómez were concerned, "There is no sympathy wasted upon General [Alvaro] Obregón [Mexican president, 1920–1924] by this Government."[40] That had been made clear to Secretary of State Hughes in October 1923 by Dr. Don Pedro Manuel Areaya, the Venezuelan minister to the United States. During their talk the minister had expressed his distaste for Mexico, claiming that "Mexico was doing exactly what the United States refrained from doing, that she was interfering in the domestic concerns of Venezuela. She desired to dictate the domestic policy of Venezuela."[41]

Yet Gómez went far beyond merely agreeing with the United States that Mexico and Colombia were intrahemispheric troublemakers. Beginning in 1920, Gómez restructured Venezuela's oil legislation to fit the needs of foreign, and particularly American, oil interests. Guided along by willing assistance from American diplomats, Gómez demonstrated that his nation, at least, was ready to follow the American pathway for proper economic development.

In April 1920, Minister McGoodwin reported that some disturbing proposals for changing Venezuela's oil laws were circulating. One idea, to reduce the size limit of "development areas from 15,000 hectares to 400 hectares," he dismissed as "ridiculous." Another, to "prohibit foreign interests from participating actively in the exploitation of petroleum concessions," seemed more ominous. Fortunately, the minister explained, President Gómez had assured him that he "would not countenance any additional changes in the Petroleum law" and would work to encourage foreign investment. McGoodwin concluded that Gómez was "not only pursuing a necessary but an eminently wise policy not only in permitting but even in inviting the cooperation of foreign capital." Three weeks later, McGoodwin drove home these points in a message to the new secretary of state, Bainbridge Colby. Gómez had again assured him that foreign interests would be protected.[42]

When, on 26 June 1920, a new Venezuelan petroleum law was enacted, McGoodwin reported that it was very "encouraging" that due to American "representations . . . all of the more objectionable features were eliminated." Equally encouraging was the effect that the law was having: "Seven large petroleum development companies" from the United States were seeking concessions. By July the minister enthusiastically noted that over one hundred oil concessions had been "purchased by United States concerns."[43]

That was not the end of the matter, however. Within a year McGoodwin telegraphed the State Department that "officials and attorneys" for American oil companies were clamoring for the "necessity of securing changes" in the 1920 law. A month later, in May 1921, the minister once again reassured the department that Gómez would work with American interests to solve the problems and that the law "will be changed to suit the requirements of the petroleum development companies during the present session of Congress." He reiterated that point in a 31 May message. Gómez was "positive in his assurances" that the law would be changed. Furthermore, the general understood that Venezuela had, "inadvertently or otherwise, placed itself in a position of retarding seriously the development of the industry through laws that impose unnecessary hardships."[44]

Gómez once again saw to it that a new oil law was passed. According to McGoodwin, the 1920 law had "undoubtedly" been set up to discourage foreign investment (a far cry from his first reaction). The new law, passed in June 1921, included all of the changes "promised by General Gómez," and "several" U.S. oil companies were already surveying conditions in Venezuela. As McGoodwin explained, the American oil interests recognized "that all of the modifications and reforms suggested have been incorporated" into the new law.[45]

Still, the Americans were not entirely satisfied. McGoodwin informed the department that U.S. interests felt that parts of the 1921 law were "ambiguous." Two companies had left the country, and no new concessions had been opened. Gómez once again went to the drawing board. In June 1922 a new oil law was passed. Willis Cook announced that "the opinion is expressed among American oil men here that this is the best petroleum law in Latin America."[46] This was understandable, considering that they had been so instrumental in writing the law. In 1923 the Division of Latin American Affairs' response to Stanley Hornbeck's letter concerning the "lions" in Venezuela's "woods" was that it did not see a "tendency on the part of Venezuela to follow in the foot-steps of Mexico" concerning oil legislation.[47]

By the mid-1920s, Venezuela had come to be seen by American officials as offering a healthy alternative to the economic nationalism of nations such as Mexico or Colombia. When Samuel Piles, the American minister to Colombia, wrote in 1927 that the Colombians had "tendencies to look to Mexico rather than Venezuela," he implied that the nations of Latin America had two choices: the economic nationalism and financial chaos of Mexico, or the enlightened, "progressive," pro-foreign investment approach of Venezuela and General Gómez.[48]

American officials believed in the vital importance of keeping Gómez in office to save Venezuela from anti-American radicalism such as that emanating from Mexico. Surveying the political climate in Venezuela in 1923, Cook remarked that there were, unfortunately, a few anti-American advisers around Gómez. One, General Julio Hidalgo, was "rabidly anti-American and defiant of what he calls all foreign interference." Hidalgo, Cook concluded, was a likely successor to Gómez. When, in 1927, there were reports that Mexican propagandists were at work in Venezuela, Cook made it clear that only the Gómez government was keeping the situation in hand: "I believe that if the Venezuelan Government showed any laxness and permitted their activity that radical agitators would find the Venezuelan working class a fertile field." It was fortunate, he wrote later that year, that unlike many other South American nations Venezuela was not anti-American. In fact, he wrote in February 1927, relations were so cordial that the Venezuelan government newspaper, *El Nuevo Diario*, always printed the American Press articles that he forwarded.[49]

While the United States viewed Gómez as a powerful block against economic nationalism and anti-Americanism in Venezuela, it became convinced by the end of the 1920s that the aging dictator also protected his nation from the ravages of communism. Not surprisingly, this belief was most pronounced during the tenure of Frank Kellogg as secretary of state.

News about Venezuela reaching Kellogg during his term of office could not have comforted him concerning Communist infiltration of that nation. In late 1925 a prominent Venezuelan, Dr. Vicente Betancourt, wrote to the American ambassador to Mexico, James Sheffield. His reason for writing was clear: Venezuela would be threatened with "communistic ideas" and anarchy if Gómez should die or be overthrown. Cook wrote in 1928 that one of the important groups of exiled Venezuelan revolutionaries in Mexico had issued a proclamation exhibiting "semi-Bolshevist doctrines." The revolutionaries were "evidently more concerned with a complete change in the political and economic systems in Venezuela" than with simply overthrowing Gómez.[50]

Not surprisingly Gómez was happy to use the issue of communism to solidify his power. His New Year's message in 1929 pointed out the "futile . . . machinations" of those trying to unleash the "horrors of communism" upon Venezuela. He congratulated the people on their patriotism in opposing a system that would "lead to the discredit of the country and the misery of its people." While Chargé Engert cautioned the department that the speech was a bit of an "exaggeration," his lengthy report on Venezuela written in December left no doubt that the death of Gómez could indeed lead to such "horrors." Declaring that a period of chaos would follow Gómez's death, Engert warned that:

> If that period of unrest be unduly prolonged it may, however, degenerate into a conflict between the privileged classes and the common people, and the next dictator may be called upon to use his military power to check communism, or some other form of extreme radicalism, from which the country has so far been entirely free.[51]

American officials were heavily influenced in the adoption of their new and friendly attitude toward Gómez by the dictator's antithesis to Mexican-style economic nationalism, his attacks on communism, and his avowed desire to work along economic pathways defined by the United States. The continuance of Gómez in power seemed to be the only thing separating Venezuela from the ravages of radicalism, as well as the only thing keeping Venezuela within the U.S. economic and political orbit. To American eyes Venezuela had become, by the end of the postwar decade, a model of development and progress, and Gómez had become a standard for other Latin American leaders to follow. Given their dim view of the ability of the average Venezuelan to determine his or her own future, it was only natural that U.S. officials would prefer to see the destiny of that nation rest with a man who understood what the people really needed: order, stability, and "a little material prosperity." Until the Venezuelan people could be trusted to make the right decisions concerning their political and economic direction—and that time was deemed to be in the very distant future—it was best for all concerned that they be kept safe from democracy.[52]

Notes

1. Guillermo Morón, *A History of Venezuela*, ed. and trans. John Street (New York, 1963), 189.
2. Bernstein, *Venezuela and Colombia*, 52.
3. Daniel Levine, *Conflict and Political Change in Venezuela* (Princeton, 1973), 19.
4. Morón, *History of Venezuela*, 192–93.
5. Liss, *Diplomacy and Dependency*, 56.
6. Luis Vallenilla, *Oil: The Making of a New Economic Order: Venezuelan Oil and OPEC* (New York, 1975), 19; Lewis, *America's Stake*, 588.
7. Division of Latin American Affairs memorandum, 19 November 1913, 831.00/698, RG 59.
8. The most likely writer of this letter was Charles Curtis, the recently retired consul general at Santo Domingo. See "ChC" to Rutherford Bingham, 26 November 1913, 831.00/698, RG 59.
9. Bingham, memorandum on "President Gómez and the Constitution of Venezuela," 15 July 1914, 831.00/699, RG 59.
10. Preston McGoodwin to William Jennings Bryan, 18 September 1914, 831.51/39; McGoodwin to Robert Lansing, 10 April 1916, 831.00/766, RG 59.
11. McGoodwin to Lansing, 26 May 1917; Alvey Adee to McGoodwin, 8 July 1917, 831.00/792, RG 59.
12. McGoodwin to Lansing, 7 June, 16 July, 28 August, 29 September 1917, 831.00/794, /795, /798, /805, RG 59.
13. Lansing to Jordan Stabler, 10 August 1917; Division of Latin American Affairs to Lansing, 6 October 1917, 831.00/803, RG 59.
14. "Copy of Memo Prepared for President Wilson on General Conditions in Venezuela by Glenn Stewart," 7 January 1918; Ferdinand Lathrop Mayer, memo, 1 February 1918, 831.00/813, /824, RG 59.
15. Lansing to Woodrow Wilson, 5 January 1918; Wilson to Lansing, 16 February 1918, 831.00/833a, /834 1/2, RG 59.
16. Mayer to Frank Polk, 27 April 1918, Box 36, Folder 844, Polk Papers.
17. A search of the BFDC files failed to turn up Bell's report. This description, and the quote, were gleaned from memoranda in 620-Venezuela, RG 151.
18. Memorandum, 22 January 1921, 620-Venezuela, RG 151.
19. Wesley Frost to C. E. Herring, 19 March 1921; Frost to Sumner Welles, 11 March 1921; Welles to Frost, 11 March 1921, 620-Venezuela, RG 151; Lewis, *America's Stake*, 588.
20. Charles Evans Hughes to Warren G. Harding, 18 April 1921; Henry Fletcher to the secretary of the Navy, 2 May 1921, Harding Papers.
21. Leo S. Rowe to Welles, 10 May 1921; Welles, memo, 20 August 1921, 831.00/991 1/2, /1145, RG 59.
22. John C. Martin to Hughes, 14 December 1921, 831.00/1125, RG 59.

23. Willis Cook to Hughes, 27 April 1922; "Venezuela," prepared January 1923, 831.00/1150, /1200, RG 59.

24. Cook to Hughes, 14 June 1923, 831.50/5, RG 59.

25. Cook to Frank Kellogg, 6 January 1926, 831.00/1282, RG 59; Stabler to Francis White, 27 February 1927, Box 15, White Papers; Stabler to Kellogg, 22 September 1927, 832.00/1282, /1337 1/2, RG 59.

26. White to Stabler, 13 March 1928, Box 6, White Papers.

27. Halbert Watkins to O. P. Hopkins, 23 April 1929; Julius Klein to Henry Luce, 22 July 1929, 439, RG 151.

28. C. Van H. Engert to Henry Stimson, 23 December 1929, 831.00/1449, RG 59.

29. Rabe, *Road to OPEC*, 22–42.

30. See for example Van H. Manning, "Memo on Meeting of Council of National Defense, March 8, 1920," Box 32, Folder 615, Polk Papers; Newton Baker to Wilson, 9 March 1920, Baker Papers; Lewis, *America's Stake*, 588.

31. Stewart Johnson to Lansing, 3 May 1919; McGoodwin to Lansing, 25 November 1919, 831.00/907, /919, RG 59.

32. Rabe, *Road to OPEC*, 24–25; McGoodwin to Bainbridge Colby, 7 April 1920, 831.6363/22, RG 59.

33. C. K. MacFadden, chairman of the Carib Syndicate, Limited, to Colby, 3 May 1920; Adee to MacFadden, 2 May 1920, 831.6363/27, RG 59.

34. McGoodwin to Colby, 11 June 1920, 831.6363/33, RG 59.

35. Acting secretary to McGoodwin, 24 June 1920; McGoodwin to Hughes, 25 March 1921; J. H. Murray to Welles, 27 April 1921, 831.6363/33, /53, /93, RG 59.

36. Rabe, *Road to OPEC*, 27–28.

37. Robert P. Skinner to Hughes, 2 May 1922; Cook to Hughes, 23 July 1923; acting secretary to Cook, 19 September 1923, 831.6363/98, /139, /142, RG 59. In discussing this episode Hogan, *Informal Entente*, 170, concludes that "the State Department acceded to the cooperative thrust of private policy, reversing its original decision to endorse only wholly American concerns and agreeing to support cooperation and combination among British and American capital." Given the decidedly anti-British statements of U.S. policymakers prior to this event, a more likely conclusion is that, aware of the decline in British fortunes in Venezuela, they saw nothing wrong in helping a company that had only a minority American interest, especially since it appeared that it might soon become a majority interest.

38. "Report on the Economic and Financial Conditions in Venezuela," September 1923, p. 6, enclosed in Skinner to Hughes, 9 January 1924, 831.50/7, RG 59.

39. Rabe, *Road to OPEC*, 29.

40. McGoodwin to Lansing, 9 September 1919; Cook to Hughes, 26 January 1923, 711.21/499, 831.00/1177, RG 59.

41. "Memorandum of Interview with the Minister of Venezuela (Senor Dr. Don Pedro Manuel Areaya), Thursday, October 18, 1923," Box 159, Papers of Charles Evans Hughes, Manuscripts Division, Library of Congress, Washington (hereafter cited as Hughes Papers).

42. McGoodwin to Lansing, 5 April 1920; McGoodwin to Colby, 26 April 1920, 831.6363/25, 831.00/935, RG 59.

43. McGoodwin to Colby, 26 June, 24 July 1920, 831.00/942, /943, RG 59.

44. McGoodwin to Hughes, 12 April, 27, 31 May 1921, 831.00/990, /997, 831.6363/61, RG 59.

45. McGoodwin to Hughes, 30 July, 8 September 1921, 831.00/1005, 831.6363/70, RG 59.

46. McGoodwin to Hughes, 17 October 1921; Cook to Hughes, 22 June 1922, 831.6363/79, /106, RG 59.

47. H. P. Starrett to Stanley Hornbeck, 6 March 1923, 831.6363/233, RG 59.

48. Samuel Piles to Kellogg, 9 November 1927, 821.6363/345, RG 59.

49. Cook to Hughes, 11 October 1923; Cook to Kellogg, 24 January, 5 February, 7 April 1927, 831.00/1204, /1321, /1322, /1326, RG 59.

50. Dr. Vicente Betancourt to James Sheffield, 25 December 1925; Cook to Kellogg, 20 October 1928, 831.00/1287, /1393, RG 59.

51. Engert to Kellogg, 2, 3 January 1929; Engert to Stimson, 23 December 1929, 831.00B/2, /3, 831.00/1449, RG 59.

52. An interesting parallel to America's relations with the Gómez dictatorship during the postwar years can be found in David F. Schmitz, " 'A Fine Young Revolution': The United States and the Fascist Revolution in Italy, 1919–1925," *Radical History Review* 33 (September 1985): 117–38.

Chapter Seven

"Friendly Suggestion and Example": Brazil, 1914–1929

The U.S. economic and diplomatic attitude toward Brazil during and after World War I was unlike that exhibited toward many of the other nations of Latin America. There were no harsh diplomatic exchanges over property rights, oil fields, or economic nationalism, as there were with Mexico and Colombia. Nor did America reduce itself to fawning over the advantages of dictatorship, as it did in its relations with Juan Vicente Gómez's Venezuela. In Brazil the United States found everything it seemed to desire in a Latin American neighbor: a lack of economic nationalism and a real desire to work with America and its business interests to develop the Brazilian economy.

The period from 1850 to 1890 brought massive economic transformations to Brazil.[1] The seventy-five years prior to 1850 had been, as Celso Furtado points out, years of "stagnation or decay." Many traditional Brazilian exports, including sugar, cotton, tobacco, rice, cocoa, and leather, had all fallen prey to falling prices and foreign competition. During the mid-1800s, however, another product that had been grown in Brazil for a number of years and was, in fact, the nation's largest export, enjoyed a rise in its world price. Coffee became the mainstay of Brazilian exports and the vehicle for economic growth.[2]

The ascendancy of coffee production in Brazil went hand in hand with the development of new approaches to economic change and progress. As E. Bradford Burns explains, the formerly dominant sugar planters "were spokesmen for conservative doctrines, were intimately allied with the imperial government and were dependent upon protective tariffs." The coffee planters, however, had "more adaptable economic and social views" which "made them receptive, for example, to liberal trade-doctrines." Furthermore, since wage labor had become cheaper than the use of slaves, upon which the sugar plantations were built, the coffee growers favored the increased use of low-paid immigrant workers. Since immigrants, especially those from Europe, did not view slavery as a pleasing institution, the coffee planters allied themselves with abolitionist sentiment in Brazil.[3]

Historian Richard Graham has described the change in economic philosophies in Brazil, from one in which conservative, protectionist, almost feudal elements predominated, to one in which liberal, free trade, "modernizing" segments of Brazilian society held sway. An important component of that change was the impact of British ideas and actions in Brazil.[4] British entrepreneurs and investors provided the export houses, insurance firms, shipping companies, credit facilities, and port construction that eased Brazil's transition to an economy based on the export of coffee. More important, British money enabled Brazil to construct a vast railroad system facilitating the transportation of the crop.

The British presence also contributed to the economic transformation of Brazil in more subtle and indirect ways. For example, Graham claims that the British helped to convince Brazil to abolish slavery, a notorious drag on modernization. But mere contact with the British economic system led the Brazilians to adopt certain philosophies and ways of living which encouraged the change from "conservative" to "liberal" economic policies. Economic individualism, freedom from government control of the marketplace, the "gospel of work," Spencerian notions of the "survival of the fittest" in the economic jungle, and especially economic liberalism were all "imported" into Brazil. The advantages of free trade and laissez-faire were constantly drilled into the Brazilians by the British. Only the free and uninhibited flow of goods would bring Brazil the growth it desired. Coffee was to be a catalyst, and its profits would allow Brazil to modernize.[5]

Ironically, however, the Brazilian move to an export economy based on coffee, spurred by the British, had the effect of creating a closer economic relationship with the United States. The United States had received the largest share of Brazilian exports since the mid-1800s.[6] As coffee came to dominate the Brazilian economy, however, the difference between the amount of Brazilian exports to the United States and to Great Britain became spectacular. By 1850 the United States consumed 47.3 percent of Brazil's coffee, while British consumption dwindled. By 1900 the United States took 43 percent of all Brazilian exports, and Great Britain received just 18 percent. By 1918 comparisons had become almost absurd: Brazil sent 1000 bags of coffee to Great Britain, while 4.5 million bags made their way to the United States.[7] That trend continued after World War I, when the United States also replaced Great Britain as the principal source of Brazilian imports and eventually moved past the British as the major foreign investor in that nation.

Brazil also was moving toward a much closer political relationship with the United States during the late 1800s and early 1900s. The establishment of Brazil as a republic in 1889 seemed, as Graham has put it, "to signify a move toward the United States." A more valuable move was Brazil's decision in 1891 to sign a reciprocal trade treaty with the United States.[8]

Most significant for this new relationship was the appointment in 1902 of Baron de Rio-Branco as Brazil's foreign minister. More than anyone else, Rio-Branco exemplified the new Brazilian perspective on relations with the United States.[9] As Burns has written, Rio-Branco "clearly understood that the newly emerged world power, if properly cultivated, could serve Brazilian interests well." Closer relations with the United States would "tip the balance of power in South America to favor Brazil, . . . add to his diplomatic strength, and . . . increase his international maneuverability."[10] Indications that he was actively pursuing such a policy were the exchange of ambassadors between the two nations in 1905 (the U.S. ambassador was the only one in South America at that time), the renewal of trade pacts in 1904, 1906, and 1910, and Rio-Branco's work to defeat a protective tariff in Brazil in 1903.[11]

By 1914 the basis for a solid U.S.-Brazilian economic and political relationship had been established. The consensus among Brazilian leaders that economic growth required foreign investment and the development of a strong export trade took on particularly pro-American aspects with the phenomenal success of coffee and the diplomacy of officials such as Rio-Branco. American trade and investment in Brazil, however, still faced considerable opposition from Great Britain. In 1913 total British trade with Brazil amounted to over $120 million, and British investments totaled $1.16 billion. Total U.S. trade with Brazil in 1913 was over $30 million greater than that of Britain, but that figure was skewed by the massive importation of coffee into America. U.S. exports to Brazil fell $30 million short of the British figure. In terms of investment, the U.S. figure of $50 million was almost negligible.[12]

World War I did not eliminate the British economic presence in Brazil, but it did mark the end of British dominance. Through the opportunities offered by the disruption ensuing from the great conflict in Europe, American businessmen and financiers were able to expand their influence, trade, and investment. U.S. ambassador Edwin Morgan, writing to the State Department on 3 August 1914, pointed out that despite the "unfavorable economic conditions" caused by the war, "an unusual opportunity is presented for increasing the market for American products here." Furthermore, American importers were "unanimous in the opinion that the moment is most propitious for increasing our markets."[13] A month later, Morgan described the American economic interest in the Amazon valley. The area was already largely dependent on the United States for a healthy import-export trade, and "the present European war should increase that dependence."[14]

The economic crisis in Brazil engendered by the war was traumatic but short-lived. American interest in that nation, however, increased as the war dragged on. For example, Morgan sent to the department a copy of a speech made by Richard P. Strong, vice president of the AIC, to a group of Brazilian businessmen in September 1916. Strong declared that the United States and Brazil had become "increasingly necessary to one another." He stressed that it was "obvious that the United States needs your products and will need much more of them than you now produce. It is also equally obvious that you need many of our products and also further capital for the development of your marvellous [*sic*] resources." That last point was especially important, Strong noted, since the war had made it the "duty and responsibility" of the United States to furnish capital for development in Brazil and all of South America. The formation of the AIC was but one step toward fulfilling that duty. L. S. Clark of the International Advertising Corporation, writing to Woodrow Wilson in April 1917, echoed Strong's enthusiasm as he described his plans for an exposition of American products in Rio de Janeiro. The war was "the historical moment of opportunity for the United States to obtain a peaceful conquest in the name of the good ideal of our Country."[15]

As the war ground on, Ambassador Morgan chided the American government for what he perceived as its laxness in following up opportunities in Brazil. In December 1917, for example, Morgan complained that while the United States denied the sale of armaments to Brazil and assumed a greater burden of the war effort, the other Allies seemed to have no qualms about such sales and were actively attempting to "solicit and fill orders from South America." "The strides and conquests which American manufacturers have recently made in the Southern Hemisphere," he concluded, "will be ephemeral unless they are alive to this fact and are prepared and allowed to actively continue their export business." In April 1918, Morgan turned his fire on the regulations of the War Trade Board, which he charged had "hindered commercial interchange and have caused considerable irritation." That was unfortunate, since "both the Government and the people of Brazil have shown an increased interest in the United States and her affairs and are realizing the power of the American Government as never before." He concluded his letter on a pessimistic note: He was concerned about what would happen to the American position in the Brazilian market following the end of the war.[16]

The BFDC, just months before the armistice, sounded more positive in its evaluation of the situation in Brazil. The war had hit Brazil hard; funding had dried up and demand for coffee had plummeted. Yet, those hardships had beneficial effects. For one thing, Brazil had been forced to look for alternative export commodities and had sought to accelerate the development of crops such as cotton, rice, and sugar, and minerals such as iron ore, coal, manganese, and monazite sand. For another, American exports to and imports from Brazil had increased dramatically. In sum, the report stated, "We may expect, therefore, to see Brazil occupy more and more of the attention of the student of foreign trade." American businessmen had, during the preceding few years, begun to "give serious attention to the possibilities of mutually profitable commercial development."[17]

Brazil, both during and after the war, was indeed attracting "more and more of the attention" of American businessmen and government officials. The rapid development of two resources in particular, manganese and monazite sand, became very important to American industry during World War I. Consul General Alfred Gottschalk noted in April 1917 that Brazil furnished 80 percent of the manganese needed by the American steel industry. The 1918 report of the Allied Maritime Transport Council cited some impressive figures on American imports of manganese from Brazil: 72,000 tons in 1914; 541,000 tons in 1917. In 1920, U.S. Steel established the Companhia Meridional de Mineracao to work manganese mines which it claimed were "the largest known deposits of high grade manganese ore."[18]

Brazil was also the site of large deposits of monazite sand, a rare material useful for producing such items as gas mantles. Bernard Baruch, writing to Julius Lay of the Latin American Division in the State Department, asked that Lay aid the Radium Luminous Material Corporation which aimed to "get control of certain monazite sand in Brazil." He enclosed a letter from the president of the corporation, Paul Willis, enumerating the many uses of monazite sand in the war effort and other industries.[19] Brazil was, slowly to be sure, becoming something more than just a huge coffee plantation in the eyes of American officials and businessmen.

The supposed opportunities of the Brazilian market brought forth high praise from American observers. John S. Hammond of the banking house Imbrie and Company sent some of his company's ads to Lay, then in the Foreign Trade Office of the State Department, in May 1919. One, entitled "South America: American Investors Should Know about Brazil," described the varied resources of that nation. "The above facts concerning Brazil's present economic strength," it stated, "are not fully appreciated by American investors, nor are the tremendous future possibilities of this rich but underdeveloped country fully grasped by the American business public." Brazil's economic future lay in its "resources as yet untouched and unexploited." Another ad, "Brazil: The Development of Our South American Ally," was even more emphatic. The ad gushed that "the extensive fertile areas of Brazil justify a prediction that the development of her resources will be similar to that of the United States," and it went on to compare Brazil's development to that of the American West. It concluded that "Brazil's commerce and economic development are dependent upon the investment of foreign capital" and that, to keep the lead in Brazil's economy, "farsighted American investors" needed to become involved. A 1920 note from the American consul at Para, Brazil, to the commercial attaché in Rio de Janeiro was unparalleled for its description of Brazil's wealth: "I think that the large capitalist has here a field so rich that it would be dangerous to tell all the truth."[20]

While the American consul was reluctant to divulge the secrets of Brazil's wealth, trade and investment figures reveal that the word got out. From 1913, American trade with and investment in Brazil climbed steadily and in some areas spectacularly, especially during the late 1920s. The State Department was deluged with information about new loans, new factories, new mines, and new sales. In the space of just over two years, from September 1926 to November 1928, American representatives in Brazil informed the department that Chrysler was considering opening a new plant in Rio de Janeiro, American bankers were in Brazil scouting loan possibilities, Baldwin Locomotive Works had sold $1.5 million worth of locomotives to Brazil, and General Electric and Westinghouse had secured large contracts for the electrification of a railway system in the state of São Paulo. In January 1927, General Electric purchased four power companies worth $20 million; in July 1928, White, Weld and Company of New York announced a contract with the state of Rio Grande do Sul for a $41 million loan; and in November 1928, Ford announced plans to open a factory in Brazil.[21]

From 1913 to 1927 total American trade with Brazil increased by 103 percent. By comparison British trade with Brazil had declined by nearly 20 percent during that same period. U.S. investment in Brazil in 1929 totaled $476 million, more than nine times the 1913 figure. By 1930, the United States had become the foremost foreign investor in Brazil, outpacing its archrival, Great Britain.[22]

American trade with and investment in all South American countries had risen during World War I, often at higher rates than those for Brazil. Yet, for a number of very important reasons, American officials and business leaders saw that Brazil was unique. Unlike Mexico, Colombia, Chile, or Argentina, Brazil exhibited little, if any, economic nationalism. American observers were convinced that Brazil intended to work toward a closer economic and political relationship with the United States, and to work against radicalism, whether Mexico's revolutionary force or communism.

Evidence of those intentions was constantly relayed to the State Department. Reporting on the election of Conselheiro Rodrígues Alves as president in 1918, Ambassador Morgan stated with assurance that Rodrígues Alves believed strongly in "the influence which the United States should and does exercise over the American continent." Shortly thereafter, the ambassador reported on the success of the U.S. Committee on Public Information in Brazil. Its material was "widely distributed and is eagerly read." Furthermore, a Rio de Janeiro newspaper, *O Paiz*, had an "arragnement [*sic*] with the United Press, [and] continues to support American interests effectively."[23] In August 1918, Morgan summed up his views on the Brazilian attitude toward the United States:

> Although there are a few individuals in Brazil who believe that every nation has a right to be treated as an end in itself, the dependence of Brazil upon foreign nations for coal, gasoline and the majority of the manufactured articles which it consumes, as well as its belief that the United States will protect it from foreign aggression, makes it impossible for any Brazilian whose opinion is of value to separate the interests of other nations from those of their native country.[24]

Evidence from Brazil reaching American officials following the war tended to confirm Morgan's analysis. In April 1919, Vice Consul Augustus Hasskarl sent a translation of an article from the Rio de Janeiro newspaper *Monitor Mercantil* discussing Brazil's economic future. "Unfortunately," the article stated, "we do not possess the necessary funds to enable us to expand through our own efforts." Foreign funds had been the salvation of Brazil, without which the nation "would still be a miserable African colony without ports, railroads, clean cities, and the comforts of civilization which we now possess." In conclusion, the story urged that "we should accustom ourselves to realize that foreign capital is the only means at our disposal by which the latent forces of this land can be brought into play."[25]

Writing to the State Department in July 1921, Ambassador Morgan enclosed an article from *O Paiz* about closer U.S.-Brazilian relations. "This necessity," it declared, "is in fact undeniable." Due to the increasing commercial presence of the United States in Brazil, it was "evident that the formation of a continental commerce becomes indispensable." The nations of Latin America were embarked on economic development, and it was clear that "the United States, with the wealth and progress with which it is blessed, can insure success to this undertaking." During the mid- to late-1920s, when American loans to and investments in Brazil were booming, that belief gained even more credence. In April 1924, the American chargé in Rio de Janeiro enclosed another article, again from *O Paiz*, highly praising the Warren Harding administration and Secretary of State Charles Evans Hughes in particular. Referring to recent statements by the secretary, the article stated that "the policy of the United States, he said, was based upon the principle that . . . the peace and progress of the two Americas depends on the compliance with international obligations and just reciprocal treatment. This is the truth."[26]

Even more encouraging was Ambassador Morgan's 1926 report on a conversation with Brazilian president Artur Bernardes. Bernardes was disappointed with the League of Nations and especially with the "indifferent" attitude toward Brazil's interests shown by the great powers. As Morgan put it, "He wished, therefore, to return to the orbit of her American continental relations" and desired cooperation with the United States. The president's program for Brazil included "alterations in the commercial code in order to allow the association of capital and the introduction of foreign capital in connection with domestic." Early in 1927, Commercial Attaché Carlton Jackson remarked approvingly on the "extremely friendly" attitude shown by Brazilians toward the United States. Of some importance, Jackson noted, was the fact that Brazilian tourists now visited the United States instead of Great Britain, "returning with proamerican propaganda."[27]

Such "propaganda" obviously had some effect, for the positive Brazilian attitude toward the United States continued throughout the 1920s. Indeed, as Stokeley Morgan (chief of the Latin American Division) wrote to William Manning (a drafting officer in the department's Profession and Science Service) in June 1927, reports from the American chargé in Brazil indicated that influential Brazilians had been so favorably impressed by the work of the American economic expert Edwin Kemmerer in Colombia that they desired his help for their nation as well. Assistant Secretary of State Francis White summed up the situation in August 1928, when he complained of the "considerable hostility" of Argentina toward the United States and added that "there is nothing of the sort in Brazil."[28]

In 1929, when the United States informed Brazil that it would keep its tariffs on exports from that nation at the same levels as before, Brazilians reacted with pro-American praise. Ambassador Edwin Morgan recounted the reaction of Brazilian newspapers with an almost skeptical relief. The nation's press "ascribes this situation to the happy political personal relations existing between the two nations rather than to a willingness to permit the free entry into the United States of non-competing raw materials and the absence of need for protecting American manufacturers and farmers." Rudolf Schoenfeld, third secretary at the Rio de Janeiro embassy, described the delight of one Brazilian official over the American tariff in October 1929. Noting that the United States took over 40 percent of Brazil's exports and contributed $20 million to Brazil's trade balance, the official believed that "the attitude of the United States takes into account Brazil's vital needs."[29]

As far as American observers were concerned, then, Brazil showed a great desire to work with the United States in its economic and political development. Economic nationalism appeared to be a dead letter in Brazil. Historian Rollie Poppino has come to that same conclusion. In his analysis, economic nationalism in Brazil became a significant force only in the 1930s under the impact of the depression and the accession of Getúlio Vargas. During the 1920s only a small group of intellectuals, politicians, and native industrialists were drawn to that philosophy.[30]

One specific example of Brazil's attitude toward economic nationalism during the 1920s was its action on petroleum legislation. In July 1927, Ambassador Morgan informed the State Department that serious questions had been raised in Brazil about nationalizing its mineral resources. A new law being prepared would clarify Brazil's position. Morgan was optimistic since, as he pointed out, even

Brazilian newspapers that were sometimes critical of American policy were advising caution. The *Correio da Manhã* stated that the new law should not exclude foreign capital, because "without such capital the latent mineral and petroleum resources of the country cannot be developed." Nonetheless, nationalist elements in the Brazilian congress continued to introduce bills prohibiting foreign ownership of the nation's mineral deposits. Still, Morgan was not unduly concerned. In February 1928 he confided that early action on the legislation was not probable, as there was "little agitation for immediate action thereon." He admitted, however, that earlier action on a petroleum bill might take place.[31]

Assistant Secretary of State White made the department's views emphatically clear. A law excluding foreign participation would be "disadvantageous to American interests" and would also be "distinctly contrary to fundamental principles for which this Government stands, namely, freedom of access to raw materials and equality of commercial opportunity." In addition undeveloped nations needed foreign capital to exploit their natural resources, just as the young United States had needed such funds. Morgan quickly calmed White's fears. In August 1928 he reported that the Brazilian senate's finance committee had defeated a new petroleum law excluding foreign participation, because it would have been too costly to Brazil's export tax on oil. Later that month Morgan relayed to the department that the director of Brazil's geological and mineralogical service had severely criticized the bill. His major argument was that Brazil was in no position to develop its oil resources by itself; it needed foreign capital. In addition, Brazil's minister of communication and public works had offered similar criticisms of another bill that had called for the building of "Brazilian-owned petroleum refineries."[32] Unlike the troublesome nations of Mexico, Colombia, and others in Latin America, Brazil required little effort on the part of the United States to convince it to ignore the siren song of economic nationalism. Happily enough, Brazil policed itself.

Brazil also policed itself in another vital area. When, during the tenure of Frank Kellogg as secretary of state, the conflict between the United States and Mexico became interwoven with American fears of Communist penetration into Latin America, Brazil let it be known that its sympathies were with the United States. Even the newspaper of the reformist Democratic party in Brazil, *O Journal*, sided with the Americans. In a June 1925 editorial, it stated that "the conflicts between the United States and Mexico only arise from the fact of North American statesmen being more fully aware of the danger which threatens the continent." Mexico's attitude toward the United States was both dangerous and unreasonable: dangerous because it undermined continental solidarity, unreasonable because Mexico needed American capital to develop.[33]

Communism never became a problem in Brazil in the 1920s. As Ambassador Morgan explained in August 1926, there were some tiny

Italian groups in Brazil, more antifascist than Communist, but they were "under control." "There are," Morgan concluded, "probably few countries where the Communist or Socialist Parties find less terrain in which to operate successfully than in Brazil." Because of the largely agricultural population of Brazil, there was not much of an industrial work force into which communism might bore. Morgan also mentioned, in a report later that month, that the official stance of the Brazilian government toward communism was encouraging. He claimed that Uruguay's recognition of the Soviet Union had caused "apprehension and annoyance" in Brazil. The Brazilians were especially fearful that the other nations of Latin America might now "find that Uruguayan recognition will give the Soviet anarchic and communistic elements an opportunity for activity which has not hitherto existed." Morgan was relieved to note, however, that Dr. Helio Lobo had become the Brazilian minister to Uruguay, "for he will be alert to the necessity of preventing the prarie [*sic*] fire from spreading."[34]

Late in 1928 a report from Consul Randolph Carroll intimated that perhaps the "prairie fire" was spreading to Brazil. In a report on "Signs of Soviet Influence in Brazilian Labor Circles," Carroll noted celebrations by certain groups in Brazil commemorating the Russian Revolution. *A Noite*, a Rio de Janeiro newspaper, reported that the Soviet Union had allotted thousands of dollars "for the spread of communist activity and propaganda in Brazil," part of a Soviet plan for "the formation of a Soviet union of the States of South America." Most State Department officials seemed to find more believability, and certainly more comfort, in reports such as that from Major Lester Baker, military attaché in Brazil, in 1929. Conceding that Communist elements did exist in Brazil, he dismissed them as small and confused. The Brazilian government was harsh in its opposition, and Baker doubted that communism would have much appeal for the "individualistic" Brazilians.[35]

Brazil's ready acceptance of foreign participation in its economic development, its avowed preference for working with Americans, and its antipathy to radicalism, in the form of either economic nationalism or communism, all contributed to positive American attitudes toward that nation. Not that U.S. officials thought any more highly of Brazilians personally than they did of any of the other people of Latin America. A report by Major Baker in 1929 on the political situation in Brazil (which was called "the best discussion of that subject that I have seen" by a member of the State Department) contained a far from complimentary assessment of Brazil and its leaders. He dismissed out of hand the majority of Brazilians, as 80 percent of them were illiterate, and he noted a "pessimistic contempt for politics on the part of the really well educated elements." Popular will was lost in the shuffle of elections that were run to keep a "self-perpetuating" group of politicos in power. Fraud was pervasive. "Principles" and "platforms" meant little, as "neither side is sincere." Government in Brazil was inefficient at best;

congressmen were good only for long, dull speeches; and Baker noted that they carried guns at times.[36]

Outweighing such skeptical evaluations, at least in the eyes of American officials, was the fact that Brazil behaved well and seemed to accept its place in the world economic order. It was not necessary to twist Brazil's arm to accept American notions of development, as it was with Mexico and Colombia. Nor was it necessary to work with odious dictators and cynically rationalize the relationship, as it was with Venezuela. The United States needed only to reinforce and constantly encourage the pro-American attitude of Brazil, while at the same time increasing the American presence and influence there.

Encouraging U.S. bankers to make loans to Brazil was one action taken by American officials to ensure the growing closeness between the two nations. Ambassador Morgan set out what benefits the loans would bring to the United States in September 1916, following the visit of Richard Strong of the AIC. In a report prepared on 12 September, Morgan stated that he believed "that any loan to Brazil at the present moment is good." Such transactions would help Brazil, and they also were desirable "both with the object of consolidating American political and commercial influence and of strengthening the interests of the International Corporation." After all, the ambassador noted, "A country with such rich and rapidly developing resources and with several of the principal European bankers deeply interested in its financial solvency, cannot become bankrupt." Two days later, Morgan was more explicit about why American bankers had to move quickly in Brazil. British and French bankers were pressing Brazil to accept their loans. Furthermore, the Brazilian minister of finance had been sounding out Morgan about a $25-million loan. Brazil had in the last two years "conducted business honestly, had reduced expenditures, and established new taxes." Therefore, the ambassador concluded, "An American loan which would free Brazil from dependence upon European bankers . . . would have important political consequences, would consolidate American influence, and would place her under obligation to us."[37]

Otto Wilson of the BFDC pointed out another advantage of American loans to Brazil in a January 1917 letter to Frederico Lage of William Morris Imbrie and Company. He was certain that Lage understood "the close connection existing between the investment of capital in a foreign country and the increase of our trade with that country." To help that "connection" along, William Manning of the State Department explained to Assistant Secretary White in 1922, "The Department has made it a point to request that as much of the money as possible obtained from these loans be spent in the United States. The bankers have usually stated that every effort would be made toward this end."[38]

The importance of these loans can be seen in the ways in which U.S. officials described the problems of securing loans to Brazil. One major problem facing them was a relative lack of interest in making loans to Brazil on the part of some American bankers. According to State Department records, this mainly stemmed from the bankers' uncertainty about Brazil's ability to repay and the relatively low returns they would receive from the loans. To observers in State and Commerce, such as Alfred Gottschalk, such attitudes were frustrating. In March 1915 the consul general reported that he had approached a local branch of National City Bank of New York about a $10- to $15-million loan for Brazil. The bank "demurred" and appeared "for a while to have thought with our characteristic American bluntness to simply 'turn the project down,' " Gottschalk complained. Finally, "wiser counsels . . . prevailed," and the bank told the Brazilians that it would have to consult with the Rothschilds, as the French banking house had already made a loan to Brazil on the condition that no other foreign loans be contracted without its consent. There was little hope for the American loan, but at least the bank had not been so "blunt."[39]

The BFDC's Otto Wilson also was dissatisfied with the performance of American bankers. Writing to George Brist of the State Department's Office of Foreign Trade Advisor in May 1915, Wilson discussed a possible $25-million loan to São Paulo which had been described by a BFDC special agent on the scene as a good opportunity. Unfortunately, U.S. bankers had little enthusiasm for such a loan, because they regarded the 5 percent return as insufficient. Wilson's displeasure contrasts with the favorable report on the activities of Harris Forbes and Company written by the acting chief of the Latin American Division, J. Butler Wright, in December 1915. That banking house had asked the State Department to discuss loan opportunities that existed in Brazil, and Wright exulted that this was "the first firm to take an intelligent interest in loans by American financiers to South American governments."[40]

A further problem that complicated matters was the interdepartmental, and sometimes intradepartmental, feuding that arose around charges that someone had missed a valuable opportunity for securing an American loan to Brazil. One heated exchange took place in mid-1915. In his May 1915 letter to Brist concerning the $25-million loan to São Paulo, Otto Wilson had suggested that Brist write the American consul, Maddin Summers, for his opinion, although he sarcastically remarked that the consul had probably "sidetracked" the whole matter. Wilbur Carr, director of the State Department's Consular Service, fired off a note to Summers chastising him for not reporting the opportunity and added that in the future he hoped that the consular officers would "keep themselves currently informed." In his reply Summers informed the department that he had not reported the loan possibility because it was a poor opportunity. Furthermore, the BFDC's commercial attachés were not reliable sources; unlike the consuls, they spent only a few days in a country and knew nothing of the nation or its people. He haughtily concluded that "when there are real trade opportunities the Consuls themselves seldom fail to see them and report them."[41]

Another incident occurred in 1917. In January, Frank Polk of the State Department sent to Secretary of Commerce William Redfield, as requested, a paraphrase of Ambassador Morgan's cable of 14 September 1916, in which Morgan had argued for American loans to Brazil. Redfield was furious. "The delay in receiving this message," he wrote, "prevented this Department from taking steps which would probably have resulted advantageously to our trade and trade relations with Brazil." He condescendingly explained to Polk that "foreign loans are, however, so essential a part of our own financial stability in the near future that we desire to encourage them within due reason."[42]

Members of the State Department and the BFDC took a variety of actions to spur the interest of American bankers. Some, like Wilbur Carr, tried to make sure that news of loan opportunities quickly reached the ears of the bankers. Obviously still stinging from what he perceived as Consul Summers's lackadaisical reporting in May 1915, Carr personally cabled American consuls in Brazil asking that any and all information on projected loans be sent to the department for use by American bankers.[43]

More effort was put into urging the bankers to themselves investigate loan possibilities in Brazil. Ambassador Morgan, recounting Richard Strong's visit to Brazil in September 1916, urged that the department contact the AIC and "express to the Corporation the benefit to American interests which it believes would accrue" from making a loan to Brazil. He was personally of the opinion that the AIC had not shown the "interest which the matter merits." The State Department moved into action. On 28 September, J. Butler Wright wrote to Roger L. Farnham of National City Bank about getting together to discuss Brazil so that "your institution may become, by this means, acquainted with other and more important aspects of the case." Two months later Wright cabled Morgan, telling him that he had given some of the ambassador's information to Farnham, who was "practically the expert of that institution on Latin-American affairs and who has a great voice in that institution's foreign loans and plays no small part" in the AIC. In March 1917, Jordan Stabler wrote a memorandum discussing information he had received from Morgan. According to the ambassador a group of American banking institutions, including National City Bank, Equitable Trust, J. P. Morgan and Company, Kuhn and Loeb, Lee, Higginson and Company, and Guaranty Trust, was interested in "taking over all of the finances of Brazil."[44]

Another approach was to guarantee help in securing loans to Brazil. As Otto Wilson wrote to Lage in January 1917, "You can be assured of our hearty support of any action you may take looking to the assistance of financially worthy South American governments and municipalities."[45]

Whether these methods influenced American bankers to work for loans to Brazil is uncertain. It is clear, however, that by the end of the 1920s American loans to Brazil and the trade that was intimately connected with those loans had increased dramatically. While Great Britain had not been entirely replaced in the Brazilian marketplace, the United States had clearly taken first steps toward a dominant position. Yet the United States did not act only along economic lines to gain influence in Brazil. There was also a steady American effort to gain influence with a particular group of Brazilians: the naval officer corps.

The navy in Brazil had held an important position since the 1889 revolt. The establishment of the Brazilian republic had not met with the approval of the navy's officers, who, as E. Bradford Burns has stated, harbored "aristocratic disdain for the republic." Two revolts by the navy, in 1891 and 1893, had not been successful, however, and divisions between the army and the navy led to an apparent loss of the military's voice in national politics. Yet that appearance was illusory: After 1894 the military did not abandon its political power, it simply "manipulated it more discreetly." After the 1910 election of Marshal Hermes da Fonseca as president, the military more openly used its position as the "most important single national institution."[46]

American officials were not blind to this. Consul Gottschalk summed it up in June 1916: "As the Department is doubtless aware, the Navy is not only a military arm but is a political force of importance in this Republic." When, in April 1914, Ambassador Morgan reported a request by the Brazilian minister of marine for two naval officers to serve as instructors at his nation's naval war college, the State Department swung into action. Robert Lansing, then counselor for the department, immediately contacted Secretary of the Navy Josephus Daniels to convey the request, adding that "the Department would be gratified if the Navy Department should find it possible to comply."[47]

Daniels was happy to comply, but he believed that the Brazilian proposal to grant the instructors honorary ranks and pay them salaries might violate the Constitution. Rutherford Bingham sought advice from the department's solicitor's office, suggesting that "from the point of view of fostering cordial relations with Latin America, it would be of great value if our officers could accept offers similar to this one." In his reply, Frederick K. Nielsen agreed with Daniels, but he noted that if the officers were not titled or paid there might not be a problem. With that in mind, Secretary of State William Jennings Bryan wired Morgan in June 1914 that the State and Navy departments would be "glad to respond" to Brazil's request if "special authority" were granted by the U.S. Congress.[48]

The ambassador then cabled the department, asking that the American naval attaché in Brazil be detailed as one of the instructors because of the "desirability of securing for the United States at the earliest possible date the positions of tactical instructor." Bingham found Morgan's argument compelling, and he advised William Phillips, third assistant secretary of state, that Morgan's plan should be put into effect. He stressed the delay involved in waiting for congressional approval and noted that "if our Naval Attaché can be detailed to this duty immediately it will give the United States possession of the field." The letter was marked "Approved, Long" (Boaz Long, chief of the Latin American Division).[49]

Accordingly, in September 1914, Morgan announced to the department that Commander Philip Williams had "begun his service" but needed official authorization to perform his duties effectively. He requested that the Navy Department secure authority from a higher source. When, by October, no answer was forthcoming, Morgan sent a more urgent message advising fast action on his September request. While World War I made the transfer of instructors from a European nation a remote possibility, a new Brazilian minister of marine would be coming to office in November. If authorization could be quickly secured, it would "safeguard him [Commander Williams] and the influence of the American navy against a possible change of policy by the new Minister of Marine." The Navy Department took this warning to heart, and three weeks later it informed the State Department that it had asked President Wilson to officially designate Williams as an instructor. Two days later, Acting Secretary of the Navy Victor Blue asked Secretary Bryan to inform Morgan that the president had officially authorized Williams to serve in the Brazilian naval war college.[50]

That news must have pleased Morgan enormously, but other news from the State Department was discouraging. On 21 November 1916, Secretary of the Navy Daniels informed Secretary of State Lansing that Commander Williams's leave of absence would end in January 1917 and that a shortage of officers "precludes the detailing of an officer as Commander Williams' relief." After America's entry into World War I in April 1917, it was difficult even for Morgan to argue with Daniels's point, but by November 1917 the ambassador was again on the offensive. On 9 November, Morgan cabled the State Department about reports that the British were interested in providing instructors for the vacancy created at the naval war college, and Daniels did a complete about-face on 16 November. He now agreed that an American replacement should be named, not because the United States "would look unfavorably upon an invitation to a British Naval Mission," but rather "on account of our desire to further the interests and welfare of the Brazilian Government." The Department of the Navy would immediately appoint an American naval mission to Brazil.[51]

Morgan responded in December 1917 that a formal naval mission would probably not be invited by Brazil. Instead, the minister of marine had been authorized to engage the services of five American naval officers, two as instructors and three as "fire control officers." Furthermore, Brazil desired to send a six-ship squadron "to Southern European waters to cooperate with the fleet of one of the Allies." It would be a good idea, Morgan went on, if that squadron could join an American naval contingent, "even should military advantage prove insignificant." The real advantage, he concluded, would be in offsetting the "effect of French purchase of ex-German ships [from Brazil, where they had been impounded] by some visual demonstration of Brazilian-American solidarity which would appeal to the poorest mind." The idea obviously appealed to Secretary Lansing, who immediately replied that the Department of the Navy would supply the five officers and that Morgan should ask the Brazilian squadron to join American ships "operating against the enemy."[52]

Having settled those issues, Morgan pressed forward with some other criticisms and suggestions. In December 1917 the ambassador caustically commented on America's denial of the sale of armaments to Brazil, while its "European Allies" had no such objections to the same kinds of sales. A month later Morgan reported the arrival of four British naval noncommissioned officers in Brazil to train enlisted men in gunnery. He expressed surprise and confusion at Secretary Daniels's 16 November letter stating that the United States would not "look unfavorably" on a British naval mission to Brazil. Morgan stated:

> This office has understood that it was a basic principle of our South American policy that all American navies as much as possible should be brought under the influence of the navy of the United States. No more practical method could probably be devised than by accrediting American naval missions to the navies of the leading South American Powers. . . . The possibility [would] be increased of the future construction in our shipyards of their naval vessels and of orders for naval materials being placed with our steel works.[53]

The responses to Morgan's criticisms from both the State and Navy departments indicated unanimous support for his position. In the month following the ambassador's letter about his confusion over American policy concerning naval missions to Brazil, Daniels and Lansing cleared up any lingering doubts. Daniels, on 16 January 1918, wrote that "I appreciate fully the importance of military and naval commissions to South American states." He also appreciated "the marked political and commercial effect that these commissions have produced in the interest of nations sending them in the past and which they may well produce in the future." He would begin action on the appointment of more officers for Brazil's naval war college. Lansing was even more direct. He informed Morgan that the United States "regrets . . . the sending of British instructors to Brazil" and "desires to confirm your understanding of the Department's policy" that naval missions to Brazil should come "exclusively from the United States." As an American gunnery office was soon to be sent to Brazil, Lansing hoped that the British NCOs would "be shortly disposed of." Finally, concerning Morgan's criticism of withholding armaments to Brazil, Daniels believed that perhaps one submarine could be spared. As the secretary concluded, "The Department is of the opinion that everything possible should be done to foster the relations now existing between Brazil and this country."[54]

With the support of Washington behind him Morgan continued to press for a closer relationship between the U.S. and Brazilian navies. In September 1918 he suggested that Admiral William Caperton be sent to attend the inauguration of Brazilian President Rodrígues Alves. That would, according to Morgan, "serve to emphasize the importnace [*sic*] of the relations of the American and Brazilian navy which in itself would be helpful and which should be brought home to the Brazilian people on all occasions." Lansing responded that Caperton would be sent as requested.[55]

The change in presidential administrations in Washington in 1921 did not change Morgan's position, but the ambassador did face a problem in 1922, a crucial year in the American-Brazilian naval relationship. In February 1922 the director of Naval Intelligence informed Sumner Welles that, due to the expense and lack of manpower, replacements for the American naval officers in Brazil would probably not be forthcoming. Once again Morgan moved to change some minds. In March he reported that Brazil was deciding between the United States and Great Britain for a new naval mission. A British mission would mean that American "naval prestige would be lowered," and, Morgan added, "There would be slight possibility of American firms securing contracts for dry-dock, arsenal and new naval units which would be established, upon the advice of the mission head." Secretary of State Hughes was suitably impressed, and he quickly notified Secretary of the Navy Edwin Denby. "In view of the importance of this matter," Hughes wrote, "and of the value of the opportunity which the situation presents," he hoped that new officers could be assigned to Brazil. The Commerce Department also got into the act, cabling to Denby a message from the commercial attaché in Rio de Janeiro. The attaché had sent to Commerce a cable from the American Chamber of Commerce in Brazil which claimed that England was "making every effort to send Naval Commission to train Brazilian Navy." If successful, this would be "destructive to American Commercial, Naval and Diplomatic prestige." A short time later Hughes informed Morgan that "as special recognition of the close relation" between the United States and Brazil, the Department of the Navy would send a "distinguished" officer to serve in Brazil.[56]

Despite Hughes's assurance, actions by the Department of the Navy were not wholly encouraging, although they were at times humorous. One example was a 25 March 1922 letter from Theodore Roosevelt, Jr., assistant secretary of the navy, to the State Department expressing Navy's regret that it could not release Captain Carl T. Vogelgesang for service in the Brazilian "Naval Museum." State Department officials had a field day with Roosevelt's mistake. One memorandum asked: "What *are* we sending anyway? A *Mission*, or a *Museum*, or a *Missionary*?" Another memorandum answered that "this refers to a naval *Mission* and has no reference to any *Museum*, though that is probably the proper place for it." In the meantime messages from Americans in Brazil continued to press for quick action. Sheldon Crosby, a consul, reported in April 1922 that the Brazilian minister of marine had "intimated to local representative of Bethlehem Steel Corporation that we should show more activity toward securing naval mission." Contracts for port work worth $80 million would presumably be awarded to the nation that provided the mission. Commercial Attaché William Schurz stressed this point when he wrote just a few days later that "the existence of an American naval mission would practically assure to us the market for naval materials of all kinds." Furthermore, the attaché noted, the majority of naval officers in Brazil, especially the younger men, favored the United States as the source of the naval mission.[57]

Secretary Hughes promptly sent a cable marked "Urgent" to Ambassador Morgan. If Brazil desired a naval mission, Hughes wrote, then the United States would be "very glad to designate officers of the American Navy for this purpose." A "distinguished" officer would be chosen to head the mission. The secretary concluded that "it would give this Government great gratification if it were able to assist the Brazilian Government in this respect." A few weeks later, Assistant Secretary Roosevelt's regrets notwithstanding, Hughes informed Secretary Denby that he had instructed American officials in Brazil to offer Captain Vogelgesang, since the Brazilians had expressed a preference for him, if they "felt that such action was necessary" to secure the acceptance of the American naval mission. On 24 July 1922, Consul Crosby informed Hughes that Brazil had offered the naval mission contract to the United States and still wanted Vogelgesang as the head of the mission. He urged rapid approval and received it a few days later, when Hughes wired that the United States was pleased to accept the contract and would send Captain Vogelgesang as the Brazilians desired.[58]

Perhaps the best analysis of what the American naval mission in Brazil meant came from its foremost competitor, Great Britain. An article carried in the 20 September 1922 issue of *The Times* in London was entitled: "Brazil's Navy. An American Mission. British Prestige Waning." The article stated that "the infiltration of American ideas amongst the younger Brazilian naval officers has been steady and progressive" and that "the United States Government and the United States Navy have personally identified themselves with the Brazilian Navy, and this has borne golden fruit."[59]

American observers were also aware of the results of the American naval mission. The past year, Morgan reported in January 1925, had witnessed a revolt of army officers in São Paulo. He was happy to report that "the Brasilian Navy . . . did good work," and "the discipline which he [Vogelgesang] and his officers have inculcated, bore fruit." In that same month the American Chamber of Commerce for Brazil wrote to Secretary Hughes, enclosing a resolution praising Vogelgesang and his work.[60]

Ambassador Morgan continued his efforts throughout the late 1920s. In March 1926, noting that the mission was due to expire that December, Morgan stated that it would "be scarcely loyal" to leave the Brazilians in midstream. The mission should only end after the Brazilian officers had mastered the "scientific and administrative methods which they have learned." "But until that time comes," the ambassador concluded, "our hands should not be withdrawn from the plow." Months later Jordan Stabler summed up the importance of maintaining the mission and, especially, of selecting an able officer to head it. With characteristic bluntness and racism Stabler pointed out that "the post in Brazil is very important for the United States. It needs a person of the greatest tact and ability to get along with Latin races. The Mission's success must be based on what it can induce the Brazilian naval officers to do by friendly suggestion and example."[61]

Ambassador Morgan had worked tirelessly to achieve U.S. dominance of the Brazilian navy. By 1926 his goal had largely been achieved, and the rewards for the United States, in a variety of ways, were potentially great. Economic rewards there doubtless were. Having an American naval mission "educating" the Brazilian navy probably increased the flow of naval materials from the United States to Brazil, but it does not appear that it ever reached the bonanza proportions that some observers believed it would during the 1920s. Figures for the sales of military equipment prior to World War II are sketchy, but the hearings of the U.S. Senate Special Committee to Investigate the Munitions Industry held during the mid-1930s are enlightening. According to testimony from U.S. officials and munitions company representatives, Brazil busily purchased not only guns and ammunitions, but also bombs, airplanes, submarines, and other weaponry during the 1920s. A 1936 Senate report noted that from December 1935 to February 1936 total U.S. arms sales to Brazil amounted to $152,208 (more than was sold to Mexico, Japan, or Germany).[62]

More important, the American naval mission was a most visible sign of the increasingly dominant position of the United States in Brazilian political and economic life. By 1929, U.S. investment in Brazil had increased by over 852 percent since 1913; British investment, while still greater than the U.S. figure, had risen by only 23 percent. U.S.-Brazilian trade had risen by over 100 percent during that same period, while British trade with Brazil had declined by nearly 20 percent.[63]

Recognizing that the Brazilian navy was a political as well as a military force, the United States had moved to "Americanize" it. The Brazilian navy had exhibited a strong desire to work with the United

States, and the American mission had fostered a "discipline" in its pupils which had counteracted disruptive revolts. As a relatively inexpensive investment, the American naval mission had indeed "borne golden fruit." Using "friendly suggestion and example" the United States had been able, with its naval mission and its increasing economic presence, to influence Brazil to stay in the U.S. political and economic orbit, away from the dangers of economic nationalism and other forms of radicalism.

Notes

1. The works most relied upon in writing this brief survey of Brazilian economic and political development during the nineteenth and early twentieth centuries were Celso Furtado, *The Economic Growth of Brazil: A Survey from Colonial to Modern Times*, trans. Ricardo W. de Aguiar and Eric Charles Drysdale (Berkeley, 1968); E. Bradford Burns, *A History of Brazil* (New York, 1970); Rollie Poppino, *Brazil: The Land and People* (New York, 1968); Graham, *Modernization in Brazil*; and Frank, *Capitalism and Underdevelopment*.

2. Furtado, *Economic Growth*, 119–26.

3. Burns, *History of Brazil*, 134–35; Bernstein, *Contemporary Latin America*, 349–51.

4. Graham's work perhaps overemphasizes the importance of external (that is, British) forces in bringing about such changes. For books that more fully consider the internal forces at work see Halperín-Donghi, *Aftermath*, and especially Cortés Conde, *First Stages of Modernization in Spanish America*.

5. Graham, *Modernization in Brazil*, 1–276.

6. Furtado, *Economic Growth*, 41.

7. Graham, *Modernization in Brazil*, 73, 75.

8. Ibid., 304–6.

9. For the best work on this subject see E. Bradford Burns, *The Unwritten Alliance: Rio Branco and Brazilian-American Relations* (New York, 1966). For a shorter evaluation see Burns, *History of Brazil*, 232–39.

10. Burns, *History of Brazil*, 237.

11. Ibid.; Graham, *Modernization in Brazil*, 311.

12. Winkler, *Investments in Latin America*, 274–85.

13. Edwin Morgan to William J. Bryan, 3 August 1914, 832.51/71, RG 59.

14. Morgan to Bryan, 23 September 1914, 832.00/127, RG 59.

15. "Address Delivered by Dr. Richard P. Strong, Vice-President of the American International Corporation, to a Group of Brazilian Capitalists and Manufacturers Invited to Luncheon with Him by the American Ambassador, Rio de Janeiro, September 5, 1916," in Morgan to J. Butler Wright, 12 September 1916; L. S. Clark to Woodrow Wilson, 23 April 1917, 832.51/129, 832.607/original, RG 59.

16. Morgan to Robert Lansing, 8 December 1917; Morgan to Lansing, 12 April 1918, 832.34/121, 832.00/181, RG 59.

17. U.S. Department of Commerce, BFDC, *Circular of the Latin American Division*, no. 42, "The Brazilian Trade Balance and Foreign Exchange," 26 August 1918, 832.51/196, RG 59.

18. Alfred Gottschalk to Lansing, 8 April 1917, 832.635/10, RG 59; Allied Maritime Transport Council, American Section, Statistical Division, "Relations between United States and Other Countries regarding Important Materials," c. 1918, Box 9, Folder 226, Auchincloss Papers; Winkler, *Investments in Latin America*, 88.

19. Bernard Baruch to Julius Lay, 10 May 1918, RG 59, SD 832.602R11/original.

20. John S. Hammond to Lay, 21 May 1919, 832.51/196, RG 59; George S. Pickerell to J. E. Philippi, 15 April 1920, 432-Brazil, RG 151.

21. Thomas L. Daniels to Frank Kellogg, 15, 29 September 1926; Morgan to Kellogg, 22 December 1926, 5 January 1927, Morgan to Kellogg, 2 July, 21 November 1928, 832.00/591, /594, /608, /611, 832.00 General Conditions/8, /13, RG 59.

22. Winkler, *Investments in Latin America*, 274–85; Burns, *History of Brazil*, 286.

23. Morgan to Lansing, 6, 29 July 1918, 832.00/155, /182, RG 59.

24. Morgan to Lansing, 10 August 1918, 832.00/154, RG 59.

25. Augustus Hasskarl to Lansing, 26 April 1919, 832.51/196, RG 59.

26. Morgan to Charles Evans Hughes, 12 July 1921; Sheldon Crosby to Hughes, 30 April 1924, 832.00/212, /335, RG 59.

27. Morgan to Kellogg, 23 June 1926, 832.00/583, RG 59; Carlton Jackson to BFDC, 9 March 1927, 400-U.S.-Latin America, RG 151.

28. Stokeley Morgan to William Manning, 30 June 1927, 832.51/487, RG 59; Francis White to F. Lammot Belin, 23 August 1928, Box 4, White Papers.

29. Edwin Morgan to Henry Stimson, 5 June 1929; Rudolf Schoenfeld to Stimson, 8 October 1929, 832.00 General Conditions/20, /25, RG 59.

30. Poppino, *Brazil*, 242.

31. Morgan to Kellogg, 24 July 1927; Schoenfeld to Kellogg, 1 February 1928; Morgan to Kellogg, 15 February 1928; Morgan to State Department, 18 February 1928, 832.00/632, 832.00 Political Reports/2, 832.6363/27, 832.00 Political Reports/3, RG 59.

32. White to Morgan, 22 May 1928; Morgan to Kellogg, 21 August 1928; Morgan to Kellogg, 29 August 1928, 832.6363/27, /31, 832.00 General Conditions/10.

33. Editorial enclosed in Morgan to Kellogg, 24 June 1925, 832.00/520, RG 59.

34. Morgan to Kellogg, 6, 28 August 1926, 832.00B/Original, /1, RG 59.

35. Randolph Carroll to Kellogg, 19 December 1928; Lester Baker to Stimson, 8 November 1929, 832.00B/7, /8, RG 59.

36. Report contained in Manning to Dana Munro, 14 October 1929, 832.00/649, RG 59.

37. Morgan to Wright, 12 September 1916; Morgan to Lansing, 14 September 1916, 832.51/129, /122, RG 59.

38. Otto Wilson to Frederico Lage, 9 January 1917, 640-Brazil, RG 151; Manning to White, 21 June 1922, 832.51/284 1/2, RG 59.

39. Gottschalk to Bryan, 18 March 1915, 832.51/90, RG 59.

40. O. Wilson to George Brist, 28 May 1915; Burnett Walker, of Harris Forbes and Company, to Maddin Summers, November [?] 1915; Wright to Wilbur Carr, 1 December 1915, 832.51/95, /108, RG 59.

41. O. Wilson to Brist, 28 May 1915; Carr to Summers, 4 June 1915; Summers to Lansing, 2 July 1915, 832.51/95, /101, RG 59.

42. Frank Polk to William Redfield, 23 January 1917, 640-Brazil, RG 151; Redfield to Polk, 27 January 1917, 832.51/141, RG 59.

43. See, for example, Carr to Arminius T. Haeberle, consul, Pernambuco, 14 March 1916, 832.51/116, RG 59.

44. Morgan to Wright, 12 September 1916; Morgan to Lansing, 14 September 1916; Wright to Roger Farnham, 28 September 1916; Wright to Morgan, 21 November 1916; Jordan Stabler, memorandum, 15 March 1917, 832.51/129, /122, /143, /148, RG 59.

45. O. Wilson to Lage, 9 January 1917, 640-Brazil, RG 151.

46. Burns, History of Brazil, 212–14, 270.

47. Gottschalk to Lansing, 14 June 1916; Morgan to Bryan, 8 April 1914; Lansing to Josephus Daniels, 11 April 1914, 832.34/105, 832.30/1, RG 59.

48. Josephus Daniels to Bryan, 15 May 1914; Rutherford Bingham to Frederick K. Nielsen, 23 May 1914; Nielsen to the Latin American Division, 26 May 1914; Bryan to Morgan, 2 June 1914, 832.30/3, RG 59.

49. Morgan to Bryan, 5 June 1914; Bingham to William Phillips, 8 June 1914, 832.30/5, /1, RG 59.

50. Morgan to Bryan, 4 September, 6 October 1914; Department of the Navy, Bureau of Navigation to Richard Pennoyer, 29 October 1914; Victor Blue to Bryan, 31 October 1914, 832.30/6, /7, /8, RG 59.

51. Daniels to Lansing, 21 November 1916; Morgan to Lansing, 9 November 1917; Daniels to Lansing, 16 November 1917, 832.30/14, 832.20/13, 832.30/19, RG 59.

52. Morgan to Lansing, 1 December 1917; Lansing to Morgan, 3 December 1917, 832.30/22, RG 59.

53. Morgan to Lansing, 8 December 1917; Morgan to Lansing, 4 January 1918, 832.34/121, 832.30/27, RG 59.

54. Daniels to Lansing, 16 January 1918; Lansing to Morgan, 7 February 1918; Daniels to Lansing, 18 [?] January 1918, 832.30/25, /27, 832.34/124, RG 59.

55. Morgan to Lansing, 11, 24 September 1918; Lansing to Morgan, 18 October 1918, 832.00/156, /157, RG 59.

56. Captain L. McNamee to Sumner Welles, 9 February 1922; Morgan to Hughes, 4 March 1922; Hughes to Edwin Denby, 13 March 1922; Hughes to Morgan, 24 March 1922, 832.30/46, /47, RG 59; Acting Secretary of Commerce to Denby, 22 March 1922, 432, RG 151.

57. Theodore Roosevelt, Jr. to Wright, 25 March 1922; Memo, Wright to Charles Curtis, n.d. (emphasis in original); Memo, Curtis to Wright, n.d. (emphasis in original); Crosby to Hughes, 15 April 1922, SD 832.30/52, /53, RG 59; William Schurz to BFDC, 17 April 1922, 432, RG 151.

58. Hughes to Morgan, 17 April 1922; Hughes to Denby, 12 May 1922; Crosby to Hughes, 24 July 1922; Hughes to Crosby, 5 August 1922, RG 59, SD 832.30/53, /63.

59. Article enclosed in Post Wheeler to Hughes, 22 September 1922, 832.30/72, RG 59.

60. Morgan to Hughes, 20 January 1925; American Chamber of Commerce for Brazil to Hughes, 22 January 1925, 832.30/120, /121, RG 59.

61. Morgan to Kellogg, 31 March 1926; Stabler to Kellogg, 28 October 1926, 832.30/132, /145, RG 59.

62. U.S. Congress, Senate Special Committee to Investigate the Munitions Industry, Hearings before the Special Committee to Investigate the Munitions Industry, 13 vols., 73d Cong., 2d sess. (vols. 1–4), 74th Cong., 1st sess. (vols.

1–9) (Washington, 1934–1943). Testimony concerning the selling activities of U.S. arms dealers is spread throughout the hearings. The figure for total arms sales to Brazil is found in U.S. Congress, *Senate Reports*, 74th Cong., 2d sess., 1936, 944:3:62-63.

63. Winkler, *Investments in Latin America*, 284–85.

Chapter Eight

Conclusion: "The Symbols of Our Wealth"

The period from 1917 to 1929 was a critical time in the evolution of American foreign policy. New opportunities and new challenges faced the United States around the globe. Although historians of American diplomacy have recently done yeoman work in analyzing and interpreting the events of those years, their almost exclusive focus on U.S.-European relations has unintentionally obscured the fact that the United States confronted different opportunities and challenges in other parts of the world.

The obvious similarity between the European and Latin American policies of the United States is that, just as American policymakers and businessmen sought to expand into the markets of the former, so too did they look to the latter area for its economic possibilities. The markets of Latin America, virtually abandoned during the war by the battling Europeans, were tempting. Their place in the postwar world economy was analyzed by both government and commercial leaders.

But there were a number of important differences between the ways in which American policymakers set out to accomplish their goals in Latin America and in Europe. To begin with, the "cooperative" nature of U.S. government-business efforts at economic expansion that was so prevalent in dealings with Europe was noticeably less so in the case of Latin America. Especially in American dealings in Brazil, U.S. government and business seemed to be complementary but not really cooperative—a "division of labor," if you will. The government's role was simply to make opportunities available for American business and banking in Latin America. Having secured those opportunities, government officials were quick to point them out to businesses and financial institutions and to encourage them to take advantage of them. The government usually then let American business follow its natural course.[1] And neither the U.S. government nor American business concerns showed much interest in cooperating with foreign competitors such as the British in developing the Latin American market.[2]

This situation often led to recrimination and suspicion by both government and business. Government officials often accused businessmen of missing opportunities that they had assiduously worked to develop. Businessmen complained that diplomats were not aggressive enough in opening up markets. On the whole, however, the analysis presented in this study supports the conclusion that the achievement of U.S. economic dominance in Latin America was neither particularly "elusive" nor, once achieved, was that dominance exercised in an "awkward" fashion, terms used by Melvin Leffler and Frank Costigliola to characterize American efforts in Europe.

American policymakers did not seem to face the problems in Latin America described by historians of the U.S.-European relationship. The relative lack of interest and power to pursue economic expansion in Europe that Melvyn Leffler describes is certainly not apparent in the U.S. attitude toward Latin America. Although Leffler is correct in stating that the export market was not looked upon as a panacea by American officials, the United States was nonetheless tremendously interested in establishing such markets in Latin America. Furthermore, American diplomats and businessmen were equally, if not more, interested in establishing secure and reliable sources of raw material imports. Latin America was seen as a virtual storehouse of resources necessary to the economic health of the United States.

In addition, the United States was undeniably in a much stronger economic, political, and military position vis-à-vis Latin America than it was toward Europe. Uncertainties relating to power were almost totally absent from policy discussions concerning the achievement of U.S. goals in Latin America.

To be sure, American policy toward Latin America was not conducted with what Joan Hoff-Wilson calls "conspiratorial efficiency." Analyses of U.S. efforts in Colombia, Venezuela, and Brazil reveal policy discussions that sometimes bordered on comedy. But, while differences did erupt between government departments, between government and business, and between businessmen themselves, both groups generally did their work well. The U.S. government worked actively and energetically to open Latin America's markets and to secure access to its natural resources. Business and banking interests, while not always interested in the particular opportunity presented, generally rushed to exploit what was there. This was not due to any careful cooperation between the groups; rather, it was because of their shared outlooks. Both saw the acquisition of export markets and raw material sources as vital to the continued healthy functioning of the American capitalist system (which, despite discussions of the interdependent nature of the world economy, was their primary concern).

The years between 1917 and 1929 brought both triumph and frustration in U.S. relations with Latin America. The triumph was self-evident; by 1929, the United States had expanded its dominant economic role beyond the Caribbean and Central America into the more developed nations of South America. American trade and investment there reached heights that would have been unimaginable a mere fifteen years earlier. Taking advantage of the withdrawal of European money and commerce from Latin America during World War I, American officials and businessmen worked tirelessly to first extend and then strengthen commercial ties to Latin America.

Those ties were not viewed as simply profitable, although they certainly were. By the end of the war Latin America was seen as both a "natural" market for American industrial overproduction and an "indispensable" supplier of important raw materials, a vital gear helping to drive the U.S. economy. American observers were also convinced that Latin America was part of an increasingly interdependent world economic system; its role was to provide raw materials to the industrialized nations. Indeed, Latin America had acquired heavy "responsibilities" as a functioning member of the world capitalist order.

The frustrations faced by United States officials came from an apparently unimagined source—the Latin Americans themselves. The burdens imposed by their world economic "responsibilities" had begun to create a nationalistic backlash in the more economically advanced nations of Latin America. In Mexico, Chile, Uruguay, Argentina, Colombia, and elsewhere a deepening resentment resulted in various programs of economic nationalism. Some were revolutionary, as in Mexico; others were less dramatic, such as in Colombia.

Whatever the form of those programs, they were unpleasant surprises for the United States. Between Mexico's promulgation of Article 27 in 1917 and the coming of the Great Depression in 1929, American officials and businessmen attempted with mixed results to form clear pictures of just what was going so seriously wrong in Latin America. U.S. observers perceived that, whatever one might call what was going on in Latin America, it posed a serious and potentially fatal threat to the postwar domestic and international economic orders they hoped to achieve.

Economic nationalism ran directly contrary to every tenet of economic development held sacred by American leaders: the value and role of private property, the proper role of the state, and the truest pathway of economic growth. Economic nationalism also promised to wreak havoc not only on the prosperous trade with Latin America which had developed so tremendously during the war and postwar years, but also on the U.S. vision of how the postwar world economic structure should function. "Withdrawals" from that structure in the form of economic nationalism were not matters to be taken lightly.

Antibolshevism and racism also played significant roles in shaping U.S. leaders' views of economic nationalism. For a number of reasons economic nationalism in Latin America was increasingly viewed as an outgrowth of the alien philosophy of communism. First, the belief that communism was an inherently expansionistic force and that Russia had designs on areas such as Latin America was deeply ingrained in such important policymakers as Secretary Frank Kellogg. Second, as Assistant Secretary Robert Olds's comments indicated, it was good politics to cast the situation in Mexico (and elsewhere in Latin America) in that light, since it provided a good propaganda springboard for defending U.S. actions against economic nationalism. Third, it was inconceivable to most U.S. observers that the people of Latin America could not perceive the "good intentions" of U.S. policy, so anti-Americanism in that region was pinned on "outside agitators" spreading their usual dose of trouble and chaos. Finally, racist attitudes made it difficult for U.S. officials to accept the notion that the "Latinos" would or could buck the system on their own. These perceptions turned the battle from one in which the United States was confronted by troublesome, but wholly indigenous, economic policies adopted by some nations of Latin America into one in which the United States was fighting the incursion of an alien and hostile philosophy into the Western Hemisphere.

Racism's role was not as publicly evident, but it was important nevertheless. Viewing the Latin Americans as generally lazy, ignorant, and perhaps subhuman, it was not surprising that U.S. officials and business leaders were flabbergasted at their attempts to run their own economies. Convinced that any attempts by the Latin Americans to develop their own economic systems were doomed to failure because of their inherently low intelligence, those same U.S. observers were equally convinced that only foreign (preferably American) economic and technical assistance could adequately exploit the riches of Latin America. Racism provided a convenient, and perhaps even necessary, bulwark for sustaining the international division of labor.

Alarm over economic nationalism, fueled by concerns over Communist machinations and by racist assumptions, naturally sparked debates among American government and business figures about effective countermeasures. In its first contact with economic nationalism, in Mexico, the United States ran the gamut of possible responses. Military intervention, diplomatic pressure, economic coercion, and even some wishful thinking on the part of people like Elihu Root concerning another dictatorship for that nation were all considered, and some were eventually implemented in efforts to steer Mexico away from economic nationalism.

U.S. policymakers were well aware, however, that the problem did not end with the protection of American oil companies in Mexico. Economic nationalism may have begun there, but American officials were convinced that it would spread elsewhere in Latin America. When it did (and even in some cases when it did not), the U.S. perceptions of and responses to the recent events in Mexico naturally influenced its policies toward other Latin American nations viewed as infected by, or susceptible to the virus of economic nationalism.

When, in 1919, Colombia seemed to be following in the nationalistic footsteps of Mexico, a variation on the diplomatic pressure previously applied to the latter was tried. By holding the treaty dealing with Panama in diplomatic limbo, the United States hoped to force Colombia to revise its 1919 oil legislation. Secretary of State Robert Lansing also instructed that the Colombians be warned in no uncertain terms about the probable losses in U.S. trade and investment if his "suggestions" were not followed. Temporarily victorious when Colombia bowed to pressure and revised its oil laws in 1921–22, the United States soon found itself confronting more nationalistic legislation during the late 1920s. American officials resorted to economic coercion, releasing a damaging assessment of Colombia's economic strength and reliability as an international debtor and allowing the Colombians to believe that the assessment was an official statement of U.S. policy. Once again the efforts of the United States were successful, and Colombia gave up on its new oil legislation.

The U.S. view of Colombia reflected many of the opinions concerning economic nationalism in Mexico. As with Mexico, U.S. officials were perplexed by Colombia's nationalistic attitude. Colombia was deemed to be a resource-rich nation with logical economic ties to the United States. Efforts by the Colombians to gain a greater voice in their own economic development were judged to be naive, misguided, and ultimately destructive, since the Colombians were obviously incapable of understanding such complex matters. And fears of communism's role in Colombia, while not expressed as dramatically or as often as in the case of Mexico, were nonetheless present in the U.S. assessment of economic nationalism in Colombia.

In addition to pressuring Latin American governments that did not share its economic philosophy, the United States encouraged governments it believed were more in line with its goals for Latin America. The despotic regime of General Juan Vicente Gómez in Venezuela was one such government. During World War I, Gómez had been castigated as a tyrant and a pro-German hemispheric troublemaker. Just over two years after the war was ended, however, the American government had decided to work with Gómez, who now seemed to have a number of previously unnoticed admirable qualities. Why such a dramatic turnaround? U.S. officials believed that Gómez was a bulwark against the economic nationalism and other forms of radicalism running amok in Latin America. The dictator also showed every indication of wanting the United States to develop Venezuela's vast oil resources, confirming the American belief that Gómez was valuable, even indispensable, to his nation's economic development. The people of Venezuela, deemed on the whole to be ignorant and racially inferior, needed such a ruler; without Gómez, they would be easy prey for radical, even Communist, rabble rousers.

Brazil also found favor with American policymakers. In some ways it was superior to Venezuela, for not only was its government equally receptive to American economic policies, but also it did not carry the unfortunate odium of dictatorship. Nevertheless, Brazil presented some problems, for, like Venezuela, its population was made up of illiterate and possibly dangerous masses. Unlike Venezuela, however, Brazil had no Gómez to keep those masses in check, and some U.S. officials fretted over the possibility of radical ideas infecting the Brazilian populace. Brazil's leaders were viewed as inefficient at best, so Washington sought ways to encourage their desire to work with American business while looking for methods to better control the Brazilian masses.

Loans sustained the pro-American feelings of the Brazilian government and drew Brazil more tightly into the U.S. economic orbit. Controlling the masses required a somewhat more sophisticated solution. Realizing that the conservative officer corps of the Brazilian navy was a political force in that nation, U.S. officials worked energetically to instill proper values through American naval missions and military trainers. Washington hoped to build the Brazilian navy into a hedge against possible outbreaks of anti-Americanism.

In the short run such policies seemed to achieve success. Mexico apparently backed down on the issue of expropriation during the late 1920s. Colombia reversed its subsoil legislation, once in 1921–22 and again in 1928–29. Venezuela was free of nationalistic problems, and American money inundated its oil industry. Brazil became a rich area for American trade and investment, while U.S. relations with the Brazilian navy seemed to be harvesting "golden fruit" for American interests.

By 1931, Norman Davis, chairing a meeting on Latin America at the Council on Foreign Relations, could speak glowingly of the American accomplishment in Latin America:

> To millions of peons, miners, workmen, in Latin-America, the United States and its people are today most immediately represented by the plow which they hold in their hand, the automobile which brushes them by on the road, the mining manager who gives them orders, the smoke stacks of the power plant that turns the narrow streets of their home town into lanes of light. The properties of our civilization are offered to their purses. The symbols of our wealth are before their eyes.[3]

Davis's optimistic appraisal was premature, however. Economic nationalism did not disappear in Latin America; indeed, its force seemed to grow in the years after 1929 as a number of the smaller nations of South America, Central America, and the Caribbean also began to express their discontent with the world market system. Bolivia nationalized its oil fields in 1937; Mexico followed suit in 1938. In 1952, Bolivia went even farther by nationalizing many of the tin mines in the nation. Guatemala, during ten years of democratic rule from 1944 to 1954, stripped hundreds of thousands of acres from the United Fruit Company. Cuba, following its 1959 revolution, began under the leadership of Fidel Castro to nationalize lands and utility companies, hotels and casinos. Salvador Allende, in 1970, brought to Chile the first democratically elected Socialist government in Latin America. More recently Grenada and Nicaragua also embarked, with varying intensity and success, on programs of economic nationalism deviating strongly from the American notion of proper economic development.

U.S. policymakers still struggle to comprehend the reasoning behind such actions. While they are not much more successful than their predecessors in this regard, they share with them a distinct dislike of economic nationalism in any form. They continue to view Latin America as a marvelously rich storehouse of natural resources just waiting for the right expertise and technology to free them. Indeed, the notion that many parts of Latin America, especially Brazil, are like the Old West in the United States continues to hold sway. And, not coincidentally, Latin America is still considered to be an important market for American consumer goods. True economic "development" for the region "someday" is still discussed in rather hazy terms. Considering all of this, it is not surprising that economic nationalism still perplexes American officials; the need for U.S. economic "guidance" is still assumed. "Free enterprise" and "private sector initiatives" are the proper prescriptions for the problems of Latin America.

The issue of Communist involvement in Latin America has, obviously, become more important in U.S. policy toward that region. Especially since the end of World War II, American officials have been much quicker to paint governments in Latin America that enact programs of economic nationalism in the vivid red tones of communism. Guatemala, for example, during the years 1944 to 1954, found itself pictured as either being in the hands of Communist dupes, or as serving as a base for Communist penetration into the Americas.[4]

Racism on the part of U.S. officials has become less vocal and has lost some of the viciousness exemplified by Ambassador James Sheffield during the 1920s. Nevertheless, the paternalistic nature of American policies toward Latin America is still evident: The Latin Americans seem to be pleasant enough people; one just has to tell them what to do.

In its responses to economic nationalism the United States continues to employ many of the same actions as it did in the 1920s, although some policies have undergone revision. Diplomatic pressure is still used, but it no longer results in the "isolation" of the target nation; in today's world, one can look elsewhere for allies. Military intervention has not lost its allure completely, especially for dealing with the more powerless Latin American nations. Grenada learned that lesson in October 1983, when American Marines landed to oust its Marxist government. Increasingly, however, the United States has fought its battles by proxy. Under the auspices of the Central Intelligence Agency (CIA), "rebel forces" have been created, trained, and supplied by the United States. The results have been mixed. In Guatemala in 1954 the CIA's private army was able to topple the government of President Jacobo Arbenz with relatively little trouble. In 1961, however, things did not turn out quite as well at the Bay of Pigs. And the "freedom fighters" who have operated in Nicaragua since 1981 have been completely ineffective in ousting the Sandinista government.

America's economic power to entice or coerce Latin America into following its economic policies has been used consistently but with uncertain effect. The enticements have usually been in the form of "intrahemispheric" economic programs which have promised much but delivered little. The Export-Import Bank, the International Monetary Fund, and the Alliance for Progress have been set up with much fanfare. Despite them all, Latin America's dependent status remains largely unchanged. Since its loans to Brazil in the 1920s, the United States has loaned billions of dollars to the Latin Americans, resulting in the current morass of unpaid debts, rising interest payments, and U.S. calls for "austerity programs" in an already strapped region. As a weapon America's economic strength remains powerful, to which Allende's Chile could attest. Yet economic blockades of Cuba and Nicaragua have not had the results hoped for by American officials.

Another policy of the 1920s, that of working with conservative military forces in Latin America to head off outbreaks of radicalism, has blossomed since World War II. The training and supplying of Latin American armies, navies, and air forces has become the norm. The fall of Anastasio Somoza in Nicaragua in 1979, in spite of his U.S.-trained and -supplied national guard, has apparently not damaged that notion too severely. The training of armed forces in nations such as El Salvador continues.

Perhaps the most enduring, and costly, legacy of the U.S.-Latin American relationship of 1917 to 1929 has been the continued American support of dictatorships in Latin America. In the January 1981 issue of *Commentary*, Jeane Kirkpatrick (who was Ronald Reagan's first ambassador to the United Nations) published an article entitled "U.S. Security and Latin America."[5] This critique of Jimmy Carter's human rights policy blames it for the deterioration of the political situation in Latin America, particularly in Central America and the Caribbean. According to Kirkpatrick, Carter's policy had resulted in the overthrow of pro-American regimes (such as the Somoza dictatorship in Nicaragua) and their replacement by Marxist-Leninist governments. The article's similarities to the reports and views of American officials during the 1920s are uncanny, and they serve as first-rate examples of how little U.S. policies toward Latin America have changed since that time.

According to Kirkpatrick the United States should have adopted a much more "realistic" approach to problems in Latin America and supported the pro-American governments in that area whether they were dictatorial or not. Her analysis is based on three key points. First, dictators such as Somoza are to be expected in Latin America. "The nations of Central America (including Mexico) and the Caribbean suffer from some form of institutional weakness," such as low electoral participation, poor economies, or weak leadership. "All," she concludes, "are vulnerable to disruption, and must rely on force to put down challenges to authority." The typical "force" is a strong dictator backed by the armed forces.

Second, the old dictatorships of Latin America were not as bad as had been portrayed in the press and elsewhere. They offered stability and some economic progress. Again using Nicaragua as an example, Kirkpatrick explained that "the government was moderately competent in encouraging economic development, moderately oppressive, and moderately corrupt." Furthermore, dictators such as Somoza did not last forever. Since their regimes were personalist, their repression lasted only as long as they lived or could stay in power. Once they were removed, the nation could hypothetically move toward a more democratic form of rule.

Third, Kirkpatrick notes that even if U.S. support for these dictators was sometimes distasteful, it was far better than the alternative. Deprived of support, the dictators would fall and the country would be thrown into chaos. Such chaos was an open invitation to the forces of communism: the Soviet Union and its puppet state of Cuba. Not only would the establishment of Communist governments in the other nations of Latin America threaten the interests of the United States, but also they would be far worse than the "authoritarian dictatorships" which had come before.

This was the theory behind Kirkpatrick's controversial distinction between "authoritarian" and "totalitarian" governments. In a later issue of *Commentary* Max Lerner stated that Kirkpatrick had "brilliantly broken the mold that had settled around liberal thinking on dictatorships and human rights."[6] What Lerner failed to appreciate, however, was that the "liberal mold" had been broken over sixty years earlier by the American relationship with Gómez in the 1920s.

For U.S. policymakers economic nationalism, whether in name or in fact, remains at the core of the problems they are trying to solve through convincing the Latin Americans to accept American plans for economic development and growth. Part of the flaw that Latin America has seen in these plans was described, unwittingly, by Norman Davis in 1931: For many Latin Americans, being "brushed by" and given orders was unsatisfactory in the 1920s and 1930s; it in many cases has become intolerable. The "symbols of our wealth" always seem to be just "before their eyes," close enough to see but never near enough to grasp. John Keith, an American living in South America, also put his finger on the problem when he wrote in 1927 that "it is a far cry between the wail of poverty and distress and Bolshevism. It is not

Bolshevism in Mexico and Central and South America that is a potential
menace to the United States—it is industrialism."[7] Perhaps, as Frank
Polk confided to Chandler Anderson in a 1917 discussion on Mexico,
the United States was "getting into an issue . . . for which they could
find no solution."[8]

The obvious importance of better relations between the United
States and Latin America should preclude us from accepting Polk's
pessimistic evaluation, the present state of those relations
notwithstanding. The problem is not that solutions cannot be found, it
is simply that since the 1920s the United States has relied on much the
same solutions to a situation that it never clearly understood in the first
place. The first step toward a reevaluation of American policy must be
recognition of the obvious fact that it is no longer the 1920s. Continued
U.S. interference in the political and economic development of Latin
America will only widen the chasm that has grown in the past six
decades. More Mexicos and Colombias, more Cubas and Nicaraguas lie
in the future. Too many nations in Latin America are now determined to
chart their own development, regardless of U.S. goals. For those
nations, the lion in the woods is the United States.

Notes

1. Discussions of the level of "cooperation" between the state and business
in the expansion of America's economic presence during the 1920s is at the core
of the recent debate concerning the applicability of corporatist theories to
American foreign policy. Thomas McCormick, "Drift or Mastery? A Corporatist
Synthesis for American Diplomatic History," *Reviews in American History* 10
(December 1982): 318–30, argues that using corporatism as a theoretical
framework for analyzing American diplomacy both resuscitates the field and gives
a clearer understanding of the forces that make policy in the United States.
John P. Rossi, "A 'Silent Partnership'?: The U.S. Government, RCA, and Radio
Communications with East Asia, 1919–1928," *Radical History Review* 33
(September 1985): 32–52, makes a convincing argument against corporatism.
According to Rossi, the corporatist focus on the role of the state overlooks the
fact that "the primary agent of modern American imperialism has not been and is
not the state; it is the modern corporation." In his reply, "Corporatism: A Reply
to Rossi," *Radical History Review* 33 (September 1985): 53–59, McCormick
argues that one cannot generalize from a single case study. Although the value of
corporatism to the study of American foreign policy is not yet proven, this work
assumes that, while the corporate industrialism of the United States is indeed the
primary force behind America's economic expansionism, the state plays the vital
role of facilitating that expansion.

2. See Chapter 6 for a response to the notion that the U.S. government
encouraged "cooperation" between American and British oil interests in
Venezuela during the 1920s.

3. Norman Davis, "Study Group Reports: Relations with Latin America. First
Meeting. Development of Conservation in Latin America, 19 February 1931,"
Records of Groups, vol. 3, Archives of CFR.

4. The two best studies of the U.S. campaign to brand the Guatemalan government Communist are Richard Immerman, *The C.I.A. in Guatemala* (Austin, 1982), and Stephen Schlesinger and Stephen Kinzer, *Bitter Fruit: The Untold Story of the American Coup in Guatemala* (New York, 1983).

5. Jeane Kirkpatrick, "U.S. Security and Latin America," *Commentary* 71 (January 1981): 29–40.

6. Max Lerner, "Human Rights and American Foreign Policy: A Symposium," *Commentary* 72 (November 1981): 45.

7. John Keith to Charles Deller, enclosed in Malcolm Davis to Dr. Isaiah Bowman, 8 March 1927, Records of Groups, vol. 2, Archives of CFR.

8. Anderson diary, 22 January 1917, Anderson Papers.

Bibliography

Manuscript Collections

Archives of the Council on Foreign Relations, New York, New York
  Records of Groups
  Record of Meetings
Baker Business Library, Harvard University, Cambridge, Massachusetts
  Thomas Lamont Papers
Manuscripts Division, Library of Congress, Washington, DC, Papers of
  Chandler P. Anderson (microfilm)
  Newton D. Baker (microfilm)
  Bainbridge Colby
  Norman Davis
  Leland Harrison
  Charles Evans Hughes
  William Gibbs McAdoo
  John Bassett Moore
Minnesota State Historical Society, Minneapolis, Minnesota
  Papers of Frank B. Kellogg (microfilm)
Record Group 59, General Records of the Department of State, National
    Archives, Washington, DC
  Papers of Francis White
Ohio State Historical Society, Columbus, Ohio
  Papers of Warren G. Harding (microfilm)
Yale University Library, New Haven, Connecticut, Papers of
  Gordon Auchincloss
  Edward House
  Arthur Bliss Lane
  Frank Polk
  James R. Sheffield
  Henry L. Stimson (microfilm)

Government Documents

National Archives, Washington, DC
    Record Group 43. Records of U.S. Participation in International
    Conferences, Commissions, and Expositions
    Record Group 59. General Records of the Department of State
    Record Group 151. Records of the Bureau of Foreign and Domestic
    Commerce
U.S. Congress. House and Senate. *Congressional Record.* 1919–1929.
    Washington, DC: Government Printing Office, 1919–1929.
————. Senate Special Committee to Investigate the Munitions Industry.
    Hearings before the Special Committee to Investigate the Munitions
    Industry. 13 vols. 73d Cong., 2d sess. (vols. 1-4); 74th Cong., 1st
    sess. (vols. 1-9). Washington, DC: Government Printing Office, 1934–
    1943.
————. Senate. *Senate Reports.* Report no. 944, 74th Cong., 2d sess.
    Washington, DC: Government Printing Office, 1936.
U.S. Department of Commerce. *Annual Report of the Secretary of*
    Commerce, 1921–1928. Washington, DC: Government Printing
    Office, 1921–1928.
————. *Reports of the Department of Commerce, 1914–1920: Reports of*
    the Secretary of Commerce and Reports of Bureaus. Washington,
    DC: Government Printing Office, 1915–1921.
————. Bureau of Foreign and Domestic Commerce. *Colombia: A*
    Commercial and Industrial Handbook. By P. L. Bell. Special Agents
    Series, no. 206. Washington, DC: Government Printing Office, 1921.
U.S. Department of State. *Papers Relating to the Foreign Relations of the*
    United States, 1906–1929. Washington, DC: Government Printing
    Office, 1909–1943.
————. *Papers Relating to the Foreign Relations of the United States:*
    The Lansing Papers, 1914–1920. 2 vols. Washington, DC:
    Government Printing Office, 1939–40.
U.S. Department of the Treasury. *Proceedings of the First Pan American*
    Financial Conference. Washington, DC: Government Printing Office,
    1915.

Books

Aguilar, Luis E., ed. *Marxism in Latin America.* New York, NY: Alfred A.
    Knopf, 1968.

Albert, Bill. *South America and the First World War: The Impact of War on Brazil, Argentina, Peru and Chile.* Cambridge, England: Cambridge University Press, 1988.

Alexander, Robert J. *Arturo Alessandri: A Biography.* 2 vols. Ann Arbor, MI: University Microfilms International, 1977.

Baerresen, Donald, Martin Carnoy, and Joseph Grunwald. *Latin American Trade Patterns.* Washington, DC: Brookings Institution, 1965.

Bailey, Samuel L., ed. *Nationalism in Latin America.* New York, NY: Alfred A. Knopf, 1971.

Baker, Ray Stannard, and William E. Dodd, eds. *The Public Papers of Woodrow Wilson.* 6 vols. New York, NY: Harper and Brothers, 1925–1927.

Bergquist, Charles. *Coffee and Conflict in Colombia, 1886–1910.* Durham, NC: Duke University Press, 1978.

Bernstein, Harry. *Modern and Contemporary Latin America.* New York, NY: Russell and Russell, 1965.

———. *Venezuela and Colombia.* Englewood Cliffs, NJ: Prentice-Hall, 1964.

Brandenburg, Frank. *The Making of Modern Mexico.* Englewood Cliffs, NJ: Prentice-Hall, 1964.

Broesamle, John J. *William Gibbs McAdoo: A Passion for Change, 1863–1917.* Port Washington, NY: Kennikat, 1973.

Burgin, Miron. *The Economic Aspects of Argentine Federalism 1820–1852.* Cambridge, MA: Harvard University Press, 1946.

Burns, E. Bradford. *A History of Brazil.* New York, NY: Columbia University Press, 1970.

———. *The Unwritten Alliance: Rio Branco and Brazilian-American Relations.* New York, NY: Columbia University Press, 1966.

Cardoso, Fernando, and Enzo Faletto. *Dependency and Development in Latin America.* Translated by Marjory Mattingly Urquidi. Berkeley: University of California Press, 1979.

Cockroft, James. *Intellectual Precursors of the Mexican Revolution, 1900–1913.* Austin: University of Texas Press, 1968.

Cortés Conde, Roberto. *The First Stages of Modernization in Spanish America.* Translated by Tony Talbot. New York, NY: Harper and Row, 1974.

Costigliola, Frank. *Awkward Dominion: American Political, Economic, and Cultural Relations with Europe, 1919–1933.* Ithaca, NY: Cornell University Press, 1984.

Davis, Harold E. *Makers of Democracy in Latin America.* New York, NY: Coopers Square Publishers, 1968.

Duncan, W. Raymond, and James Nelson Goodsell, eds. *The Quest for Change in Latin America: Sources for a Twentieth-Century Analysis.* New York, NY: Oxford University Press, 1970.

Ellis, L. Ethan. *Frank B. Kellogg and American Foreign Relations, 1925–1929.* New Brunswick, NJ: Rutgers University Press, 1961.

Fitzgibbon, Russell H. *Uruguay: Portrait of a Democracy.* New Brunswick, NJ: Rutgers University Press, 1954.

Fontaine, Roger W. *Brazil and the United States: Toward a Maturing Relationship.* Washington, DC: American Enterprise Institute for Public Policy Research, 1974.

Frank, André Gunder. *Capitalism and Underdevelopment in Latin America: Historical Studies of Chile and Brazil.* New York, NY: Monthly Review Press, 1969.

Furtado, Celso. *Economic Development of Latin America: Historical Background and Contemporary Problems.* 2d ed. Translated by Suzette Macedo. Cambridge, England: Cambridge University Press, 1976.

———. *The Economic Growth of Brazil: A Survey from Colonial to Modern Times.* Translated by Ricardo W. de Aguiar and Eric Charles Drysdale. Berkeley: University of California Press, 1968.

Gardner, Lloyd. *Safe for Democracy: The Anglo-American Response to Revolution, 1913–1923.* New York, NY: Oxford University Press, 1984.

Gilderhus, Mark. *Pan American Visions: Woodrow Wilson in the Western Hemisphere, 1913–1921.* Tucson: University of Arizona Press, 1986.

Graham, Richard. *Britain and the Onset of Modernization in Brazil, 1850–1914.* Cambridge, England: Cambridge University Press, 1968.

———. *Independence in Latin America.* New York, NY: Alfred A. Knopf, 1972.

Grieb, Kenneth J. *The Latin American Policy of Warren G. Harding.* Fort Worth: Texas Christian University Press, 1976.

Halperin, Ernst. *Nationalism and Communism in Chile.* Cambridge, MA: MIT Press, 1965.

Halperin-Donghi, Tulio. *The Aftermath of Revolution in Latin America.* Translated by Josephine de Bunsen. New York, NY: Harper and Row, 1973.

Harbaugh, William. *The Life and Times of Theodore Roosevelt.* New York, NY: Oxford University Press, 1975.

Hawley, Ellis. *The Great War and the Search for a Modern Order: A History of the American People and Their Institutions, 1917–1933.* New York, NY: St. Martin's, 1979.

Herring, Hubert. *A History of Latin America: From the Beginnings to the Present.* New York, NY: Alfred A. Knopf, 1961.

Hill, Lawrence. *Diplomatic Relations between the United States and Brazil.* Durham, NC: Duke University Press, 1932.

Hodges, Donald, and Ross Gandy. *Mexico, 1910–1976: Reform or Revolution?* London, England: Zed, 1979.

Hoff-Wilson, Joan. *American Business and Foreign Policy, 1920–1933.* Lexington: University of Kentucky Press, 1971.

Hogan, Michael. *Informal Entente: The Private Structure of Cooperation in Anglo-American Economic Diplomacy, 1918–1928.* Columbia: University of Missouri Press, 1977.

Hoover, Herbert. *American Individualism.* New York, NY: Garland Publishing, 1979.

Horsman, Reginald. *Race and Manifest Destiny: The Origins of American Racial Anglo-Saxonism.* New York, NY: Cambridge University Press, 1981.

Hunt, Michael H. *Ideology and U.S. Foreign Policy.* New Haven, CT: Yale University Press, 1987.

Immerman, Richard. *The C.I.A. in Guatemala.* Austin: University of Texas Press, 1982.

Johnson, Harry G., ed. *Economic Nationalism in Old and New States.* Chicago, IL: University of Chicago Press, 1967.

Katz, Friedrich. *The Secret War in Mexico: Europe, the United States and the Mexican Revolution.* Chicago, IL: University of Chicago Press, 1981.

Kaufman, Burton I. *Efficiency and Expansion: Foreign Trade Organization in the Wilson Administration, 1913–1921.* Westport, CT: Greenwood, 1974.

Keen, Benjamin, and Mark Wasserman. *A Short History of Latin America.* Boston, MA: Houghton Mifflin, 1980.

Kinsbruner, Jay. *Chile: A Historical Interpretation.* New York, NY: Harper and Row, 1973.

Klein, Herbert. *Bolivia: The Evolution of a Multi-Ethnic Society.* New York, NY: Oxford University Press, 1982.

Kline, Harvey F. *Colombia: Portrait of Unity and Diversity.* Boulder, CO: Westview, 1983.

Lael, Richard L. *Arrogant Diplomacy: U.S. Policy toward Colombia, 1903–1922.* Wilmington, DE: Scholarly Resources, 1987.

LaFeber, Walter. *The New Empire: An Interpretation of American Expansion, 1860–1898.* Ithaca, NY: Cornell University Press, 1963.

———. *The Panama Canal: The Crisis in Historical Perspective.* New York, NY: Oxford University Press, 1978.

Leffler, Melvyn. *The Elusive Quest: America's Pursuit of European Stability and French Security, 1919–1933.* Chapel Hill: University of North Carolina Press, 1979.

Levin, N. Gordon. *Woodrow Wilson and World Politics: America's Response to War and Revolution.* New York, NY: Oxford University Press, 1968.

Levine, Daniel. *Conflict and Political Change in Venezuela.* Princeton, NJ: Princeton University Press, 1973.

Lewis, Cleona. *America's Stake in International Investments*. Washington, DC: Brookings Institution, 1938.

Link, Arthur, ed. *The Papers of Woodrow Wilson*. 36 vols. Princeton, NJ: Princeton University Press, 1966–1982.

Liss, Sheldon B. *Diplomacy and Dependency: Venezuela, the United States, and the Americas*. Salisbury, NC: Documentary Publications, 1978.

Lynch, John. *The Spanish American Revolutions, 1808–1826*. 2d ed. New York, NY: W. W. Norton, 1986.

Masur, Gerhard. *Nationalism in Latin America: Diversity and Unity*. New York, NY: Macmillan, 1966.

Mayer, Arno. *The Political Origins of the New Diplomacy, 1917–1918*. New Haven, CT: Yale University Press, 1954.

———. *Politics and Diplomacy of Peacemaking: Containment and Counterrevolution at Versailles, 1918–1919*. New York, NY: Alfred A. Knopf, 1967.

McGreevey, William. *An Economic History of Colombia, 1845–1930*. Cambridge, England: Cambridge University Press, 1971.

Morón, Guillermo. *A History of Venezuela*. Edited and translated by John Street. New York, NY: Roy Publishers, 1963.

Nunn, Frederick M. *Chilean Politics, 1920–1931: The Honorable Mission of the Armed Forces*. Albuquerque: University of New Mexico Press, 1970.

Parks, E. Taylor. *Colombia and the United States, 1765–1934*. New York, NY: Greenwood, 1968.

Parrini, Carl. *Heir to Empire: United States Economic Diplomacy, 1916–1923*. Pittsburgh, PA: University of Pittsburgh Press, 1969.

Pendle, George. *Argentina*. 3d ed. New York, NY: Oxford University Press, 1963.

Phelps, Clyde William. *The Foreign Expansion of American Banks: American Branch Banking Abroad*. New York, NY: Ronald Press, 1927.

Philip, George. *Oil and Politics in Latin America: Nationalist Movements and State Companies*. Cambridge, England: Cambridge University Press, 1982.

Plummer, Brenda Gayle. *Haiti and the Great Powers, 1902–1915*. Baton Rouge: Louisiana State University Press, 1988.

Poppino, Rollie. *Brazil: The Land and People*. New York, NY: Oxford University Press, 1968.

———. *International Communism in Latin America: A History of the Movement, 1917–1963*. New York, NY: Free Press, 1964.

Rabe, Stephen. *The Road to OPEC: United States Relations with Venezuela, 1919–1976*. Austin: University of Texas Press, 1982.

Randall, Stephen J. *The Diplomacy of Modernization: Colombian-American Relations, 1920–1940.* Toronto, Canada: University of Toronto Press, 1977.

Rippy, J. Fred. *The Capitalists and Colombia.* New York, NY: Vanguard, 1931.

————, José Vasconcelos, and Guy Stevens. *American Policies Abroad: Mexico.* Chicago, IL: University of Chicago Press, 1928.

Rock, David. *Politics in Argentina, 1890–1930: The Rise and Fall of Radicalism.* London, England: Cambridge University Press, 1975.

Rodó, José Enrique. *Ariel.* Translated by F. J. Stimson. Boston, MA: Houghton Mifflin, 1922.

Romero, José Luis. *A History of Argentine Political Thought.* Translated by Thomas McGann. Stanford, CA: Stanford University Press, 1963.

Rosenberg, Emily. *Spreading the American Dream: American Economic and Cultural Expansion, 1890–1945.* New York, NY: Hill and Wang, 1982.

Safford, Frank. *The Ideal of the Practical: Colombia's Struggle to Form a Technical Elite.* Austin: University of Texas Press, 1976.

Safford, Jeffrey J. *Wilsonian Maritime Diplomacy, 1913–1921.* New Brunswick, NJ: Rutgers University Press, 1978.

Schlesinger, Stephen, and Stephen Kinzer. *Bitter Fruit: The Untold Story of the American Coup in Guatemala.* New York, NY: Doubleday, 1983.

Scobie, James R. *Argentina: A City and a Nation.* New York, NY: Oxford University Press, 1964.

Seidel, Robert Neal. *Progressive Pan Americanism: Development and United States Policy toward South America, 1906–1931.* Ithaca, NY: Cornell University Press, 1971.

Smith, Robert Freeman. *The United States and Revolutionary Nationalism in Mexico, 1916–1932.* Chicago, IL: University of Chicago Press, 1972.

Snyder, Louis L. *The New Nationalism.* Ithaca, NY: Cornell University Press, 1968.

Stein, Stanley J., and Barbara H. Stein. *The Colonial Heritage of Latin America.* New York, NY: Oxford University Press, 1970.

Tancer, Shoshana. *Economic Nationalism in Latin America: The Quest for Economic Independence.* New York, NY: Praeger, 1976.

Taussig, F. W. *The Tariff History of the United States.* 6th ed. New York, NY: G. P. Putnam's Sons, 1914.

Tulchin, Joseph. *The Aftermath of War: World War I and U.S. Policy toward Latin America.* New York: New York University Press, 1971.

Vallenilla, Luis. *Oil: The Making of a New Economic Order: Venezuelan Oil and OPEC.* New York, NY: McGraw-Hill, 1975.

Van Alstyne, Richard. *The Rising American Empire.* New York, NY: Quadrangle Books, 1960.

Vanger, Milton I. *José Batlle y Ordóñez of Uruguay: The Creator of His Times, 1902–1907.* Cambridge, MA: Harvard University Press, 1963.

Weaver, Frederick Stirton. *Class, State, and Industrial Structure: The Historical Process of South American Industrial Growth.* Westport, CT: Greenwood, 1980.

Weinstein, Martin. *Uruguay: The Politics of Failure.* Westport, CT: Greenwood, 1975.

Weston, Rubin Frances. *Racism in U.S. Imperialism.* Columbia: University of South Carolina Press, 1972.

Whitaker, Arthur P. and David C. Jordan. *Nationalism in Contemporary Latin America.* New York, NY: Free Press, 1966.

Williams, William Appleman. *Empire as a Way of Life: An Essay on the Causes and Character of America's Present Predicament along with a Few Thoughts about an Alternative.* New York, NY: Oxford University Press, 1980.

———. *The Roots of the Modern American Empire: A Study of the Growth and Shaping of Social Consciousness in a Marketplace Society.* New York, NY: Oxford University Press, 1969.

Winkler, Max. *Investments of United States Capital in Latin America.* Boston, MA: World Peace Foundation Pamphlets, 1929.

Articles

Austin, O. P. "Development of the Tropics—A Probable Result of the War's Lessons." *The Americas* 4 (June 1918): 24–26.

Bath, C. Richard, and Dilmus D. James. "Dependency Analysis of Latin America: Some Criticisms, Some Suggestions." *Latin American Research Review* 11 (Fall 1976): 3–54.

Cox, Isaac. " 'Yankee Imperialism' and Spanish American Solidarity: A Colombian Interpretation." *Hispanic American Historical Review* 4 (May 1921): 256–65.

Gardner, Lloyd C. "Commercial Rivalry with One's Allies as Well as with One's Enemies." In William Appleman Williams, ed., *The Shaping of American Diplomacy*, 2:49–56. Chicago, IL: Rand McNally, 1970.

Helguera, J. León. "The Problem of Liberalism versus Conservatism in Colombia: 1849–85." In Frederick Pike, ed., *Latin American History: Select Problems: Identity, Integration, and Nationhood*, 220–46. New York, NY: Harcourt, Brace and World, 1969.

Jones, Grosvenor. "Our Stake in Latin America." *Journal of the American Banking Association* 21 (March 1929): 853–55, 925.

Kies, W. S. "Branch Banking in South American Trade." *Journal of the American Banking Association* 8 (September 1915): 280–81.

Kirkpatrick, Jeane. "U.S. Security and Latin America." *Commentary* 71 (January 1981): 29–40.

Klein, Herbert. "Social Constitutionalism in Latin America: The Bolivian Experience of 1938." *The Americas* 22 (January 1966): 258–76.

Krenn, Michael, John P. Rossi, and David Schmitz. "Under-Utilization of the Kellogg Papers." *SHAFR Newsletter* 14 (September 1983): 1–9.

Leffler, Melvyn P. "Herbert Hoover, the 'New Era,' and American Foreign Policy, 1921–29." In Ellis Hawley, ed., *Herbert Hoover as Secretary of Commerce: Studies in New Era Thought and Practice*, 148–82. Iowa City: University of Iowa Press, 1981.

Lerner, Max. "Human Rights and American Foreign Policy: A Symposium." *Commentary* 72 (November 1981): 45–47.

Little, Douglas. "Antibolshevism and American Foreign Policy, 1919–1939: The Diplomacy of Self-Delusion." *American Quarterly* 35 (Fall 1983): 376–90.

McCormick, Thomas. "Corporatism: A Reply to Rossi." *Radical History Review* 33 (September 1985): 53–59.

———. "Drift or Mastery? A Corporatist Synthesis for American Diplomatic History." *Reviews in American History* 10 (December 1982): 318–30.

Redfield, William. "The Government's Work for Trade Expansion." *The Americas* 1 (October 1914): 9–11.

———. "You and Our Foreign Trade." *Journal of the American Banking Association* 13 (February 1921): 515–16.

Roberts, George. "Unrest and Lessened Production Threaten America's Prosperity." *The Americas* 5 (August 1919): 1–3.

Rossi, John P. "A 'Silent Partnership'?: The U.S. Government, RCA, and Radio Communications with East Asia, 1919–1928." *Radical History Review* 33 (September 1985): 32–52.

Schmitz, David F. " 'A Fine Young Revolution': The United States and the Fascist Revolution in Italy, 1919–1925." *Radical History Review* 33 (September 1985): 117–38.

Williams, John H. "Our Foreign Trade Balance since the Armistice." *Journal of the American Banking Association* 13 (February 1921): 571–73.

Index